WHAT MAKES TRAINING REALLY WORK

Dr. Ina Weinbauer-Heidel
with contributions from Masha Ibeschitz-Manderbach
(English version by Ann Terry Gilman and Jutta Scherer)

WHAT MAKES TRAINING
REALLY WORK

12 LEVERS OF TRANSFER EFFECTIVENESS

Institute for Transfer Effectiveness | www.transfereffectiveness.com

© 2016 Dr. Ina Weinbauer-Heidel
Institute for Transfer Effectiveness | www.transfereffectiveness.com

Cover Design: Antoneta Wotringer Cover
Image: 123rf.com – ekinyalgin
Illustration: Katharina Trnka
Layout and Design: PEHA Medien GmbH, peha.at

Published by tredition GmbH, Hamburg
978-3-7469-4299-5 (Paperback)
978-3-7469-4301-5 (e-Book)

Bibliographic information of the German National Library:
The German National Library lists this publication in the German National Bibliography; Detailed bibliographic data are available online at http://dnb.d-nb.de.

CONTENTS

FOREWORD

by Robert O. Brinkerhoff and Paul Matthews

Robert O. Brinkerhoff

Training without transfer is like a car without an engine; it won't get you anywhere. When performance matters (as it almost always should), learning and development professionals must be able to drive transfer – being sure that training participants actually apply their learning in worthy ways. Ina Weinbauer-Heidel's clear and engaging prescriptions for managing the 12 transfer levers make this good book a must-read for anyone who wants to make sure training investments will pay off.

Robert O. Brinkerhoff, an internationally recognized expert in evaluation and learning effectiveness, is the creator of the Success Case Method; he consults widely on issues of program effectiveness and recently retired as professor, Western Michigan University, where he coordinated graduate programs in human resource development.

Paul Matthews

Apparently, elephants don't like the sound of buzzing bees, and you can stop elephants from trampling your precious crop by setting up speakers to play the chorus from a swarm of bees. A simple solution, yet powerful and effective. I have long described 'learning transfer' as one of the elephants in the room that Learning & Development people habitually ignore, in part because they don't know how to handle the elephant, and so the precious crop they sow with their training gets trampled. After reading this book, this is no longer an excuse. It is full of a buzzing chorus of simple and effective methods to manage the learning-transfer elephant.

Sustainable, competitive advantage is not so much based on what the organisation and its people know, but on what they do with what they know. Sure, training creates potential, but it does not drive performance until it is implemented. Josh Bersin, in a June 2018 article, states that globally, the corporate training market is worth over $200 billion, but how much of that actually 'lands' and makes a difference? If you are reading this book, you already know the answer: 'Not nearly enough'.

One of the things I welcome most about this book is that it is based on research. It gives you the findings from a meticulous review of the transfer-of-training literature and turns these findings into practical steps, supported by wise advice on the truths and traps of transfer. Building this bridge – between scholarly studies and the 'real' world – is no mean feat, and Dr. Weinbauer-Heidel demystifies the transfer complex deftly and well. In effect, she leaves no room for claims of 'not knowing what to do' and avoiding the issue of learning transfer. After reading this book, you WILL want to make changes to your training courses, and the explanations from the research will give you the credibility you need to enlist others for help along the way. You'll want to give them this book to read as well!

Thomas Edison said, 'The value of an idea lies in the using of it'. So, get people using the ideas they gain in your training courses by using the ideas you gain from this book.

Paul Matthews, People Alchemy's founder and managing director, is also a sought-after speaker and the author of Capability at Work and Informal Learning at Work.

THE ESSENCE OF TRANSFER RESEARCH – AN INTRODUCTION

"Seminars are useless – they're a waste of money." This is, in a rough translation from German, the title of a best-selling business book by Richard Gris. Quite a startling claim he made there. After all, companies in Austria and Germany invest around 30 billion euro each year in training their employees.[1] An enormous investment indeed. Can it really be true that these training efforts don't accomplish anything? That they only waste time and money? Are trainings really pointless?

Take a rough guess – how much of what people learn in trainings is actually put into practice? Many HR developers and trainers – even participants themselves – think it's only 10 to 30 percent. Which is exactly the figure given by transfer researchers, too. Let me run that by you once more: According to transfer research, only 10 to 30 percent of what people learn in training is put to profitable use in the workplace.[2] Not exactly an impressive return on investment, is it?

> Training transfer is the extent to which trainees effectively use the knowledge, skills and attitudes they have acquired in the training context in the work context.[3]

Professor Robert O. Brinkerhoff, one of the leading experts in the field of effectiveness and evaluation, has found that, on average, only two out of twelve trainees manage to transfer what they have learned into everyday life. Another eight try to apply their learnings but fail. And two don't even try.[4] In view of the enormous investments involved, transfer success should definitely be much higher.

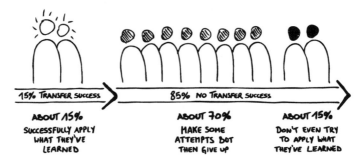

Fig. 1: On average, only two out of twelve trainees succeed in transferring what they have learned into practice

10

Are trainings simply ineffective?

Does it have to be like this? Could it be that the instrument "training" just doesn't work anymore? Should we simply forget about it? Actually, in many cases this is an excellent idea. Like any other instrument, the instrument of training is not a cure-all for all organizational problems and challenges. When sales numbers go down, what is needed in some cases might just be a better product, not training. And when burnout rates skyrocket, the solution often lies in extra staffing, different organizational structures, or less bureaucracy – not stress management training.

And yet they still exist: the challenges for which trainings are an optimal solution (Note that we will come back to the question of when training is the right solution when we deal with the lever "application options," see pages 191 ff.). They do exist: those trainings that are tremendously effective. You've probably experienced this before, as a trainee, an HR developer, or a trainer: an ingenious training program in which you have given or received the key idea that made all the difference. It is an unforgettable experience when, years after a training session, one of the participants comes to you and tells you, "Your training was such a great help! I still use your model XYZ." Yes, these are the moments that make trainers glow with pride: the experiences that prove that training can definitely be efficient and effective. An observation, by the way, that is corroborated by science: The effect training can have on various criteria such as outcome, behavior, and knowledge varies enormously (from d = 5 to d = 0 or even d = -1.5) – where the numbers mean that training can have a tremendous effect, no effect at all, or even unwanted effects. Why is that so? What influences transfer effectiveness? And how can we make training more effective?

The essence of transfer research

Transfer researchers have been working on this question for more than a hundred years, conducting empirical studies in which they iteratively manipulate various factors, then measure the change in transfer results. There is a broad consensus that three elements are crucial for transfer effectiveness: training participants (trainees), training design, and training organization

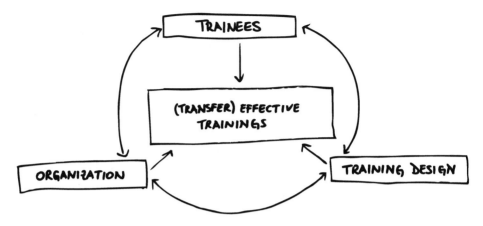

Fig. 2:   Three elements need to work together to make training transfer-effective

Each of these three areas comprises a variety of factors. Lots of factors! Transfer researchers are truly hard-working people. As many as 100 factors have been identified that are believed to influence transfer effectiveness.[5] Are you now tempted to put this book down, thinking, "What am I supposed to do with 100 factors?!" You are absolutely right: 100 factors are hardly convenient to work with, let alone work effectively. And you don't have to. Many of these factors are nice to know but offer no practical help in controlling transfer effectiveness. Let me give you an example. Take one of the factors from the area of training participants. Numerous studies have revealed a significant correlation between intelligence and transfer success.[6] But what are we to do with this information? Are we supposed to make participants take an intelligence test before each training session, and admit only those whose IQ promises significant transfer success? Probably not. As you can see, some of the factors transfer researchers have looked into are interesting but no great help when it comes to making training transfer-effective NOW – simply because we can't influence those factors at all, or not enough, or not fast enough. For practical purposes, what we need are only those factors that we can influence, and only a handful of them: only the most important ones to keep things manageable. – Well, here they are: the 12 levers of transfer effectiveness:

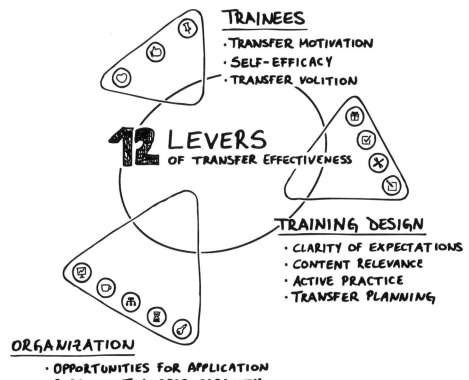

TRAINEES
- TRANSFER MOTIVATION
- SELF-EFFICACY
- TRANSFER VOLITION

12 LEVERS
OF TRANSFER EFFECTIVENESS

TRAINING DESIGN
- CLARITY OF EXPECTATIONS
- CONTENT RELEVANCE
- ACTIVE PRACTICE
- TRANSFER PLANNING

ORGANIZATION
- OPPORTUNITIES FOR APPLICATION
- PERSONAL TRANSFER CAPACITY
- SUPPORT FROM SUPERVISORS
- SUPPORT FROM PEERS
- TRANSFER EXPECTATIONS IN THE ORGANIZATION

Fig. 3: The 12 levers of transfer effectiveness

Who pulls the levers?

Whose job is it to set the levers to "transfer effectiveness"? As an HR developer, you may say, "What do I care about things like training design? That's up to the trainers." As a trainer, you may think, "I don't have any leverage over organizational issues, so why bother?" So, could it be an option for you, depending on your role, not to get to know all the levers and focus on those within your area of responsibility? Let me tell you straight out: No, this is not an option.

Why? Because this is one of the main reasons for poor transfer success: a lack of clear responsibilities. Effective transfer is always the outcome of a joint effort. Several people need to work together, each making his or her specific contribution – an effort that needs to be organized and managed. Yet there's also a risk when several stakeholders are responsible for overall transfer success: Whenever many people are jointly responsible for something, often none of them really feels responsible. Everyone assumes that someone else will make sure that everything is done properly – especially when tasks are not clearly defined and/or clearly assigned to individual people or roles. Which is exactly what happens with transfer improvement. Who is responsible for defining and selecting the right training content? Who develops and implements measures to ensure that participants' supervisors will support the transfer? Who can – and should – make sure participants are motivated to implement what they've learned, and to keep pursuing their plans in everyday work? If you ask different people, you'll get a range of answers. As a result, these questions remain unsolved and responsibilities unclear, and often they are not addressed or even considered at all. The transfer process remains unmanaged – and transfer success fails to materialize.

After having read this book, this won't happen to you. You'll be familiar with the levers of transfer effectiveness and raise the questions that are essential. You'll have an overview of what is important, and a toolbox full of ideas on how to drive and promote transfer.

If you are an HR developer, you will benefit from knowing the levers of transfer effectiveness in that you'll be able to look very specifically for trainers that meet your transfer requirements. In addition, with this model in mind you will find it easier to make executives in your organization aware of their importance for transfer success and to request their participation. Last but not least, the levers of transfer effectiveness will enable you to get the necessary commitment in your organization and convince decision makers to budget the necessary funds for training and, in particular, for transfer activities and interventions.

If you are a trainer, you'll find that knowing the levers of transfer effectiveness will help you become a strong sparring partner and conceptual adviser to your clients. You'll be able to point out to them what needs to be done and who needs to be involved in order to achieve transfer success. By doing that, you will make them aware that successful transfer is not your sole responsibility but that the organization must do its share. Not only will this gradually strengthen your reputation as a trainer with very special transfer abilities and results – it will also help you secure additional business as, in your role as a consultant and partner for creating transfer-effective development programs, of course you can also provide your clients with the appropriate tools, activities, and interventions.

Ultimately, the question of which levers are relevant for you depends on your perspective on your own role and positioning: As an HR developer, do you see yourself as an organizer of seminars – or as a business partner that contributes to a company's success? The latter implies, of course, that you are also responsible for transfer management, the coordination of transfer success, and, consequently, all of the levers. And in your role as a trainer or training provider, do you want to be someone who conveys content in a methodically-didactically appealing way – or do you see yourself as someone guiding and facilitating development, someone determined to help training participants and organizations make progress in their respective fields? In that case you'll need all levers, not just some of them.

In a nutshell, whenever you ask yourself this question: "Is this lever really relevant for me as a trainer, as a training provider, or as an HR developer?" it may be a signal to revisit your own (possibly narrow) perspective on your role.

The first step towards transfer-effective training

So, let's get down to business. What's the first step to increase transfer effectiveness? The answer is: setting goals. If you are now tempted to skip the next pages, stop right here. Of course, we start with goals. In fact, it's something so obvious we often don't devote enough care and attention to this step.

How do we define goals so they will be transfer-effective? Let's take a brief look at the definition of transfer. Training transfer means putting acquired knowledge, skills, and attitudes into practice. So, acquiring new knowledge as such is not considered "transfer" and is therefore not the goal of training. As Goethe once put it succinctly: "Knowing is not enough; we must apply. Willing is not enough; we must do." A transfer-effectiveness goal (or transfer goal, for short) describes exactly this "doing." A transfer goal describes an action that leads to the desired business success – a critical behavior, as Kirkpatrick, the grandmaster of evaluation, calls it.

When we describe transfer goals in this way – as actions, that is –, they automatically become clearer. Here's an example. In descriptions of sales trainings, we often find goals such as: "Improve your sales skills" or "Gain confidence in dealing with customers." Are these goals clearly defined? Are they phrased clearly enough to allow everyone involved in the transfer (training participants, trainers, executives, etc.) to understand them the same way? Are they measurable? Not really. So, let's give this another try. Let's find wording for a tangible critical behavior; a transfer goal. In the case of our sales training, it could be this: "Participants will increase their closure rates by 20 % by using closing techniques in their sales talks." This wording makes it very clear what the outcome – the benefit for the organization and participants themselves will be (+20 % – awesome!) and what concrete behavior will achieve it (applying closing techniques). Transfer goals ensure that everyone involved knows where they are headed and what's in it for them. And that is the starting point of transfer-effective training.

Time for transfer! How to increase your personal transfer success

What holds true for participants in training is also true for your own personal transfer success with this book. Knowing is not enough; you need to apply what you learn. Reading is not enough; you need to act. You will achieve maximum transfer effectiveness if you immediately put what you have learned to the test and into practice. Not in an abstract way, but by applying it to exemplary cases from your own practice. This way, you'll get the most out of your precious time (using it for both reading and conceptualization) and can immediately check whether what you've read really works for you.

Specifically, I recommend you take a real-life training session or program that you're planning or developing at the moment and write a transfer concept for it, lever by lever. Which training session or training program are you going to choose?

> As I read this book, I will develop a transfer concept for this training or development program:
> _____

Let's start with the first key step: setting transfer goals. What should this training accomplish in practice? What will participants do differently or better, based on the training? What behavior will be key to success and what should be the result? Write down whatever ideas and cue words come to mind.

Transfer goal(s) of my training:

If you've just realized that your transfer goals are not as clear and unambiguous as they should be, this is an important insight, too. In the course of the book you will learn about various tools and interventions to sharpen your goals (for example, the Transfer Goals Workshop or the Needs Assessment, see pages 196 ff.). If your goals are clear-cut and tangible already, so much the better.

So, let's get started. Let's look at what levers affect transfer effectiveness, and what tools and interventions will help you increase the transfer success of your training.

[1] In Germany, around €27 billion is invested annually in in-company training, according to Gris and Gutbrod, who use a biting title in German: "Keep on training, keep on lying? Why, despite all the findings, a large share of consulting and training work is still a waste of time." Gris, R., & Gutbrod, A., "Weiter bilden, weiter lügen? Warum entgegen aller Erkenntnisse ein Großteil der Beratungs- und Trainingsarbeit immer noch Verschwendung ist" in: Organisationsentwicklung, 2009, 28(3), pp. 52 – 57. Note: Richard Gris also writes in German as Axel Koch on his "transfer-strength method": In Austria, investments amount to around €1.4 billion. For details and comparisons of EU Member States, see the regular Eurostat survey (Vocational Education and Training Statistics – CVTS) and also the national reports from the Federal Statistical Office in Germany and Statistics Austria.

[2] For estimates of transfer success, see, for example, Baldwin, T. T., & Ford, J. K., "Transfer of Training – A Review and Directions for Future Research" in Personnel psychology, 41(1), 1988, pp.63 – 105 or Kauffeld: S., Nachhaltige Weiterbildung. Betriebliche Seminare und Trainings entwickeln, Erfolge messen, Transfer sichern, Springer, 2010, p.4.

[3] This, the most common definition employed in the transfer research debate, comes from Baldwin, T. T., & Ford, J. K., "Transfer of Training: A Review and Directions for Future Research" in: Personnel psychology, 41(1), 1988, pp.63 – 105.

[4] Brinkerhoff, R. O., What If Training Really Had to Work? 2006, http://www.iap-association. org/getattachment/Conferences/Annual-Conferences/Annual-Conference-2014/Conference-Documentation/19AC_P3_Discussion_Note_Pauline_Popp_Madsen.pdf.aspx (1.12.2016). The values are based on Prof. Robert Brinkerhoff's many years of personal evaluation experience. More information on his work can be found at www.brinkerhoffevaluationinstitute.com

[5] For a fully comprehensive description of the transfer determinants, see, for example, Meißner, A., Lerntransfer in der betrieblichen Weiterbildung: Theoretische und empirische Exploration der Lerntransferdeterminanten im Rahmen des Training off-the-job, Josef Eul Verlag GmbH, 2012, pp. 96 ff.

[6] For intelligence (cognitive abilities) as a determinant of transfer, see, for example, the meta-analyses of Colquitt, J. A., LePine, J. A., & Noe, R. A., "Towards an integrative theory of training motivation: A meta-analytic path analysis of 20 years of research" in Journal of Applied Psychology, 85(5), 2000, pp. 678 – 707, and also the meta-analysis of Blume, B. D., Ford, J. K., Baldwin, T. T., & Huang, J. L., "Transfer of Training: A Meta-Analytic Review" in Journal of Management, 36(4), 2020, pp. 1065 – 1105.

LEVERS FOR TRAINEES

> I want – I can – I will
> In the end, transfer is a trainee's decision

Lever 1
Transfer Motivation

Lever 2
Self-Efficacy

Lever 3
Transfer Volition

In this section, you will learn:

- How to increase training participants' transfer motivation,
- What the magical four-minute mile has to do with transfer,
- How our "willpower muscle" works,
- What you can do to set the three trainee levers to "transfer-effective."

LEVER 1 – TRANSFER MOTIVATION

TWO REAL-LIFE EXAMPLES

A week ago, Christina and Martin each completed an in-house Leadership Excellence program. From reading their accounts, what do you think: who is more likely to have greater transfer success?

Martin, 38, manager in the automotive industry

When my boss nominated me for the Leadership Excellence program, I was proud. I had heard from my colleagues that the program would really help me get ahead. The top management team was even present at kick-off to tell us about the purpose of the program, and how it benefits both me and the business. Our company spends quite a bit of money to ensure we'll be able to put into practice what we learn. During the program, I felt I was in the right place. The issues I raised were addressed, the coaches treated us all as equals, no one patronized us. We, the trainees, were actively involved most of the time, not just sitting and listening. With each exercise, we talked about benefits and possible applications. At the end of the program, I had very straightforward plans for how to implement what I have learned. I discussed them with my boss, who gave me some valuable advice. It's so great to see how she takes an interest in my issues. Her appreciation is a real motivator. Plus, by achieving my own goals, I contribute to her success. I look forward to implementing more, to seeing the outcome – and, of course, to my next training!

Christina, 36, manager in the public sector

After three years, I could no longer avoid it. I had to sign up for our so-called "Leadership Excellence" program. I already knew that it wouldn't help me get ahead – a waste of time, like most of our trainings. All that happens there is that people from outside tell you how management works. As if they knew how the wind blows or what I am dealing with. A big presentation and some run-of-the-mill group exercises. What they were good for, I still don't know. What will I implement from the program? Well, nothing. But, of course, I can't tell that to my boss when I get back. At first, I had hoped he'd forget about it, like all the other times – but no. This time there was an actual debrief because HR insisted on getting a report. I felt like a little kid during this conversation: "Do this, but don't do that, it doesn't work anyway!" – That's my boss for you. Well, I sat through it all, then jotted down something for the record. I hope they'll leave me alone now for the next few years with all that training hassle!

Well, what's your take on transfer success? Who do you think will implement more? What's the key difference between the two?

Christina considers training programs to be useless, a waste of time. Ditto for the Leadership Excellence program. The benefits of the overall program, its individual modules, and the exercises were not evident to her and did not seem relevant or applicable. As a result, she has zero motivation to apply what she's learned. Unlike Martin. He feels honored to be nominated for the Leadership Excellence program ad appreciates the opportunity. The benefit of the program was clear to him, both personally and for his organization. There is no question he wants to implement what he has learned. Researchers refer to this strong desire to actively use and implement what one has learned in one's everyday work as "transfer motivation."[1] Participants with a pronounced transfer motivation will leave their training with a strong feeling of commitment: "Yes, I want to put this into practice." As we will discuss later, training design and organizational elements are additional key factors for transfer success. Here, I'm focusing on the "I want" of transfer motivation, which, as we will see in the next chapters, has to be reinforced by "I can" (self-efficacy) and "I will" (transfer volition).

For transfer effectiveness as a whole, it is the participants themselves who make a very crucial decision: whether they want to apply what they have learned or not. Quite obviously, this decision – this transfer motivation – plays a key role. If participants have no interest in applying what they have learned, transfer success is virtually impossible. If they are determined to put their new knowledge into practice, a great deal has been achieved. Not surprisingly, this is confirmed by empirical studies in transfer research: High transfer motivation is a key factor for successful training transfer.[2]

TRANSFER MOTIVATION – YES, I WANT IT!

	Transfer motivation in a nutshell
Trainees say	"Yes, I want this!"
Definition	Transfer motivation is defined as the desire to implement what has been learned.
Guiding question	How can you ensure that trainees have a strong desire to put into practice what they have learned?

So, being motivated means wanting something very strongly. But when or why do we want something strongly? Generations of researchers have been looking into this question. Motivation research is a vast field with virtually inexhaustible amounts of publications, studies, and theories. I assume you've come across names such as Herzberg, Maslow, Murray, or Alderfer, as well as technical terms from motivational psychology such as motives, drives, need pyramids, motivators, hygiene factors, and extrinsic and intrinsic motivation. If someone decided to write just an overview of the theories and insights in the field of motivational research, the resulting book would probably run to 500 pages or more. Here, we will therefore focus on just a few motivational theories that provide a particularly good basis for developing measures to drive transfer.

Second-class motivation?

If you ask your three-year-old if and why she wants to play in the afternoon, she will probably answer, "Because I want to. Because it's fun!" If you ask your twelve-year-old why he plans to study chemistry in the afternoon, he will give you the same answer – in an ideal world, mind you. It is much more likely that you will get very different replies, such as, "because I have a test on Monday" or "because you said I could play on my PlayStation if I do."

So, it seems there's a fundamental difference here. Your three-year-old is willing because the activity in itself is fun; your twelve-year-old is willing because he is hoping for a reward, something other than the activity itself. This difference even occurred to none other than Aristotle – perhaps because he, too, had two children. Much later, it was re-discovered, and, in 1918, Robert S. Woodworth, a renowned American psychologist, described this difference as intrinsic and extrinsic motivation.[3] Intrinsic means "on the inside" and describes the motivation to do something for its own sake (as your three-year-old wants to play). Extrinsic means "from the outside," referring to the kind of motivation that occurs when people expect something desirable when the task is completed successfully (PlayStation as a reward for studying – yay!!).

All in all, both types of motivation seem useful and meaningful when it comes to motivating people to do something specific or act a certain way. It's just that in the second case, we have the problem that the desired behavior quickly stops once the rewards are no longer there or can no longer be controlled. Consequently, there seems to be a "genuine, better, more sustainable" kind of motivation – the intrinsic one – and second-class kind that is "false, not quite so good, and less sustainable": the extrinsic kind. Which comes back to the advice often found in guides to a happier life: Do what you enjoy doing! Meaning: only things for which you are intrinsically motivated. But let's be honest – how realistic is it to expect that you can only do the things you enjoy doing every minute of your (working) life, and stop doing them when you stop enjoying them? And how realistic is that in terms of training transfer? Is it really false, second-class motivation when trainees apply what they've learned because they hope for good results, achievements, or rewards (extrinsic motivation), rather than simply enjoying the activity itself (intrinsic motivation)? Also, the solution can hardly be to offer rewards every time (for example, a promotion or salary increase) to motivate participants for training transfer. Or to have bosses threaten them with consequences if people don't apply what they've learned. Somehow it seems this distinction between intrinsic and extrinsic isn't quite enough ...

What follows after extrinsic and intrinsic

Intrinsic and extrinsic motivation were long regarded as a pair of opposing, incompatible concepts. A common undertone in motivational literature has been that intrinsic motivation (doing what you enjoy doing) is better than extrinsic motivation. However, within the field of extrinsic motivation, there are important differences. For instance, while studying or tidying up the garage isn't always fun, the result (passing an exam, looking at a clean and tidy garage) gives you a deeply satisfying feeling that makes the commitment worthwhile. It's quite a different story when parents "force" their children to study, or your partner "tells you" to clean out of the garage. Instant reluctance sets in, an uneasy feeling. So, what makes the difference in motivation quality? It's self-determination, according to Deci and Ryan, who have developed this into a proper theory.[4] Their self-determination theory of motivation became popular through Daniel Pink, along with his TED talk and his bestseller.[5] According to him, the self-determination theory is the treasure chest of motivational research; he claims that in forty years we will consider Deci and Ryan to be the most influential social scientists of our time. Have I kindled your curiosity? Then let's take a closer look at the self-determination theory.

As the name implies, the lynchpin of their motivation theory is self-determination. At its core, the question "Is the act in itself fun or not?" is replaced by "Do I want it for myself, or do others want it?" This theory assumes that humans have an innate basic need for autonomy and self-determination. Like Maslow's theory, which places self-realization at the top of the hierarchy of needs, this theory also holds that we humans pursue what we ourselves want to do; that it is conducive – but not essential – to this pursuit if the activity itself gives us pleasure (intrinsic motivation); and that we tend to tackle things with great (and sustainable) motivation if they have positive and desirable consequences for us.

Why are we discussing all of this? What are the benefits of this theory with regard to transfer motivation? The answer is: It increases our options for action and motivation. Let's take, for example, a training in telephone marketing. One of the targets could be for participants to call five potential customers per week. So how could we promote transfer motivation? Or, put differently: How could we get the trainees to say, "Yes, I want to do that!"? Here are three possible approaches:

Promote extrinsic controlled motivation	Promote extrinsic autonomous motivation	Promote intrinsic autonomous motivation
Show **that others want this to be done**	Show **how desirable the results and consequences will be**	Show **how much fun it is to do this**
Trainees will say: I'll call five customers a week because that's what my boss wants me to do	Trainees will say: I'll call five customers a week because I'll sell more – which I think is great	Trainees will say: I'll call five customers a week because I enjoy making phone calls

We know from empirical studies that all three versions of both autonomous and controlled transfer motivation increase transfer success.[6] In other words, transfer success also increases when external pressure is exerted (e.g., by supervisors, by the organization, by the coach, etc.). However, gut instincts and common sense tell us – and so does the self-determination theory – that controlled motivation is not necessarily optimal, appropriate for adults, and sustainable. Which is why I recommend placing greater emphasis on the autonomous forms of motivation.

> Motivate trainees by offering clear, tangible benefits. Even if it isn't always fun to apply what has been learned, this approach will enable them to develop sustainable transfer motivation. Make sure you keep stressing the benefits and desired outcome of putting things into practice.

What does this mean in practice? How can you promote and enhance autonomous motivation? Here are some examples you might want to explore further.

You promote autonomous transfer motivation by ...	Examples
Giving reasons for decisions instead of making them without explanation	• Discuss with people why they were chosen to undergo a training
Communicating benefits and purposes rather than taking them for granted	• Communicate the benefits of the training to trainees (e.g., in the training description, during kick-off, in the pre-training talk, etc.) • In the training itself, communicate the benefits of each topic and each exercise
Letting people choose instead of imposing things on them	• Before the training, let participants have a say in determining the content and methods • During the training, give people options (e.g., offer a choice of thematic areas from which they can choose what to work on)
Promoting explorative/ discovery learning instead of passive receptive learning	• During the training, focus on active, problem-based learning methods rather than "lecturing" people classroom-style (also see Lever 6 – Active Practice)

Using language that implies autonomy rather than control	• Before, during and after the training, make sure you replace control-related phrases ("You must ..." or "It has been decided that..." or "It's not done that way!") with wording that expresses autonomy ("I encourage you to ..." or "It's been my experience that ..." or "Another option would be to ..." etc.). • As a trainer and supervisor, support people by expressing your recognition, giving positive feedback, and assuming a coaching attitude, rather than acting as an authority who exerts control (for more on this, see Lever 10 – Support from Supervisors).
Strengthening people's sense of responsibility instead of making others responsible for transfer	• Point out before, during, and after training that trainees – not trainers or other people – are responsible for their learning and transfer success.

This approach to interacting with learners, promoting their self-determination, has become quite common. It is a basic attitude that is also a key factor for successful transfer.

"Hands up or I'll shoot!" – Transfer under pressure

"Basic attitude" is a key word that has gotten us to a very intriguing and basic issue of transfer promotion. Let's summarize what we've said so far. Transfer motivation exists when trainees say, "I want to do this." After having talked about controlled and autonomous motivation, we can get more precise now. What we want is trainees who say, "I want to do this (apply what I've learned) because it is my will" rather than "I want to do this because others want me to." This insight illustrates something fundamental and important. Transfer interventions should never be controlling or coercive, but always take the form of offering support and fostering self-determined learners. In other words, promoting transfer doesn't mean making people apply what they've learned, but enabling them and making it as easy as possible for them to apply it. The purpose of every transfer intervention is to pave the way for transfer success and remove barriers wherever possible. This way, we enable both the organization and the trainees themselves to get the most out of the training investment (money, time, commitment, etc.) and benefit sustainably. This is in the interest of both the organization and the trainees.

What follows from this basic attitude is that all other levers in this book, and the ideas to promote transfer that are derived from them, support not only transfer success but transfer motivation as well. It's a natural consequence. Transfer interventions are offers of support and enablement, not pressure. Offers of support and enablement require and ensure that self-determined learners want both the offer (the intervention) and the result (the transfer success). Transfer successes and all transfer interventions are always based on a high degree of transfer motivation, of "I want to apply this." Unfortunately, the reverse doesn't work: Transfer motivation is not a guarantee for transfer success.

> Transfer motivation - the individual will – is necessary but not sufficient – a key requirement but not a guarantee for transfer success.

Wanting to do something is not enough to really do it. We will discuss this in more detail when we talk about the other levers. The key message here is that transfer interventions are always offers of support and enablement, paving the way for transfer success – and that we should keep that in mind when designing our transfer interventions and finding the right words.

> Transfer-promoting measures make the development and application of what is learned easy, attractive, and barrier-free for trainees. Such steps are offers of support and enablement for self-determined, benefit-oriented adult learners.

So, are only volunteers motivated?

What about self-determination and the pressure to participate in a training? Following the logic of autonomous motivation, should training always be offered on a voluntary basis? After all, it is quite a common phenomenon for trainers and HR developers to be faced with participants who've been "sent" to a training and clearly appear bored. Even worse, some openly vent their frustration, which sometimes affects the mood of the whole group. So, are trainees who've been sent to or "nominated" for a training generally less motivated? A good question that is well worth discussing, in particular as research confirms that transfer motivation is significantly influenced by the level of motivation before and during training.[7] So, should there only be voluntary training from now on? Several studies have shown that voluntary participation results in higher motivation[8] – but there have also been other studies that failed to confirm this point,[9] and even proved the opposite: trainees who were obliged to attend were the most motivated.[10] So, which of the findings are true? What's the explanation for these contradictory results?

As a matter of fact, the two factors that make the difference are (1) participants' subjective assessment of the importance and significance of the training and (2) their previous training experiences. Let's explore this in a thought experiment: Imagine a trainee who's had very positive experiences with past training programs in your organization. The training programs he has attended so far have been extremely meaningful and useful, applying what he learned has helped him advance in his career. How will this person react to the news that he is to attend yet another training? Obviously, he'll view this as yet another opportunity, and tend to feel chosen or "nominated" rather than obligated or "pressured" to attend. Rather than an obligation, it will be an opportunity, a reward, an honor to him. So, in this case, the nomination will tend to increase motivation. If, on the other hand, someone is nominated (and thus obliged) whose past experiences have made her feel that training was ineffective and meaningless – a waste of time, the opposite will be true: Upon being nominated, that person's motivation will decrease further. In short, our motivation strongly depends upon our past experiences.

Another key factor is the importance we attach to the training. Imagine you're a member of the HR development team in an organization. Every three years there's this major conference in Washington, D.C., where the world's most renowned experts present the latest insights from employee research. Everyone in your team wants to go, because every time someone returns from that conference, they bring back innovative ideas that are very valuable for the HR teams' work. The boss is deeply interested in these ideas and highly committed to supporting their introduction and implementation. Then, at the next jour-fixe, the announcement: This year, the boss is going to send you to that conference! You will go to Washington, you will learn exciting new things, and come back with brilliant new ideas. What do you think that will do to your motivation? How high will it be? Pretty high, right? Although – or because – you were nominated to go. Well, the same is true for the attendees of a training: If they consider that training to be significant and important, being "sent" will increase their motivation. If it is just another one of those trainings that they need to attend because that is the rule, being sent is likely to lower their motivation. Past experiences and perceived importance make all the difference.

Even trainees who've been selected or nominated for training can be highly motivated for transfer. Key factors are (1) what previous experience participants have had with training, and (2) how significant and valuable they consider the training to be ("honor and opportunity" versus "onerous duty").

Imagine at the next human resource development conference you meet a colleague who's struggling with the issue of voluntary attendance. "Our executive development program is mandatory," she says. "Everyone has to attend. But that's demotivating! So, what am I supposed to do? I'd like people to be motivated for this, but my boss insists that all managers must attend that training." What advice would you give her? Correct: Asking "How can I push voluntary attendance?" is not the right question. Instead, she should ask herself, "How can we make our training program more meaningful and attractive for candidates?" and "How can we make it so that trainees will gain positive experiences, so they'll find our training effective and useful?" When employees see a training as an opportunity they are grateful for and eager to take, they will perceive their nomination (or being "sent") as a sign of appreciation, which will motivate them even more.

> Work on the image you want your trainings to have. Make sure your training programs are perceived in the organization as significant, desirable, useful, and effective.

A critical look at voluminous educational programs

The issue of significance, value, and exclusiveness brings us to another interesting point: What makes training meaningful, desirable, and exclusive? Let me give you two extreme examples.

Company No. 1 offers its employees a comprehensive development program. Those interested can choose courses from a voluminous 100-page training catalog, in line with what new recruits ask for in job interviews. This educational program is sent out to all employees every year. Key figures for the company's HR development team are "training days per employee per year" and "number of training courses offered." In HR, these figures are used as performance metrics. Let's forget for the moment that physical presence is, of course, not an indicator of either transfer success or training effectiveness (we will go into more detail on that when we get to Lever No. 12, "Transfer Expectations of the Organization"). Instead, let's focus on what this company's huge training catalog and its focus on the number of training days achieve. In some cases, trainings are well attended; for others, the HR development team wonders how to fill the slots. As a consequence, the HR team uses every opportunity to advertise those trainings: They send out emails encouraging people to sign up; they emphasize making full use of the training allotment available to each employee; they remind managers to send their people to attend. Due to the number of free slots, it may then happen that, for instance, secretaries are sent to a training on "visualizing concepts on flipchart" – fully aware that they've never used a flipchart in their lives and probably never will. But since the training is about "general presentation skills" and those slots need to be filled, they follow HR's recommendation. In this company, employees are faced with an oversupply of training offers. So, rather than feeling elated because they get the chance to attend a training, they feel they should/must use up two more training days this year. Do you realize what this means in terms of significance, value, and, above all, motivation? They all drop! "Training fatigue" is a phenomenon known all too well to the extremely dedicated HR development team, especially when it comes to leadership training.

Here's the other extreme. A distribution company has a very compact employee training program in place. To qualify, employees must achieve certain goals (for example, with a certain annual sales figure you are entitled to attend a training called "Active Selling II"). Or if you have been nominated for the next career step, you're eligible to participate in "Leadership I." In order to attend, you need to apply for a training slot by submitting a letter of motivation. Key figures for the HR development team are "transfer rate" and "number of transfer projects implemented." These figures are published in the half-yearly employee magazine, together with interviews with participants talking about the training and their implementation success and experiences. In addition to the fact that this organization has a much lower training budget, the term "training fatigue" is virtually unheard of there.

What's the difference? It lies in a proven economic principle: the principle of scarcity. Oversupply reduces value. And when training is not considered valuable or meaningful, trainee motivation decreases. Mind you, this does not mean that all educational programs should be radically trimmed down. Rather, I want to encourage you to do as you would with your rosebush: prune individual shoots so the overall plant can grow better. From a transfer perspective, neither a comprehensive educational program nor the number of trainings held are quality criteria for successful HR development. Fewer offers, clearly tailored to company, employee, and transfer needs – this will help you not only free up some of your budget but also to enhance motivation and thus increase transfer success. Plus, the experience of effectiveness in a previously completed training fosters a positive attitude towards the next training.

> A comprehensive training program and the number of training days completed are no indicators of transfer-effective HR work. Have the courage to offer less training. Focus on transfer quality not the quantity of training.

Summary

Transfer motivation is a key factor for transfer success. There are different types of motivation. A less sustainable kind is extrinsic, controlled motivation (such as a supervisor or HR department who monitor implementation through reports and evaluations). This form of motivation usually only exists as long as there is strict control. A much more sustainable form is autonomous motivation – the kind that we feel when applying the new knowledge is fun (intrinsic) or the consequences of applying it are desirable and positive (extrinsic). We can promote this kind of motivation by highlighting the individual benefits of a training and each individual exercise, by providing choices and opportunities to co-decide, by facilitating self-determined learning, and by enhancing transfer through praise and feedback. Self-determination should become the key principle in all transfer interventions. Transfer interventions should always be offers of support and enablement, never pressure or control. Therefore, effective transfer interventions addressed to adults increase both transfer success and transfer motivation. This does not mean, however, that voluntary participation is mandatory for motivation. If trainees consider a training to be attractive and meaningful and have also gained positive experiences with effective training in the past, their nomination or selection for training will further increase their motivation. To enhance the importance of a training, it is advisable to leverage the economic principle of scarcity: offer less training rather than more, but make sure it is tailored to existing needs and supported by appropriate interventions to promote transfer.

HOW TO PROMOTE TRANSFER MOTIVATION

**At a glance:
Ideas for reflection and implementation**

Frame transfer interventions as useful and beneficial
- Real-life examples for benefit-oriented versus controlling wording

Enhance the importance and reputation of your training offers
- Signals from management to reinforce performance
- Testimonials from those who have successfully completed courses
- Reports on transfer successes and interventions
- "Formal" application for programs branded as "transfer-level" trainings

Highlight the purpose and benefits
- Define and communicate transfer goals
- Use transfer goals as a starting point for the training concept
- Explain the benefits of each training component (exercise, input)

Encourage self-initiative and self-responsibility
- Ask the trainees what benefit they want to gain from the training
- Evaluate the self-responsibility trainees take on
- Work with real-life case studies and active learning
- Address theory separately to provide enough time for practical work and realistic learning experiences

Frame transfer interventions as useful and beneficial

Trainees tend to embrace transfer measures (such as trainer hotlines, pre- and post-training discussions, follow-ups, focus groups, practice assignments, etc.) when they find them useful and meaningful. Signs of reluctance or even boycotting of transfer interventions usually indicate that people do not see the point or feel controlled in inappropriate ways. Actually, it's completely logical and under standable, don't you think? What this means for us is that, whenever we plan and implement transfer interventions, we need to pay attention to how we frame and communicate them to the participants. Our communication about the transfer and our transfer-promoting efforts determine how committed people will be and how successful and effective the transfer will be. The rule of thumb, in line with self-determination theory, is: Avoid control-based wording – use supportive and benefit-oriented wording.

Examples: Control-based wording	Examples: supportive, benefit-oriented wording
Management has decided that we need to ensure effective transfer through the following measures ...	It is a key concern of management that you get the most out of this training – both for the company and for yourself. The purpose of these activities is to support your implementation and increase your success.
As of today, we'll have pre-training meetings for everyone delegated to X. Please use the following form ...	In a meeting with your supervisor, you will jointly define how you can optimally use what you have learned. Enclosed is a discussion guide for use as support for a brief pre-training meeting.
We have reached the end of our training. I'll distribute this test sheet so you can review what you have learned ...	We have reached the end of our training. It has been a long and intense day. I now want to invite you to review what we have discussed in a relaxed setting, using this quiz ...
To ensure that the content of the training is effectively transferred into your work, there will be a two-day follow-up meeting. Please bring a presentation on your key implementation successes and difficulties.	Implementation is the most important phase of the training. This is where you will see whether your time investment pays off. We'll therefore have a follow-up meeting to discuss our successes and some aspects of failing, clarify open questions, and jointly tackle implementation challenges. I'd like you to share your experiences and tell us about them in a brief presentation.

Three months ago, you attended my training XY and set yourself the following transfer objectives. [...] This is to remind you about the implementation of your plans. You haven't started yet? Then this is the time to start! Make your first call, enter an appointment in your calendar, ...	Three months have passed since our joint training. I am very curious to learn how you have experienced the implementation so far. Among the many ideas and points discussed, there was one that ended up on your notepad as your key objective: [...]. So, have you been able to put that plan into action? Then I'm very happy for you and congratulate you on your transfer success. Or haven't you had an opportunity to implement it yet? Then I'd encourage you to take the first step right now – make that first phone call, make the first appointment in your calendar, or collect some initial thoughts on your personal division of work time and leisure time. Don't wait for opportunities to arise – create them yourself!
Transfer success is critical to the overall success of our company. We therefore take this opportunity to evaluate it for the training you completed three months ago ...	It is our key concern to offer you top-quality education opportunities with a maximum of practical value. We are therefore interested in knowing how well you have been able to apply what you have learned in your daily work. By participating in this survey, you will help us continuously improve our services to you.

You may wonder, "Is this window dressing, deception, manipulative marketing?" Well, the answer depends on your overall attitude towards promoting transfer. The answer is yes, if you perceive transfer interventions as mere control mechanisms to ensure that trainees will put into practice what they have learned. An attitude from which I firmly distance myself. The above phrases express quite precisely the attitude I prefer: understanding efforts to increase transfer success as a form of support and enablement for self-determined, adult learners. We should never forget that in our communication.

Strengthen the significance and reputation of your training

When participants perceive and experience training as meaningful, their motivation increases. What exactly can we do to make training desirable, valuable, and meaningful? A proven tip from marketing: let opinion-leaders and influential decision-makers contribute their words. How about if, at your next kick-off for your leadership program, the CEO explains why this program is critical and meaningful for the company? How about if the invitation e-mail for the internal sales training is sent by the Head of Sales? Let the board and/or managers express for themselves why this training program is important and useful – whether it be live, via video message, or in written form. Invite managers and/or board members to join the training group in a fireside chat or invite them to the trainees' implementation presentations. Their willingness to do so is usually high – especially for major, more expensive training programs – and will have an impressive effect, as it signals to participants: "Wow! This training (program) is really about something important!"

But what can we do for smaller training programs? The board can hardly be expected to personally get involved in each and every single-day training. No problem. Graduates can be wonderful ambassadors, too. Let participants of a previous training talk about its benefits for them personally and about their implementation successes – at kick-off, in the training description, on the intranet, in your invitation mail, wherever. Let them describe how valuable the training was for them and their work. Personalized experiences like these are especially credible to future trainees, as they will find it easy to identify with former participants (see also pages 56 ff.).

What works for certain training courses obviously also works for certain transfer tools and methods. Use the channels you have at your disposal to communicate over and over again how important, valuable, and useful certain transfer tools are; for example, the pre- and post-training discussions with the supervisor, the transfer book, a follow-up, and all the other tools you'll learn about in this book. What the proven principle "Do good and talk it up" means here is this: promote and achieve transfer success and talk about it over and over again!

What can you do if training fatigue or training inertia has begun to spread in an organization? What if training is considered to be "nice, but not really changing anything," or, worse still, a "waste of time"? How can you make sure people see a difference between the "new" training and the less effective previous trainings? The answer is: let the trainees feel the difference. How? There are countless ways to highlight this uniqueness. Perhaps participants never received personal invitations by e-mail before, with clearly defined goals? Why not start now and take that opportunity to point out that this training will be different? Why not – as mentioned above – have the board or management communicate that very specific expectations are attached to this training? Why not request applications from participants? You may even want to combine all of these elements and, within your training program, introduce a special brand for this new type of training, such as "Transfer-Level Training." Similar to other labels or quality seals, this label could indicate that this training includes transfer-enhancing modules. On a separate page in the training program, you could explain what "Transfer-Level Training" means. The label then signals to attendees that this is something new and different, which can help reduce the negative impact that previous training experiences have had on the general attitude towards this training. In addition, the label would indicate to trainees that there will be additional tasks and developmental steps (a preparatory task, pre- and post-training discussions, a follow-up, a transfer presentation, etc.). Step by step, more and more trainings can be raised to the "transfer level": a good way to gradually and continuously establish transfer interventions.

Make benefits and meaning the focus

Value and purpose are the keywords in transfer promotion. Make sure to place the value for the trainee – the transfer goal – at the center of each training. The transfer goal clearly defines what is supposed to be different in practice after the training and what behavior the training is supposed to achieve. A clearly defined transfer goal provides the basis for a transfer-effective training – both on the conceptual side and on the part of the trainee. Clarifying and sharpening the transfer goals is a challenging task and, at the same time, one of the first and most important ones in the context of clarifying requirements and orders (see also pages 15 ff.).

My advice is to communicate the transfer goals – the value and purpose – to your trainees. Make it a standard part of your training descriptions and also of your introductions to the training sessions. Trainees can only learn with motivation if they know why and what for. While at a younger age, it may still suffice to study to pass an exam or obtain a degree, adult learners become more critical and demanding with age, as far as the "why" is concerned. A certificate or a vague notion of "might come in handy some time" is typically not enough to motivate. Increasingly, it's the content that should be enriching, exciting, and useful in people's work environment. For our training context, this means you should make sure from the start that your trainees have a clear idea of precisely what benefits they will derive from this training, why making the effort will pay off, and what the transfer goals are (see also Lever 4 – Clarity of Expectations).

On the trainer's side, clear transfer goals with significance for the trainees form the key starting point, the logical basis for every transfer-oriented training concept for adult trainees. Unfortunately, it often happens in practice that trainers begin designing a training by determining the content. For example, they begin by listing all the content elements that come to mind with regard to a broadly defined training topic, or with which they have gained experience. They often do this in the form of a "mindmap," placing the training topic at the center and a collection of models, facts, and concepts around it. The result is a content- and trainer-focused concept that, unfortunately, often hardly intersects with participants' needs – in short, a disaster for transfer success and trainee motivation. What should be placed at the center instead is the transfer goal, that is, the specific benefits the training is to offer for participants. If you are a trainer and you work with mindmaps, give it a try! You will come up with completely different results and a much more benefit- and learner-focused concept.

Once the transfer goal has been established as the center of the training design and communicated in the training description, it is important to maintain this benefit focus throughout the entire training. As a trainer, ask yourself this question with every training sequence – every model you introduce, every exercise you have participants do: "How is this model or exercise useful for my participants? How does it help them achieve the transfer goal?" Be critical and be brave. If you cannot answer the question, skip the model or exercise.

If you proceed like this, it will be easy for you to make the benefits and meaning of each sequence clearer to your trainees. It is crucial for mature, self-determined learners to know and feel why this or that particular point is important and why they should deal with it. Ideally, your trainees will be frank about it, so you can respond. Worse, if they keep their questions to themselves and, at the end of the training, state that actually, there wasn't much in this training that was relevant to them. Or say nothing at all. In both cases, transfer success will fail to materialize. To prevent this, it is imperative to meet the (unspoken) need for purpose. Make it a habit to state and explain the purpose and value of each training component in advance.

A highly recommendable model for communicating the meaning clearly and effectively is the Golden Circle, developed by Simon Sinek.[11] Just google it – who knows, it might be the best intro for your next training!

Encourage self-initiative and self-responsibility

Self-determination is a motivator. So, make sure to enable participants to learn for themselves while having them take responsibility for their own learning and transfer success. (Not all responsibility, but a significant part of it.) Exactly how can you do this in the training context? Encourage participants to think about their motivation, for example, by introducing motivational letters as a prerequisite for participation. Ask for specific issues or cases that participants would like to resolve in the training. (On the question as to how you collect and use these so-called "critical incidents," see pages 119 ff.) Address the issue of self-responsibility at the beginning of the training. Ask the group: "How much value do you want to draw from this training?" or "What take-aways are you looking for in today's training session?" At the end of the training, ask how participants have taken responsibility for their own learning success (e.g., in the feedback form). Try to have participants try out things right there in the training sessions, using their own real-life cases and challenges, rather than making up artificial situations. Use a minimum of classroom-format lectures; instead prefer active learning and exercises, shifting the theory part to preparatory work or elements of "blended learning" – a learning style that combines the benefits of face-to-face and e-learning. This way, you can make the time and space needed for the essential things – exercising in the sense of practicing, trying out, getting feedback, and gaining experience. Give trainees as many practical exercises as possible (see also Lever 6 – Active Practice, pages 133 ff.). The more concrete and realistic the learning experience, feedback, and tips, the better the training will be for transfer motivation and transfer success. Last but not least, give trainees some space and time to exchange experiences and, above all, to individually plan their transfer intentions (many ideas for this can be found in Lever 7 – Transfer Planning, pages 171 ff.). With each of these steps, you will help participants to act independently, which provides the basis for the desired feeling of "I am doing this because I want to" – the transfer motivation.

Time for transfer!

Your turn. How could you, in your specific situation, support trainees' transfer motivation? How can you encourage trainees to say, "Yes, I want to apply what I've learned!"? What's the next step you need to take? Write down all ideas and thoughts that come to mind.

This is how I can promote transfer motivation:

[1] Gegenfurtner, A., "Dimensions of motivation to transfer: a longitudinal analysis of their influence on retention, transfer, and attitude change" in: *Vocations and Learning,* 6(2), 2013, pp. 187 – 205.

[2] For correlations between transfer success and transfer motivation see, for example, the meta-analysis of Blume, B. D., Ford, J. K., Baldwin, T. T., & Huang, J. L., "Transfer of Training: A Meta-Analytic Review" in: *Journal of Management,* 36(4), 2010, pp. 1065 – 1105.

[3] Woodworth, R., *Dynamic psychology,* Columbia University Press, 1918.

[4] For a detailed account of self-determination theory, see Deci, E. L., & Ryan, R. M., *Handbook of Self-determination Research,* University of Rochester Press, 2002.

[5] Pink, D. H., *Drive: The Surprising Truth About What Motivates Us.* Riverhead Hardcover, 2009.

[6] Gegenfurtner, A., "Dimensions of motivation to transfer: a longitudinal analysis of their influence on retention, transfer, and attitude change" in: *Vocations and Learning,* 6(2), 2013, pp. 187 – 205.

[7] For the influencing factors and predictors of transfer motivation see, for example, Chiaburu, D. S., & Lindsay, D. R., "Can do or will do? The importance of self-efficacy and instrumentality for training transfer" in: *Human Resource Development International,* 11(2), 2008, pp.199 – 206; Kontoghiorghes, C., "Predicting motivation to learn and motivation to transfer learning back to the job in a service organization: A new systemic model for training effectiveness" in: *Performance Improvement Quarterly,* 15(3), 2002, pp.114 – 129; Rowold, J., "The impact of personality on training-related aspects of motivation: Test of a longitudinal model" in: *Human Resource Development Quarterly,* 18(1), 2007, pp. 9 – 31.

[8] A positive correlation between motivation and voluntary participation can be found in, for example, Cohen, D. J., "What Motivates Trainees?" in: *Training and Development Journal,* 44(11), 1990, pp.91 – 93, and Hicks, W. D., & Klimoski, R. J., "Research Notes. Entry into training programs and its effects on training outcomes. A field Experiment" in: *Academy of Management Journal,* 30(3), 1987, pp. 542 – 552.

[9] There was no significant correlation found between motivation and voluntary participation in, for example, Mathieu, J. E., Martineau, J. W., & Tannenbaum, S. I., "Individual and situational influences on the development of self-efficacy: Implications for training effectiveness" in: *Personnel psychology,* 46(1), 1993, pp. 125 – 147.

[10] A negative connection was found between motivation and voluntary participation in, for example, Baldwin, T., & Magjuka, R., "Organizational training and signals of importance: Linking program outcomes to pre-training expectations" in: *Human Resource Development Quarterly,* 2(1), 1991, pp. 25 – 36.

[11] More about the Golden Circle can be found on Simon Sinek's website www.startwithwhy.com or in his popular book Sinek, S., *Start With Why: How Great Leaders Inspire Everyone To Take Action,* Penguin Books Limited, 2011.

LEVER 2 – SELF-EFFICACY

TWO REAL-LIFE EXAMPLES

Read what Martina and Peter report after a negotiation skills training. Who is more likely to transfer what they've learned into practice?

Martina, 32, key account manager in the energy industry

When I left the training room I felt really confident. I've got a pretty good idea now of what I'm going to try to do in my next negotiation, and I'm confident I'll manage. During the training, I practiced my five favorite negotiation techniques in several role-plays. It worked: I had my negotiating partner in the bag at first try. For fine-tuning, the feedback I got from my peers was extremely helpful; also, I got to implement everything right away in another round of role-plays, which was really great. I was able to see how the outcome and also the course of the discussions got better and better. That boosted my self-confidence for the next negotiation.

Peter, 27, sales representative in the mechanical engineering industry

During the whole ride home from training, my thoughts kept revolving around the price negotiation I was having the following Tuesday. I found the trainer very impressive and admired her for her self-confidence, spontaneity, and eloquence. Negotiating seemed so incredibly easy for her. Like an eel in the water, she slithered effortlessly through the conversation, had just the right negotiating technique ready at all times, always kept charming yet firm. I paid close attention, absorbed all her explanations, and made lots of notes. But will I be able to do what she did? Am I the negotiating type at all? I've just learned these negotiating techniques – should I really try to employ them this soon, at such an important negotiation? Seems kind of risky …

So, what do you think – who is going to have greater transfer success – Martina or Peter? Why?

Peter is still unsure whether he has actually mastered what he learned and how to put it into practice. Martina, on the other hand, has that confident "I can do it" feeling that is essential. She's convinced she has acquired the skills and will be able to achieve results using the negotiating techniques she's learned. This personal conviction is crucial for transfer success. In the relevant literature, this "I can do it" feeling is referred to as self-efficacy: Self-efficacy is defined as a person's conviction that he or she is able to execute certain tasks based on his or her skills and capabilities. It is the firm conviction that one is able to create and achieve something specific. "Yes, we can," as Barack Obama put it. If you firmly believe you can make a difference your (belief in your) self-efficacy is strong. High self-efficacy helps trainees put into practice what they have learned.

SELF-EFFICACY – YES, I CAN!

Self-efficacy in a nutshell	
Trainees say	"Yes, I can!"
Definition	Selfefficacy describes the extent to which someone is convinced he or she can master acquired skills in practice
Guiding question	How can you ensure that, after a training, participants will believe in their ability to apply and master the skills they have acquired

The magical four-minute mile

Developed in the 1970s by Canadian psychologist Albert Bandura, self-efficacy is a common personality concept in psychology and neighboring disciplines. In his highly acclaimed article, Bandura[1] sums up his concept in the impressive story about the runner Roger Bannister.

In competitive sports, the "four-minute mile" was long considered an insurmountable barrier for runners. It was thought that it was physically impossible for a human being to run a mile in less than four minutes. Nobody had ever done it. A physical limit seemed to have been reached. Until Roger Bannister came along – a 25-year-old medical student from the UK. On May 6, 1954, stadium announcer Norris McWhirter announced a new world record. When he got to the time and read the word "three," the crowd broke into a tremendous cheer that drowned out the rest of the announcement. BBC reported live: Roger Bannister had cracked the four-minute mark, the new world record was 3:59.4. And there was an even greater surprise just five weeks later: John Landy broke the world record again, running the mile in 3:58.8. After that, record was followed by record. Roger Bannister's success had cracked the insurmountable four-minute barrier not only for him, but for many more athletes afterwards. The realization that it was possible led to a whole series of new records. High self-efficacy – an inner conviction that "I can do it!" or "It is doable!" – makes the seemingly impossible become possible. The key factor for those records wasn't new material, or a new technique, or other external or objective influences – it was the athletes' higher self-efficacy: the Roger Bannister effect.

As mentioned, scientifically speaking, self-efficacy is defined as "the subjective certainty of being able to cope with new or difficult requirements based on one's own competence."[2] So, the issue is not an "objective" capability but a person's own belief in his or her ability to master a certain situation. This subjective conviction ("I can…") is critical to success or failure. The concept of perceived self-efficacy occurs in various research disciplines (reflected in the fact that more than 500 scientific publications focus on the topic). And we've probably all seen self-help guides that keep emphasizing that "You just need to believe it, and it will be possible." Self-efficacy increases the success of your actions, both in life as such and with regard to training transfer – this has been demonstrated by a number of empirical studies.[3] If training participants believe they will be able to implement what they have learned, a key factor for transfer success is fulfilled.

Blame it on the weatherman

To leverage the concept of self-efficacy for our purposes, we need another concept, one that is commonly referred to as "locus of control." You've probably come across the phenomenon before. Do you know people with a tendency to blame their own failures on external circumstances? "I couldn't do anything about it; it was XY's fault." No matter what goes wrong, it's never their fault. They always blame others, or the circumstances: the weather, an unfortunate coincidence, or their bad luck in general. Psychology refers to this attitude as having an "external locus of control," as individuals concerned seek the reasons why certain things happen (or why things are the way they are) in the external world, not in themselves. Having an external locus of control doesn't necessarily have to relate to failures. Some people also attribute their own successes primarily to external causes: happy coincidences, luck, God or other people. The opposite of an external locus of control is an internal locus of control. People with this attitude believe they control things themselves; they feel responsible and accountable for their own successes and failures. When thinking about the reason why certain things happened, they don't go looking externally but instead think about how they might have contributed to the situation.

But what does locus of control have to do with self-efficacy? And why is it important for us to know? It's simple. Imagine someone thinking things "just happen" to them. They see themselves as passengers, not someone behind the steering wheel of life. People like this will obviously find it hard to believe that they can master challenges on their own. As a consequence, people with an external locus of control usually have lower self-efficacy, too. On the other hand, someone with an internal locus of control who believes that success (or failure) is in their own hands is much more likely to develop self-efficacy. They can build up the belief that their skills will enable them to master situations in practice, including training transfer.

Is it possible to change a person's locus of control and self-efficacy?

You may wonder: Are locus of control and self-efficacy stable qualities or personality traits? Aren't there people who are simply more confident than others – natural go-getters – while others have not been blessed with lots of self-efficacy or much of a sense that they're the captain of their fate, and therefore feel they can't really control anything in this world? Is it possible at all to influence such basic beliefs through a single training? Good question. The good news is, yes, we can influence them, albeit only for a very specific kind of self-efficacy and locus of control.

Both convictions exist in two forms: as a general attitude and as a task-, situation-, or action-related attitude. Regardless of walk of life, there are people who generally have a stronger belief than others in their own ability to influence situations and other people. These people have a high level of generalized self-efficacy. Their typical attitudes are reflected in statements such as the following: "I approach obstacles calmly because I can always trust in my capabilities." Or: "If a problem arises, I can master it on my own." Or: "Even when faced with unforeseen circumstances, I'm sure I can cope."[4] Then again, it's a whole different story when it comes to accomplishing specific tasks, such as quitting smoking, speaking in front of a large crowd, running a marathon, etc. – or, in other words, when self-efficacy or control conviction relates to specific situations, tasks, or actions. Of course, people with high general self-efficacy are more likely to believe in their capabilities to master specific tasks. But it does happen that people who generally have little trust in their own capabilities develops strong self-confidence when faced with a certain task. For our training and transfer topic, what this means is: While we can provide only limited support for people to help them build their general belief in themselves and their influence, what with the short time available in the course of a training, we can certainly help them strengthen their self-efficacy with regard to the training topic. And that's part of what it takes to promote transfer success.

Where does faith in yourself come from?

How can we promote self-efficacy? Where does it originate, how can it be influenced? The creator of the concept, Albert Bandura, explored this question in his research. He identified four drivers of self-efficacy, which will be very useful for our topic here:

(1) Self-efficacy through experience of mastery. A sense of achievement is a true booster of self-efficacy. When someone successfully masters a challenge, this will increase their faith in their own capabilities. They will be more likely to believe they can master similar situations in the future. Failures, on the other hand, can cause people to doubt in their own capabilities and avoid similar situations in the future. To increase trainees' self-efficacy, it is imperative to enable them to experience success – both during the training and at the workplace – and to show them that this success is the result of their own efforts and dedication. So, no matter whether it's a successful role-play, a successful test presentation, etc., let's give our trainees that invigorating feeling: "It's not luck, not just the trainer, not just the good atmosphere in the training room. It's my own merit that allowed me to achieve this!" Based on achievements like these, trainees can and will be just as successful in their everyday work.

> Enable trainees to experience success both in the training and in everyday work. Show them that their achievements are not the result of coincidence or luck but occur because of their own actions.

(2) Self-efficacy through vicarious experience. Here, Albert Bandura's research has produced a particularly remarkable finding: Other people's achievements can also enhance our self-efficacy. In other words, the feeling of "Yes, I can" may also be generated by seeing others successfully master the situation in question. If your sister can speak to a crowd of a thousand people, why shouldn't you be able to? When your child watches you chop wood, he or she will think they can do it, too. And when people see how others have become YouTube stars, they believe that they can do the same. Amazing, isn't it? Our faith in our own abilities increases when we see others

successfully accomplish the tasks or challenges in question. Self-efficacy is promoted by vicarious or "proxy" experiences.[5]

Well, doesn't that sound tempting: You just need to watch successful people and you'll believe in your own abilities!? A Frank Sinatra or Beyoncé concert, and there you go believing in a singing career for yourself? A day with Didi Mateschitz, the founder of Red Bull, and you'll be convinced you can build a globally successful brand? You probably sense there is a catch somewhere. Observing others – gaining experience vicariously or by proxy – only works as a catalyst for our self-efficacy if we can identify with the person we observe. The more we believe we are like that person, the more likely it is that our observation will have a positive impact on our self-efficacy. So, surrounding ourselves with successful people to become successful ourselves does work – but only if these people are, to some extent, like us.

> Watching others successfully complete a task can increase trainees' self-efficacy. The important thing is that they can identify with the people they watch.

(3) Self-efficacy through verbal persuasion. Persuasion helps people believe in themselves. It is easier to believe in ourselves when someone else tells us, "You can do this!" Verbal persuasion from others who trust in our ability to manage a particular task increases our faith in our own capabilities. This also works, by the way, when we do this ourselves – through autosuggestion, that is. There are numerous guidebooks that tell us to stand in front of the mirror twice a day and tell ourselves, "I can do XY." Autosuggestion is a key element of autogenic or mental training. But there are limits even to verbal persuasion, whether it comes from ourselves or others. Actual experiences of success or failure have a much stronger impact. For instance, using the mirror exercise to tell yourself over and over again that you will get a certain job will lose effect if you keep receiving rejections. Also, the verbal persuasion must feel reasonably credible and realistic. Even if your father keeps telling you, say, that you'll become the next Nobel laureate, or the next Steve Jobs, it won't help if you yourself consider this extremely unrealistic. To some up: Verbal persuasion from others increases our self-efficacy, provided we consider the messages somewhat realistic and we don't keep experiencing the opposite.

> Verbal persuasion from others or even themselves helps trainees develop self-efficacy. It is crucial, however, that they consider the statements realistic and don't see them as contradicting their personal experiences.

Unfortunately, this also works very effectively in the opposite direction. Negative language inhibits trainees' self-efficacy and thus transfer success. This is true of destructive self-talk ("I can't do that!"), killer phrases ("It doesn't work like that in our company"), and exercises in defeatism or helplessness ("I'd like to, but I can't …"). It is therefore advisable to pay close attention to verbal persuasion and discouragement in your training, and to intervene as appropriate.

(4) Self-efficacy through emotional arousal. Finally, our gut instincts also play a crucial role in fostering self-efficacy. When we think of an impending task, the though is usually accompanied by physical and emotional signals. And they are very important in determining whether we have that "Yes, I can" feeling or not. Let's put ourselves in the position of a trainee in a negotiating skills training. As a participant, you think of a sales negotiation and the new techniques you've learned and that you now want to use. At the very thought of it, an unpleasant, sinking feeling rises in your throat, your heart beats faster, your hands grow moist, and your knees go weak. Within seconds, your brain concludes, "I'm not going to manage this." That message from your brain fuels your fear even more. Its interpretation of your bodily signals lowers your self-efficacy. In a worst-case scenario, this leads to a vicious circle. Your low self-efficacy leads to physical discomfort (palpitations, sweating, etc.), which, in turn, further reduces your self-efficacy, leading to even stronger physical reactions. You will be less and less inclined to believe that you can master your price negotiations using the new techniques. You will do everything you can to avoid it. Training transfer? Zero. Of course, the same thing also works the other way around. When the thought of doing something triggers a positive gut feeling, a sense of anticipation, a pleasantly tingling excitement, this boosts self-efficacy and thus transfer success. Interestingly, re-interpreting the physical signals can also produce a positive result. After all, wet hands and weak knees don't necessarily have to mean "I can't handle it." In a training setting, trainees might hear from other participants – perhaps successful negotiators – that they, too, have or had these physical signals and that they are completely normal. Trainees could get tips on how to deal with them or some help in re-interpreting them. When that happens, wet hands and trembling knees could be read as a sign that you are leaving your comfort zone and taking a huge development step. Or the physical tension could be interpreted as the body bracing itself for an important battle, and so on. The point is that gut instinct (referred to in psychology literature as "somatic markers") is a crucial factor we should never underestimate in the context of training and transfer. So, give gut instinct some room in your training setting, and the attention it deserves. Help participants work on and resolve negative gut feelings, as self-efficacy and thus transfer success can only occur when participants' gut feeling is positive.

Give gut feelings some room in your training and transfer settings. Help trainees develop a positive gut feeling about the targeted learning activity.

Summary

Roger Bannister gave the world faith: the belief that a mile could be run in less than four minutes. Once he had accomplished that – all of a sudden, others could do it, too. Just because they suddenly had that feeling of "Yes, I can do it!" That feeling is something that training participants also need. For transfer success to occur, we need trainees to believe that they themselves can make a difference (internal locus of control) and that they will be able to implement what they have learned at their workplace. What does this require? It requires an organizational setting that promotes rather than prevents transfer (the organizational levers). It takes a sense of achievement – through trainees' own achievements and/or those of other people with whom trainees can identify. It takes verbal persuasion, both through others' words and through our own positive and supportive thoughts and words. And it takes a positive gut feeling when we think of the upcoming task. Next, let us look at how we can implement these insights into training and transfer practice.

HOW TO PROMOTE SELF-EFFICACY

At a glance:
Ideas for reflection and implementation

Facilitate successful experiences in training
- Have trainees talk about successes they've experienced
- Incorporate exercises of increasing difficulty
- Give praise and feedback

Promote successful experiences in the application phase
- Assign transfer tasks of increasing difficulty, or have people plan them for themselves

Integrate demonstrations into training
- Demonstrate in class what successful behaviors look like
- Contrast positive with negative examples
- Show videos of successful / less successful actions

Tell success stories
- Use stories about individual people instead of anonymous studies
- Have former training participants give testimonials

Work in "What if?" mode
- Integrate and work on real and perceived implementation barriers from trainees' work environment

Have people talk about their successes

Experiences of success are a boost for self-efficacy. We can use that in our training sessions! Design your training in such a way that participants will be able to experience several personal successes during the training itself – personally or in proxy. This may begin with a preparatory task beforehand or in the round of introductions. Why not start a negotiating skills training with trainees introducing themselves not merely by name, but also by giving a brief account of a successful negotiation, or introducing their personal success formula? And bingo – there you'll have several success stories at once, and the "What if?" mode will be activated.

Also, incorporate exercises of increasing levels of difficulty. In your negotiating skills training – to return to this example – you might have people develop a range of answers to typical objections raised in negotiations. Afterwards, the trainees each select the answers that suit them best and are given the opportunity to practice these answers with "standard" objections. The next level of difficulty could be to have objections raised in random order, not the predictable sequence, so participants will also be able to parry them with their prepared answers – another success experience. Work your way towards a real-life negotiation situation, step by step. In a final walk-through, allow your trainees to experience how well the things they've learned can work. Experiencing numerous successes and observing others' success – this is what drives people's self-efficacy and thus transfer success.

By the way, remember what we said about verbal persuasion? By giving constructive feedback and lots of praise, or encouraging other participants to give it, you can enhance the positive effect of success experiences even further.

Promote successful experiences in the application phase

If your trainees leave the training with that "I can do it" feeling, you've achieved a great deal. In addition, you can help them gather more success experiences "out in the wild" step by step. For instance, by giving them transfer tasks. Design the tasks so that success is likely to materialize. Ideally, you'll give your trainees a set of different, increasingly challenging tasks. If possible, have them resolve one of those tasks during training. To illustrate what I mean, let's go back to our example, the negotiating skills training. Let's say the training consists of two all-day sessions. If you give your trainees the assignment to use the new negotiation techniques right in the next customer negotiation they will have, that may be too much for them. And since failure reduces self-efficacy, this may put the transfer at risk. So, it's a much better idea to start by giving them simpler assignments. For example, after the first training day you might ask them to observe their negotiating partners' negotiating skills and read their "negotiating style." Prepare a worksheet for participants to fill out after their next negotiation: Ask them to describe as precisely as possible the techniques their counterparts have used, consciously or not. Ideally, they should also note the wording used. Also instruct them to act the same way in that negotiation as they have before, and not to apply what they have learned. (You will probably see that many will apply some of the new techniques anyway.) After that real-life negotiation, your trainees can reflect on it calmly without pressure and think about what else they could have done. At the next training day, you can have the group discuss and reflect on these transcripts. The next and more demanding assignment could be to prepare for three specific negotiation techniques and react accordingly in the real-life situation; after that, the next assignment would be to use their own technique, etc. You can e-mail participants these increasingly difficult assignments as a standardized mail, or hand them out in class. The ideal solution, of course, is for trainees to define increasingly difficult assignments for themselves – for instance, as part of the transfer planning module (see pages 171 ff.). This way, their individual level of development is appropriately taken into account. The key is for your trainees to gain success experiences in practice, step by step, to increase their self-efficacy and thus the potential for transfer success. At the same time, this also takes care of Lever 3 – Transfer Volition, which I will introduce to you next.

Integrate live demonstrations into your training

As we have seen, self-efficacy is increased not only by people's own successes but also through success experiences by proxy, such as watching people doing things successfully. This is another insight we can leverage in training. Demonstrate to trainees what "success behavior" looks like. As a trainer, you can do it yourself. Lots of trainers talk about techniques, methods, and tips for successful negotiation, many distribute handouts with wording suggestions, note 10 Golden Rules on a flipchart, or have the group work out success factors and "dos & don'ts." Which is all very nice and helpful – but is it enough for trainees to develop that "I can do it" feeling? Hardly. Too many key points can be overlooked when you only talk about them in class (see also Lever 6 – Active Practice, starting on pages 133 ff). So, instead of just talking about successful behavior, show them what it is. In a negotiating skills training, for instance, ask one of the participants to be your negotiation partner and play through a whole negotiation talk. In a training on presentation, demonstrate what a good intro could be. In a training on "mastering difficult conversations," have a difficult conversation with one of the participants, preferably about a real-live topic – an issue one of your trainees is facing. Let trainees experience first-hand how things work in practice. This will enhance your credibility as a trainer, as it is an opportunity to show that you master your topic not only in theory but in practice, too. In addition, it helps you promote trainees' self-efficacy and increase the potential for transfer success. As mentioned before, experience has shown that both positive and negative demonstrations can promote transfer. So why not have two rounds of demonstrations? In one, you make all the mistakes one could possibly make and, in the other, you show best practice. Discussing and reflecting on these opposites will provide trainees with an optimal learning experience.

Do you feel uncomfortable demonstrating things yourself? No problem. There are many other channels for imparting proxy experience. You may want to show videos of successful and less successful negotiations, presentations, and/or debates. For millennials, YouTube videos and tutorials are a good medium for successful learning. So why not use them in class? Whichever way your trainees experience success by proxy, it will enhance their self-efficacy and increase their transfer success.

Tell success stories

"Studies have shown XY to work" – this is how trainers often explain why participants should apply XY, too. A typical response from trainees with low self-efficacy might be, "Yeah, right. Maybe it's been like that in the study – but it's different for me." Objection or an excuse? Whatever it is, it may be justified. Self-efficacy increases if we can identify with successful people – not anonymous studies (for the phenomenon of "personification," see also pages 117 ff.). It is only if we believe that we can actually be those successful people that we will be ready to believe that we can do the same. So, what we need is people who are a) similar to your trainees in some way and b) successful because they've applied the things you teach. If this is not the first time you conduct this training session, you already have those people: It's your former trainees – ideally, from the same organization. Use their achievements to strengthen your current trainees' self-efficacy. You could start, for instance, with your invitation to the training (see also pages 37 ff.): Let them describe in a few sentences what has changed since they attended the training and what they now manage to do better than before. Should a kick-off event be planned, why not invite some of these alumni? Having successful people tell their stories can also work wonders during training itself. Fireside chats or alumni as live guests create an ideal opportunity to report on successful application and strengthen both self-efficacy and transfer motivation. Should this not be possible or too time-consuming and/or costly, give those alumni a voice in your documents (your PowerPoint presentation, your handouts, etc.). Or simply tell those success stories in class. Even after the training, testimonials are a great way to enhance self-efficacy and transfer motivation. For instance, you can write to the trainees about former participants' implementation attempts and successes, or about what obstacles they faced and how they overcame them. Encourage trainees to share their success stories, too. Not only does this show that you are interested and believe in their success; it also helps you gather testimonials for the next training group.

Work in "What if?" mode

For transfer successes to take place, participants need to feel that the conditions in their work environment allow them to implement what they've learned – in other words, they need the conviction that they are in control. But what if they are convinced that they are subject to external control? What if they say, "It's not possible, because the conditions aren't there" or "… because my boss / my colleagues / time / whatever simply don't permit it"? How can we, as trainers, respond? How can we counteract such objections, resistance, and concerns? Using appropriate interventions, we can try to get trainees into the "What if?" mode – get them to move from the passenger seat to the driver's seat.

What if all of these things don't do the trick? What if the whole group thinks that what they've learned is interesting but not feasible? Well, ask them what they think should be done. This, too, puts trainees back in the driver's seat. In fact, you might even ask them whether they want to end the training. After all, this is your time – and theirs – which should be treated with great care. Let the trainees decide whether it makes sense to continue or not.

Are you feeling more and more resistance building up inside? Is your trainer's gut instinct telling you: "No way," or "I've got a job to do," or "I know this can work"? That is perfectly understandable, good, and important. Your reaction shows that you are convinced of the relevance of your training content. You've probably experienced several times that this particular training produces results. Well, no doubt about that. It's not the point here. However, as trainers and HR developers we need to be very much aware that there will never be a model, theory, or content that is universally effective, appropriate, and applicable. The only thing that determines the success of the transfer is what works for this particular organization and these particular trainees. Experience has shown that the crucial organizational conditions for transfer success are, indeed, often missing (more about this when we get to the organizational levers). Sometimes participants are simply correct about that. So, when it happens that, despite all the paraphrasing, questioning, and reflecting, trainees still see no chance to put things into practice at their workplace – whatever the reason may be – they probably won't do it. They won't even try. In such cases, it's only reasonable to stop wasting anybody's time. When dealt with in that way, these situations are often a wonderful opportunity for trainers and HR developers to finally get the issue of transfer on the table, create conditions to support transfer, clearly define the need and the mandate, and make their position on effectiveness crystal clear.

Time for transfer!

Your turn. How can you enhance trainees' transfer motivation? How can you get them to say, "Yes, I want to apply this!"? What's the next step you are going to take? Write down any ideas and thoughts that come to mind.

This is how I can promote self-efficacy:

1 Bandura, A., *Self-efficacy – The Exercise of Control,* New York, W. H. Freeman & Co., 1997, p. 396.

2 Schwarzer, R., & Jerusalem, M., "Das Konzept der Selbstwirksamkeit" in *Zeitschrift für Pädagogik,* 44, 2002, pp.28 – 53, p. 35.

3 For correlations between self-efficacy and transfer effectiveness, see, for example, Blume, B. D., Ford, J. K., Baldwin, T. T., & Huang, J. L., "Transfer of Training: A Meta-Analytic Review" in *Journal of Management,* 36(4), 2010, pp.1065 – 1105; Ford, J. K., Quiñones, M. A., Sego, D. J., & Sorra, J. S., "Factors affecting the opportunity to perform trained tasks on the job" in *Personnel psychology,* 45(3), 1992, pp.511 – 527; Machin, M. A., & Fogarty, G. J., "The Effects of Self-Efficacy, Motivation to Transfer, and Situational Constraints on Transfer Intentions and Transfer of Training" in *Performance Improvement Quarterly,* 10(2), 1997, pp.98 – 115; Machin, M. A., & Fogarty, G. J., "Perceptions of Training-Related Factors and Personal Variables as Predictors of Transfer Implementation Intentions" in *Journal of Business and Psychology,* 18(1), 1997, pp.51 – 71.

4 Schwarzer, R., & Jerusalem, M., "Das Konzept der Selbstwirksamkeit" in *Zeitschrift für Pädagogik,* 44, 2002, pp.28 – 53.

5 On sources of self-efficacy, see, for example, Bandura, A., *Self-efficacy - The Exercise of Control,* W. H. Freeman & Co., New York, 1997

6 On somatic markers, see Damasio, A. R., *Descartes' Irrtum: Fühlen, Denken und das menschliche Gehirn,* Ullstein eBooks 2014 (English title: Descartes' Error: Emotion, Reason, and the Human Brain, Penguin Books, reprint, 2005).

LEVER 3 – TRANSFER VOLITION

TWO PRACTICAL EXAMPLES

A week ago, Klaus and Sabine completed the training "Successful Acquisition by Phone." Both were very pleased with it. Read what is crossing their minds when they think back to that training. Who is more likely to enjoy transfer success in the long run?

Klaus, 42, salesman in the energy sector

> *It's 2:00 p.m. An exhausting day – and now I've got to do phone acquisition. Phew. I could hardly get ahold of anyone yesterday. And then that cold rejection. Yeah, I know, the plan was to make four calls a day. But I'm just not in the right state of mind today. Plus, I really need to review that presentation for Friday once more. The heck with it – tomorrow's another day.*

Sabine, 43, saleswoman in the energy sector

> *It's 2:00 p.m. An exhausting day – and now it's phone acquisition. My post-it note says 'Call four customers right after lunch' in big, fat letters. Okay, yesterday there was one contact I couldn't get a hold of and I got two rejections. But then afterwards I had a chat with Manuela, a peer from my training, and she really built me up again. I realized that it's completely normal to have a tremble in your voice when you start out. Plus, she gave me a great tip for my wording. Alright, so let's grab the phone – at 3 p.m. I'm supposed to call Manuela again to report back on my success!*

What do you think – what makes the difference here?

Telephone acquisition is not a pleasant task (yet) for either Klaus or Sabine. Getting out of their comfort zone, bringing themselves to do it, although more pleasant tasks are waiting, dealing with setbacks, trying again – all of these things require willpower. Klaus has a plan but, when it's time to implement it, starts having doubts, and eventually abandons it. Sabine, on the other hand, sticks to her plan. Using appropriate methods, she manages to muster the necessary willpower, stay on the ball, and follow through. Willpower is crucial for transfer success. In research, willpower is referred to as volition. Volition is needed to implement a plan in general, and the same holds true for transfer goals and plans that training participants have set for themselves. While motivation describes our desire to act or implement a plan ("I want ..."), volition describes our dedication to making the necessary effort ("I will do this – come what may"). As illustrated by Klaus's example, motivation may subside when the implementation situation draws closer or when setbacks throw us off course ("I really wanted to, but ..."). When motivation wanes (temporarily), volition is the battery, the power generator that helps us to pursue our plan nevertheless ("Although I don't really feel like it, I'm going to do this anyway"). In most cases, motivation comes back when success materializes or when the activity gradually gets easier and more fun to do, as a result of the experience gained. So, it takes volition to stick to a plan, stay on the ball, try over and over again, and not let setbacks keep you from reaching your goal in the end. Without volition, participants will hardly be able to achieve their transfer goals and implement their plans. Volition is a crucial ingredient for transfer success.[1]

TRANSFER VOLITION – ACHIEVING TRANSFER SUCCESS WITH WILLPOWER

	Transfer volition in a nutshell
Trainees say	"Yes, I'll stay on the ball and follow through"
Definition	Transfer volition is trainees' ability and willingness to dedicate their attention and energy to the implementation of the transfer plan even when there are obstackles and difficulties.
Guiding question	How can you help tranees to develop the ability and willingness to persistently work on implementing their transfer plan?

Why we don't keep our New Year's resolutions

Scientific research long failed to recognize the power and significance of volition. In motivational psychology, people's goal-oriented action was long explained as follows: If something is really important, desirable, and somehow doable for someone, this person will do anything to achieve it. In other words, if we really want something and consider it halfway feasible, we'll do it – or so goes the theory.[2] Sounds plausible and fits with what the world's leading motivational trainers keep preaching: Sufficient motivation is all we need, and we can achieve anything. However, enticing as this may sound (and familiar as it may be by now), it doesn't always stand the test of reality. Perhaps you've experienced, as I have, that motivation alone is often not enough. Think back to your last New Year's resolution. Perhaps you resolved to exercise more, take better care of yourself, eat healthier, make more time for your family and friends, or stop smoking. You were probably really motivated to implement your plan this year. It was definitely what you wanted. It was also achievable, actually. So, according to the "old school" of motivational psychologists, you should have achieved your goal by now. High motivation = implementation success. If you did, congratulations! Great job! If not, here's a pat on the back: We are in the same boat. Even for me, a lot of motivation does not automatically result in success – lamentably. Over the past years, this insight has spread in motivation and action research, too. Heinz Heckhausen, an influential researcher in this field, called this gap between motivation and implementation the "action gap".[3] To explain this action gap, willpower was (re-) introduced into the scientific debate – rephrased as "volition." While motivation is primarily about choosing and setting goals, it takes volition to turn these goals into results. It is the power that ensures that, despite possible feelings of displeasure, discomfort, fear, listlessness, distractions or temptations, we stay on the ball and implement our plan. Volition is the standby power generator that provides us with energy when our main power supply (motivation) fails.

> To implement a plan, motivation usually isn't enough. Volition is the standby power generator we can use when our main supply (motivation) is down.

What this also shows is that, although volition and motivation are two different things, they are interrelated. If motivation is not particularly high, or if it concerns the implementation of projects where there are competing motivational tendencies, a lot of volition is needed. Consider, for example, people studying for exams. While they often have a strong and pronounced desire to pass that test (motivation), they also want to enjoy their leisure time, not neglect their day job, go to dinner with their business contacts, or just relax on the weekend (competing motivations). If motivation is temporarily low or spread across competing activities, volition – our back-up power generator – is needed for people to sit down and study. Numerous theories, models, and strategies have been created to explain and promote volition, such as the Rubicon Model,[4] the compensatory model of motivation and volition,[5] and the theory of action control.[6] The topic is worth familiarizing yourself with – not only to create transfer interventions for your trainings but also to make sure you'll implement your New Year's resolutions next time around.

Like psychology, transfer research initially mixed up volition with motivation. After what you have read so far, you probably realize that motivation and willpower are two separate things, including when it comes to implementing transfer projects. In a longitudinal study with 1,755 participants, Seiberling and Kauffeld[7] provided empirical evidence that transfer motivation and transfer volition are two separate factors, and that both are crucial to transfer success.

Radishes and the willpower muscle

What about volition, what about willpower? On the one hand, we have professional cyclists, marathon runners, and Ironman participants accomplishing extraordinary athletic achievements, Tibetan monks performing impressive stunts, and our neighbor effortlessly (or so it seems) losing 40 pounds. On the other hand, we all know someone who finds it extremely challenging to go without chocolate even for a day. Why do some people have so much willpower while others seem to have none? And if volition is distributed so unevenly, do we have to accept the amount we've been dealt, or can we change, learn, and "train" it? Scientific studies have shown that it is actually possible to influence one's willpower, albeit with some limitations. Here, the exercising metaphor is particularly apt. The American social psychologist Roy Baumeister compares willpower to a muscle – a muscle that can be trained but has limited capacities, depending on its training status.[8] There is no such thing as a biceps that can go on lifting dumbbells forever, or a thigh muscle able to put up with stairclimbing without ever tiring. Muscles get exhausted; they need to regenerate and recharge to be able to perform again. The same is true of willpower. Once you use it, you can exhaust it – this is an undisputed scientific finding. Roy Baumeister was the first to monitor the limits of willpower systematically. He later became a bestselling author – thanks to radishes! In his almost cruel social experiment, test subjects were told not to eat anything all day. When they got to the lab, ravenous, there was a smell of freshly baked cookies.

The test subjects then sat at a table with three bowls of food: one was filled with fragrant, warm cookies, one with chocolate, and a third with radishes. One group was encouraged to help themselves to the cookies and gorge to their heart's content, another group was only allowed to eat radishes. A control group did not get anything to eat. Even when the scientists left the room, further adding to the temptation, the radishes group continued to resist. What marvelous willpower! But the actual test was yet to follow: Next, the test subjects were taken to another room and given what they were told was an intelligence test. In reality, the questions asked were unsolvable. The purpose of the exercise was to see how long subjects would be willing to try to solve the problem before throwing in the towel – a test of willpower. The result: those who had been allowed to eat cookies and chocolate puzzled over the questions twenty minutes longer on average – and so did the control group that did not get anything to eat. By contrast, those who had had to resist the sweet temptation before – the radishes group – gave up after just eight minutes. So, this group had only 40 percent of their willpower left: their willpower muscle had been exhausted by the earlier challenge.[9]

Roy Baumeister has been carrying out experiments like this one for over 15 years. Over and over again, he conducts sophisticated experiments in his lab to test people's willpower. No matter what the challenge was – to refuse cookies, ignore distractions, suppress anger or negative thoughts, or keep their hands in ice water for as long as possible – participants' willpower decreased over time. The experiments repeatedly confirmed that willpower acts like a muscle that tires.[10] Other scientific research has confirmed this. Smokers who go 24 hours without a cigarette are more likely to indulge in ice cream; drinkers who suppress the urge to have their favorite cocktail fare worse on endurance tests, and people on a diet are more likely to cheat on their partners.[11] When we use willpower, we keep tapping the same power source. And that power source seems to wear out at some point. Just like a muscle.

> Willpower is like a muscle.
> It tires under permanent strain and needs regeneration.

This realization can be very comforting. After all, it means that if you can't give up chocolate for a day, it's not necessarily due to weakness of character. Rather, it's a sign that you've exhausted your available willpower for other things. Perhaps you've sat through a boring meeting, in which your whole body was screaming, "I want out of here!" Perhaps you've treated an annoying customer with infinite patience. Or it took all your willpower to suppress a sharp retort to your colleague, although he'd really deserved it. Being stuck in a traffic jam, having to deal with a screaming child, mustering the energy to cook family dinner, having to change tires today because you promised to do it, making yourself go to the gym, enduring a boring festivity – all of these things tap into the same source of energy, often leaving little willpower for the "really" important things. When critical minds claim our society has collectively lost willpower, perhaps they are right. The cause, however, is much more likely to be an accumulation of collective stress and increasing demands, rather than weakness of character. Stress and willpower are simply incompatible biologically.

So, does this mean that Ironman competitors, Tibetan monks, and your neighbor who's miraculously lost 40 pounds simply face no other demands on their willpower? No stress, no other challenges? Or, put differently: In our modern society, where stress and challenges are integral parts of our daily routine, do we have to resign ourselves to facing life with a shortage of willpower resources? No, we don't, researchers say. As mentioned before, we can train our willpower the same way we would train our biceps or thigh muscle: by integrating small exercises into our everyday lives – such as hiding sweets in the desk drawer and resisting them when we open it, making a habit of doing squats while brushing our teeth, or finally putting an end to all the "uhs" and "erms" when we talk, or riding the bike to work every day. Small, relatively simple, repetitive exercises strengthen our volition.[12]

As discussed before, stress is an antagonist of willpower. The logical conclusion is that if we learn to cope better with stress, we'll get better in terms of willpower, too. And that's exactly what scientific research shows. For example, as little as three hours of meditation improves attention and willpower. After eleven hours of meditation, researchers can even detect changes in the brain.[13] Also, it has been proved that sleeping enough[14] and exercising regularly increases your willpower resources. Even 15 minutes on the treadmill can help dieters stay away from chocolate, and smokers to resist the temptation to have a cigarette.[15] So, instead of viewing sleep, meditation, and exercise as unnecessary and time-consuming, we should perceive them as exercise to strengthen our willpower.

Volition can be trained and strengthened: not only with small willpower exercises, but also with activities that help us cope with stress (such as meditation, sufficient sleep, and physical exercise).

Do you still believe there's a weaker self?

Do you know what else strong-willed people do to keep that willpower? They try to use it as little as possible! Brilliant, right? And quite logical. If volition is available only in limited amounts before it needs to be replenished, it makes a lot of sense to use it sparingly. Actually, there are two kinds of volition: a dictatorial kind – self-control – and a democratic kind, which is referred to as self-regulation. Usually when we think of willpower what we have in mind is the dictatorial kind, so-called self-control. It is about using the power and control of our minds to make something happen regardless of our acute desires or needs. Not eating that cake, forcing yourself to write the darned minutes of that meeting, bringing yourself to exercise even though something inside is absolutely unwilling. We often call this something "our weaker self," and it's something that, according to many self-help guides, we need to "conquer," "fight," or "overcome." Maja Storch, a scientist specializing in willpower research, finds those terms misleading. And she is right. Why should evolution have equipped us with an inner saboteur to undermine our good intentions? A vicious antagonist we need to outsmart and manipulate? There is no evil or "weaker self" wrestling with a good self that has all the right intentions and the good brains. What we do have is two different evaluation systems – each with its own justification and meaning – that work differently.[16]

One is our mind – which is also referred to as intentional memory – where conscious thinking takes place. The other evaluation system is our gut, also referred to as emotional memory: This is where all our experiences are stored and painstakingly tagged with an emotional evaluation (a somatic marker[17]) that says, "I like" / "I don't like." So, if your mind plans a visit to the dentist, your gut may say, "I don't want to" – and justifiably so, due to previous bad experiences and lots of horror stories. Now, self-control means your mind dictates. Your mind drags your gut to the dentist. And that eats up lots of your willpower reserves! Self-regulation, on the other hand, means that your head and gut get into an inner dialogue and reach a democratic decision. This might be something like, "This time, we won't go to that dreadful doctor again, but pay the extra money for this private practice" or "The reward for this visit to the dentist will be a huge banana split." Try out different ideas until your gut says: "Yes, I can accept that" – and you won't need to tap into your willpower reserves. It will not always be possible, of course, to engage in an elaborate inner dialogue to make your mind and gut agree with each other. That's why we also need to train our willpower muscle: so, we can use it when we need it. But let's not forget to use it as sparingly as possible. In other words, the motto for successfully implementing your plans should be: as much self-regulation as possible – and self-control only where absolutely necessary.

> Encourage training participants to listen to their "gut feelings." Use self-regulation (inner dialog) wherever possible. Use self-control (the "dictator") only where absolutely necessary. This way, trainees can spare their willpower muscle.

What helps trainees persevere

What does all this look like in practice? How can volition be enhanced? Although volition research has long been neglected, it is a true treasure chest of volitional (or even self-management) strategies.[18] Let's open this treasure chest and see what it has in store for us. You'll probably smile and nod as you read, as you have probably employed many of these strategies for yourself or in a training context, consciously or unconsciously.

Deliberately focus attention – or: multitasking is a myth. Many of us have learned the hard way that Facebook and other social media don't really help us stay on our projects. We might have the best intentions, but then we are suddenly surrounded by temptations and distractions. "Just check my emails ... get a coffee ... ask my peers how their weekend went ... have a bite of chocolate ... urgently check this thing on the internet ..." TV, the internet, the phone, the people around us – everything seems more tempting than our work. Sometimes, even the vacuum cleaner can keep us from getting started on our projects. What to do? One of the fundamental volitional strategies is to control attention – that is, (1) deliberately focus it on what we've planned to do and (2) deliberately deflect it from anything that distracts us. The sooner we realize we are at risk of being distracted, the better. Recommendations such as: close your email program, turn off Facebook, don't work in a room with your TV on, clear your desk of anything potentially distracting, as unhip as they may sound, have proved to be effective ways to complete what we have set out to do. Incidentally, even the world of business has recognized the threat of distraction. A distraction-free word processor is now (again) available in the market – no apps, no surfing, no emails. Imagine that: distraction-free typing (and modern storage) for a lousy $499.[19]

Another volitional strategy aimed at our attention is environmental and stimulus control. The aim here is to change and shape the physical and/or social environment so as to facilitate our implementation of what we have planned. Practical examples include: putting your sports bag in the trunk of your car to head straight for the gym after work rather than go home first, avoiding smokers' hang-outs if you are trying to quit smoking, making fixed appointments with your peer group rather than parting with a lukewarm "Let's call each other," or moving objects into our line of sight to remind us of things we need to get done. Our habits are particularly strongly linked to situations and environments (work breaks with a cigarette or pastry are a classic here), so it can be very helpful to replace the old habit with a new one and rearrange our surroundings accordingly. Instead of passing the baked goods display in the cafeteria, you bring the apple you had strategically placed on your desk. Instead of having a cigarette during your break, you might have your toothbrush, chewing gum, or apple at hand and start your break by brushing your teeth and then spend your time in the coffee lounge rather than the smoking area.

This strategy of directing one's attention also works for training transfer. Give trainees the time and space to shape their social and physical environment in a way that will promote transfer, for example, by deliberately placing little reminders. To promote transfer, it is important to keep calling people's attention to their transfer goals and plans, even after the training. I'll introduce some tools for that a little later on.

> Strengthen your participants' volition by calling their attention to their transfer plans, over and over again.

Boost motivation – spare the willpower muscle

This chapter has already touched on the differences and interrelations between volition and motivation. We know that willpower requires a great deal of self-control, especially when motivation is low. By the same token, this means we need less willpower if we can increase motivation. Professor Julius Kuhl, willpower researcher and developer of the PSI theory and framework, calls this volitional strategy "motivation control." He describes it as the deliberate creation and strengthening of one's own motivation in relation to a specific goal or wish. In professional sports, athletes often work with mental images – that is, they imagine and visualize achieving a goal. By consciously picturing what it will be like to have achieved what we plan to do, how we will feel, how proud it will make both us and others, etc., we can increase our motivation.[20] The opposite works, too. If we imagine how uncomfortable we will feel if we do not achieve our goals, and how unpleasant the consequences will be both for us and for others, we will also increase our motivation. Provided we have made good preparations, it can help in a low-motivation phase of implementation to simply think back to why this transfer plan was so important to us – which goes to show how valuable it is to have written down those motives and have them available during down phases. (To ensure this, in the transfer planning module at the end of your training, you may want to ask participants to write down their motives in their transfer book or make an audio file (see pages 173 ff.). Another approach is to have trainees revisit how much work they have done towards their goal and what sub-goals they have already achieved (this can also be part of the relevant transfer planning module, see also pages 173 ff.). The key to this volition strategy is this: If we enhance motivation in the actual implementation situation, it will require less willpower for us to finish implementing our projects.

Methods such as imagining and mentally contrasting good and bad outcomes, or reviewing the motives for one's plans, can help increase motivation and spare the willpower muscle.

Work with your emotions – do not believe everything you feel

Another strategy for strengthening volition is to actively work with your own emotions. As mentioned earlier, the implementation of our plans doesn't always come with pleasant feelings. You face an exam – and promptly get a numbing headache or stomach pains. Your presentation is scheduled for tomorrow – and the mere thought of it makes you weak in the knees. A look at the phone you're supposed to use for making cold calls, and your pulse starts racing. To avoid feelings like these, we tend to postpone projects and eventually forget about them. That may bring emotional relief – but our plan has failed.

What can we do to stay on the ball despite these unpleasant sensations? Three things. First, accept them. Be prepared for them and have a plan for how to deal with them. Second, try to make them more pleasant. Third, attach a new interpretation to your gut feeling (this is called cognitive restructuring[21]). If the thought of the exam causes pain, try to divide the way there into small, emotionally acceptable steps. Perhaps your stomach can deal with stepping into the car? Yes? Then let's go! Can it deal with meeting colleagues for a coffee? Great! Can it deal with having a quick look at the exam sheets to decide whether to stay or go? Super! And so on. How do you get through your presentation when you're feeling weak in the knees? Perhaps it helps to identify your favorite part of the presentation and focus on it. Or to memorize the first and the last sentence, and tell yourself everything else is less important. You could practice understanding stage fright as a sign that this presentation matters to you, and you take it seriously. Or that after the presentation, you'll treat yourself to a bike ride, and you look forward to it. For your acquisition call, you might decide to sit outside in the sun to make it more pleasant. Or to make the call at the same time as your colleague does, which might make it more fun. Or you give your gut feeling a new interpretation: "I am feeling tremendous energy, which I can use for my call." The point is: We do not have to instantly believe everything we feel. We can prepare ourselves for it, actively work with it, and use it for our purposes!

In short, emotional work is about being prepared for, or changing, potential unpleasant emotions so that they will not distract us from our plans. For our transfer theme, this means – once again – that we should give our gut feelings some space. The better trainees familiarize themselves with the gut feeling that will come with their transfer plans, and the better they prepare themselves for using it constructively, the easier they will find implementation. That is why it is advisable to actively work with people's gut feelings in training, and to make the transfer palatable not only to the mind, but also to the gut (see also pages 165 ff.).

> Help trainees to prepare transfer not only with their minds but also with their "guts."

Process information sparingly – avoid "second-guessing" yourself

Perhaps you've decided at some point that you want to clear out your garage or basement or go on a twenty-minutes run every day. Everything was well thought out, deadlines fixed, the necessary conditions created. But as the deadline loomed, you started wondering more and more whether your project really made that much sense. Shouldn't you better clear out the garage with your partner present? And didn't you need something only yesterday that had been sitting in the garage forever, and suddenly came in very handy – so perhaps it would be better not to throw everything away? Or you happen to hear a TV report or a colleague pointing out that jogging isn't that healthy after all, and that other sports such as swimming and yoga are much more effective? You start revisiting your plan, and the time you had set aside for it passes unused. Willpower researcher Julius Kuhl points out that this is precisely what we should avoid: forever second-guessing our plans versus alternatives and throwing our good intentions overboard. He also recommends that we limit the amount of information we take in after making a decision, after careful consideration, so as not to let this information divert us from our plans (there will always be colleagues and studies that make one sport appear better than another). In terms of volition techniques, we can even make use of the fact that in our modern world, we will always be able to find information to confirm or refute our plans. Why not look for lots of "friendly" information and people when preparing for implementation? When we're in the process of implementation, our mind will take that step anyway – looking for confirmation, so why not take it now? Yes, from a volition perspective, it makes perfect sense to give trainees published reports that confirm their transfer plans. You can give trainees such reports as pre-reading or further reading – or have them research positive studies as an exercise. Later on, in the implementation phase, they will then be able to revisit this information and prevent themselves from carrying on another "Is that really true?" debate in their minds.

> Make sure participants have a range of information at hand that confirms the value of their transfer plans. This can help prevent second-guessing, i.e., that, once they face implementation, they will start weighing the pros and cons again.

The question of how to avoid lengthy deliberations is something you can take into account as early as in the planning phase. Studies have shown, for example, that "if-then" plans can significantly increase the probability of implementation (see also pages 162 ff.). The more specific participants are when mapping and shaping their transfer plans, the greater the odds they won't start weighing the pros and cons again. This step demonstrably helps trainees put their transfer plans into action.

Observe, evaluate, and reward yourself – "I'm the one behind the wheel"

Another volition strategy is to observe yourself with regard to the desired behavior. This helps focus your attention on the behavior you aspire to and emphasizes your responsibility for your own behavior. As such, self-observation prepares trainees for an active role in the transfer process and sensitizes them to what kind of behavior to aim for. In addition, their awareness of their actual versus their target behavior can enhance motivation. Depending on the trainees and their development level, self-observation tasks can be assigned very specifically (e.g., observe frequencies, identify emotions, etc.). Sometimes, however, a subtle, inductive form of self-observation is more appropriate (such as, "In your next meetings, you will probably notice the killer phrases you keep using yourself ..."). In most cases, self-observation is associated with informal or formal self-evaluation. Trainees who observe themselves will also assess their current behavior or their progress in goal achievement during the transfer phase. This keeps up their motivation and ensures that they will stay focused on their projects. An additional boost for motivation can result from the self-reinforcement – or rewards – people give themselves. These can be simple things like a bar of chocolate, a smiley sticker, an extra hour of online gaming, an entry on a progress chart, a beer after work, or an evening out with the training peers. Or they can be hidden motivation boosters, the kind that automatically sets in when you realize you are successful – such as self-praise, a clear conscience, or a sense of pride. All of these encourage trainees to stick to their transfer plans.

Give your trainees assignments for self-observation, self-evaluation, and self-reward. These assignments promote trainees' determination and responsibility, and thus transfer success.

User self-commitment – What will others think?

Essentially, the self-commitment strategy consists in irrevocably committing yourself to a goal and determining the path that leads to it. Methods such as making a contract with yourself have become quite common in a number of fields, including transfer effectiveness. Self-commitment is particularly effective when combined with social pressure or social recognition. What others think of us is crucial for us as humans (we will discuss this in more detail when we get to the levers "support from peers and support from supervisors"). We humans make an extra effort to be perceived as individuals who stand by their word and practice what we preach (on striving for consistency, see also pages 260 ff.). Preventing others from thinking we can't keep our word or are inconsistent provides the basis for proven tips such as: "Tell as many people as possible" that you are planning to do XYZ or "Get help from others" to finish your projects. You've probably heard about (or been given) the recommendation to make regular appointments with a training partner to go to the gym. It will make it rather unpleasant for you to skip your exercise – after all, there is social pressure. In digital times, social pressure can quickly build up to much higher levels. The writer Drew Magary offers a somewhat extreme example: Determined to lose weight, he invented what he called the "public humiliation diet," including the announcement that he would tweet an update on his weight once a day. Another example is the software "Covenant Eyes." To help people spend less time surfing the internet, the app registers every single web site a person visits and sends the results to people that person has chosen, e.g., his or her boss or partner. Users of "stickK.com" can set their account so that the software will send an automatic email to their friends (or enemies) if they fail to achieve their plans. Whether you agree or disagree with these somewhat bizarre forms of self-commitment – one thing's certain: the basic idea works. Self-commitment in combination with social pressure or social recognition helps us persevere. For our topic here, promoting transfer effectiveness, the power of social pressure and social recognition results in a variety of tips and tools, such as the transfer journal or transfer coaching, transfer partnership, the presentation of transfer achievements to management, and many other tools we will discuss at a later point.

> Promote participants' self-commitment to their transfer plans. Reinforce it by integrating elements that add some social pressure and social recognition.

Manage barriers – come what may

With the strategies mentioned so far, trainees will be well equipped and prepared in terms of volition. That is, provided that everything happens the way the trainee intended. And this is the snag – because in practice, things often don't go according to plan. Real life holds its surprises and obstacles, expected or unexpected, physical or social. Suddenly there's that urgent customer request that eats up all the energy trainees need for their implementation task. Or someone has a boss who likes to drop the occasional snide remark about the transfer plan. Or someone's child falls ill, and after taking two weeks off to take care of the little patient that person first needs to clear the backlog of work before he or she can even think of tackling the transfer plan. Or perhaps there are inner barriers, such as the tendency to postpone the project over and over again.

Trainees can prepare for these barriers – foreseeable or not. Above all, they can learn to deal constructively with setbacks and relapses into old, unwanted behavioral patterns that could otherwise cause them to abandon the project entirely. The factors that make it difficult for people to persevere or cause them to give up are highly individual. One person might be left devastated by colleagues mocking their new behavior, another might feel even more motivated to prove them wrong. To find out what obstacles threaten an individual's transfer success, it can be helpful to ask questions such as "What would be the worst thing that could happen now?" or "What would you say could distract you from following through with your plan?" Even just considering the possibility that obstacles may get in the way will help trainees prepare themselves by developing counter-strategies for the biggest obstacles right there in the training session.

> Have your participants develop strategies for dealing with obstacles, both expected and unexpected. To identify the most important ones, ask them questions such as: "What could keep you from following through with this?" Or: "What could make you drop this plan?"

At this point it should be noted that dealing with obstacles and/or cases of relapse can, unfortunately, have side-effects – for instance, a negative effect on self-efficacy. When people think about why something they want to do might not work, it does prepare them for reality – but it may also affect their belief in their ability to implement their plans. So, addressing obstacles makes sense only with individuals whose self-efficacy is fairly well-developed. Hence my recommendation: address obstacles only if participants' self-efficacy permits it; also, encourage trainees to focus intensely on those of their resources and strengths that they will need to overcome potential obstacles.

Summary

"If trainees are truly motivated, then they will apply what they have learned." Really? Nice and simple as this may sound – especially given that it's what motivational trainers keep telling us – it usually does not work that way in practice. Even when trainees' spirits and motivation are high at the end of a training, transfer plans often fail because of what is commonly (and unjustly) referred to as "the weaker self". Training participants need volition to stay on the ball, even when they don't feel like it, when other things seem more enticing, when they're not in the right mood, or when they've forgotten all about it. Willpower is like a muscle. A muscle that tires when we overwork it. So, let's help trainees require as little as possible of their precious willpower resources. The way this works is by working with their gut feel rather than against it, and by using one of several proven volition strategies. With suitable measures, we can keep directing people's attention back to their transfer projects, even after training. We can help them convince not only their head but also their guts of the benefits of their transfer plans. We can assist them by providing information and clean transfer plans, so they won't start weighing the pros and cons over and over again, and put them in control of their activities through self-observation, self-evaluation, and self-reward. We can also use social pressure and barrier management to help them follow through. Next, we'll take a look at what this looks like in practice.

HOW TO STRENGTHEN TRANSFER VOLITION

**At a glance:
Ideas for reflection and implementation**

Keep trainees' attention on their transfer plans
- Send reminder emails
- Send letters / mails / voice messages to yourself
- Ask about implementation successes
- Share success stories and other tips with the group via social media
- Send reminders based on symbols and tools already deployed in training (or develop new ones)

Use follow-up formats
- Plan follow-ups with clear goals, benefits, and procedures
- Share transfer successes and progress
- Discuss and process transfer obstacles
- Prepare follow-ups effectively

Create a transfer magazine or journal
- Trainees keep a log or draft a magazine article for the participants' group journal, e.g., email newsletter, to report on transfer successes, what they've learned, and steps they took to overcome obstacles to successful transfer
- Also conceivable in other formats (blogs, videos, podcasts)

Include transfer coaching
- Trainees work with their transfer coach to implement the goals and plans that resulted from the training

Teach volition strategies
- Communicate general strategies and techniques that help trainees to implement their transfer plans
- Use the transfer-strength method to foster self-learning skills.

Keep trainees' attention on their transfer plans

We have already learned that volition depends on, among other things, the attention we dedicate to our plans – and the same is true, of course, for transfer plans: the more attention they get, the greater trainees' transfer volition will be and the greater the potential for transfer success. So, how do we ensure trainees keep their attention on their transfer projects? Well, for one thing, we can remind them repeatedly. With modern technology, reminders are not only simple and inexpensive but also time efficient. For example, send trainees reminders by email. In these messages, you can repeat particularly important points, remind them of their plans, and/or give them small implementation tasks. To make it easier and reduce the time you invest in composing the reminders, you might try the good old "letter or email to myself" technique. If you don't feel like typing yourself, try a "voicemail to myself." If you can make the time to speak to people individually, call them some time after the training and ask how their transfer efforts are coming along. Perhaps you have kept copies of written notes that trainees made for themselves during transfer planning – in that case, you can attach these to your e-mail or scan them and send them via text message. And/or create groups on WhatsApp, LinkedIn, or similar with your trainees, where you can post tips and little tasks, and have trainees share their progress with the group. Any type of reminder will focus people's attention on their transfer plans and promote transfer success.

According to attention control research, haptic memories such as items or symbols can work, too. If your trainees learn some of these techniques, one idea is to develop symbols for each techniques and print them on workplace objects such as mousepads and mugs. Reminder symbols such as a pyramid, a cube, or a T-shirt (as a symbol) can also be effective to remind people to implement what they have learned. Have participants record their transfer plans on sticky notes, which they stick to their screens. (These work particularly well if they also have a box to check off as "Done"). If the transfer intention is a continuous and permanent change in behavior (such as taking regular daily lunch breaks, making four sales calls per week, etc.), you can prepare a tear-off calendar to use each time the new, targeted behavior is successfully performed.

Creating reminders can also be a part of the training. For example, you can use checklists, "Ten Golden Rules," or ideal process sequences in the initial training sessions, which participants then take along to use at their workplaces. The key is to make them handy and compact – postcard or letter sizes have proved particularly useful. So, instead of giving people the usual notepad or book that will disappear in the desk drawer, prepare a blotting pad. This can be a nicely designed A2 poster or – the faster solution – half a flipchart sheet that is placed on each participant's desk or place at the table throughout the training. Its purpose is for participants to make notes on key content points and their transfer plans. Back at the office, they are to put this sheet on their desk as a blotting pad, and steady, authentic reminder of their transfer to do's. Of course, a key prerequisite for this is that participants still have a desk. For those who don't, here's a variant: a digital photo of this sheet full or notes, used as a desktop background on their PC, mobile phone, or tablet.

In the English-speaking world, "lap books" are becoming popular. This is a scrap-book-like format, typically with a "window shutter" cover. Participants gradually create their lap books during a training module or course by summarizing key content for themselves playfully and in a graphically appealing way. Google it! It can be a great tool – not only for children but also for adult learning.

Use follow-up formats

A common approach for increasing transfer volition and thus transfer success is to hold follow-up events after the actual training. Depending on the format, the participants – with or without the trainer(s) – meet again a few weeks or months later to discuss implementation progress. Unfortunately, follow-up formats often have a bad reputation, and companies are often unwilling to pay for them. Why? Because they often lack a concept or agenda – simply "Let's see what pops up." As a result, they tend to consist of long silences and poorly planned, even meaningless ad-hoc activities. Or they are used for content elements that didn't get enough time at the actual training. Sometimes they are even used to continue with the training and crammed with new content – and not as intended: to support the implementation of what trainees have learned.

Follow-up sessions eat up time and resources, so make sure they are worth the expense and design them with the same care as the training itself. The aim and focus of a follow-up session must be clearly defined, transparent, meaningful, and attractive to the client, the contractor, and the trainees. Follow-ups are not about conveying new content. They should strengthen training transfer by having participants exchange their transfer successes and obstacles, and work on finding solutions. A key prerequisite is that, at the initial training, participants have defined specific transfer plans and received clear assignments that can be reviewed at the follow-up session. It is particularly helpful to agree with participants on a process for documenting their achievements and the barriers they face in the time between the training and the follow-up session (such as transfer books/journal entries, assignments containing questions to reflect on, etc.). A week or two before the scheduled follow-up session, it is advisable to remind trainees to complete their assignments and books (an e-mail should suffice) and, if applicable, ask them to each prepare a short presentation. Once participants realize there will be a follow-up format at which they are supposed to report on their progress – in whatever form – they have another good reason to put their shoulders to the wheel and implement their transfer plans. In addition, follow-up sessions as such help people deal with setbacks in constructive and action-oriented ways and to get recognition for their transfer achievements. Properly organized, follow-up events also enhance trainees' self-efficacy and transfer motivation, and can thus be triggers for transfer success.

Create a transfer magazine or journal

Transfer magazines or journals are also ideal for multi-module training programs. A transfer journal is a small newsletter or magazine in which trainees compactly summarize their successes, failures, experiences and learnings. Between the modules of the program, the participants' homework includes describing their implementation attempts in short articles with meaningful headlines. (This can be a great task for transfer partnerships, or peer groups interviewing each other for their articles, see also the "Support from Peers" lever). The assignment for these articles is to describe what you have tried out in practice and what successes or obstacles have arisen. Plus, if possible, how to overcome these obstacles, and who can provide ideas or support. Depending on layout constraints, the ideal article length has proved to be a half to a full A4 page per participant. The inclusion of pictures and illustrations makes the transfer journal more visually appealing. Send a simple layout template before or after the module with the assignment to return the article before the start of the next module. The collected articles can be sent to all participants as a recap and additional motivation before the next module. At the end of the entire program, each participant receives the collected articles as a complete transfer journal - a great memento of the learning and transfer process.

And it can also be a great way to show future participants what they can potentially achieve through the program. Incidentally, in the age of blogs, podcasts, and YouTube video clips, transfer journals are conceivable in a wide variety of formats. And for those who are less keen on writing, there is also the "illustrated booklet" format: simply take a picture that shows, literally or symbolically, a successful aspect of implementation, with a short caption – a sentence or even just an explanatory word.

Include transfer coaching

Coaching has already been successfully established in many companies as a human resource development tool. For investment-intensive leadership programs, in particular, there is a trend towards increasing the number of accompanying coaching sessions to provide participants with individual support in their development. A future-oriented and promising form of this support is transfer coaching. Instead of initiating new development topics in a parallel coaching process - which is unfortunately the exception rather than the rule - the transfer coach should support the participant in realizing the project plans and goals set in the training. One of the most important tasks of the transfer coach: Ensure commitment. It makes a decisive difference for trainees when someone is interested in their implementation efforts and successes, asks questions, and willingly provides hints and assists, thus motivating trainees to stay on the ball. A second key task: Accompanying the individual participants in overcoming possible obstacles, supporting them in dealing with setbacks, and ensuring that they do not throw in the towel prematurely. Transfer coaching can manifest itself in various forms: face-to-face or virtual, in personal conversation, by phone or in the form of emails, social media chats, Skype conversations, WhatsApp messages, etc. The role of the transfer coach can be assumed by the trainer who designed the relevant training, or also by other external or internal coaches. It is important that no new topics are opened up during the process of transfer coaching to keep the sole focus on achieving transfer from the training.

Teach volition strategies

It pays to educate people in companies regarding volitional abilities and strategies - not just in terms of transfer, but more generally. Because when we look at research results as well as our own personal experience, many may need a few more implementation skills, for both professional and personal success. Professor Waldemar Pelz puts it this way: "We are knowledge giants, but implementation dwarfs."[22]

Many organizations already offer self-management seminars that deal with this topic. And paradoxically, the transfer problem manifests itself in such training. It would be useful for trainees to avoid looking for new individual goals and projects in such trainings, and, instead, work with what is already there and ready - for example, the transfer project. Integrate a self-management module into your program or course, in which participants learn more about the learning and transfer process (see also pages 221 ff.). Practice various volition strategies and encourage trainees to immediately use and implement them for their own transfer plans. Trainers from other modules can refer to transfer and build it up, making transfer a consistently recurring theme. Of course, the strategies learned in those other modules help not only in this course, but also in all other trainings. And more generally, when it comes to sticking to what you set out to do.

And what if you don't have a multi-module program or course, where you can integrate a test and/or module for transfer? Every trainer should have a basic knowledge of transfer-promoting strategies, which they can impart to trainees in a compact form, and with which they can help them along the way. And if there is no time to do this in training, send the trainees an email with some reading attached, such as "How to implement – The 10 strategies for your transfer success."

Time for transfer!

Now it's your turn! How could you encourage transfer volition? How do you support your trainees in sticking to their transfer plans in their day-to-day work? What is the next step that you would like to implement? Off the top of your head, write down your ideas and thoughts.

This is how I will encourage transfer volition:

[1] On the correlation between volition and transfer, see, for example, Seiberling, C., & Kauffeld, S., *Volition to transfer – Making transfer of training happen.* Paper presented at the EAWOP, Münster, May 2013.

[2] See, for example, expectation-by-value models summarized in Heckhausen, J., & Heckhausen, H., *Motivation und Handeln,* Springer, 2010.

[3] Heckhausen, H., "Neuere Entwicklungen in der Motivationsforschung," Paper on new developments in motivation research presented at the 32nd Congress of the German Psychological Society, Zürich, 1981.

[4] For the Rubicon Model, see, for example, Achtziger, A., & Gollwitzer, P. M., "Rubikonmodell der Handlungsphasen" in V. Brandstätter, & J. H. Otto (Eds.), *Handbuch der Allgemeinen Psychologie – Motivation und Emotion,* 2009, pp. 150 – 156: Hofgrefe Verlag.

[5] For the intersection model, see Kehr, H. M., *Authentisches Selbstmanagement: Übungen zur Steigerung von Motivation und Willensstärke,* Beltz, 2009.

[6] The theory of action control is described, for example, in Kuhl, J., "Motivation und Handlungskontrolle: Ohne guten Willen geht es nicht" in *Jenseits des Rubikon,* Springer, 1997, pp.101 – 120.

[7] Seiberling, C., & Kauffeld, S., *Volition to transfer – Making transfer of training happen.* Paper presented at the EAWOP, Münster, May 2013.

[8] Scientific findings on willpower are entertainingly summarized in the bestseller by Baumeister, R. F., & Tierney, J., *Willpower: Rediscovering the greatest human strength,* Penguin, 2011. (German translation Baumeister, R., & Tierney, J., *Die Macht der Disziplin,* Frankfurt: Campus, 2012).

[9] The radish experiment and others are detailed in Baumeister, R. F., Bratslavsky, E., Muraven, M., & Tice, D. M., "Ego depletion: Is the active self a limited resource?" in *Journal of personality and social psychology,* 1998, 74(5): p. 1252.

[10] Various experiments on ego depletion can be found in Muraven, M., Tice, D. M., & Baumeister, R. F., "Self-control as a limited resource: Regulatory depletion patterns" in *Journal of personality and social psychology,* 1998, 74(3): p. 774. See also Baumeister, R. F., Vohs, K. D., & Tice, D. M., "The strength model of self-control" in *Current directions in psychological science,* 2007, 16(6): pp. 351 – 355.

[11] These exciting findings can be found summarized in McGonigal, K., *Bergauf mit Rückenwind: Willenskraft effizient einsetzen,* Goldmann Verlag. e-Book, 2012, Chapter 3.

[12] For the willpower exercises, see Baumeister, R., & Tierney, J., 2012. Die Macht der Disziplin, Frankfurt, Campus, 2012, pp. 145 ff. See also McGonigal, K., *Bergauf mit Rückenwind: Willenskraft effizient einsetzen,* Goldmann Verlag, e-Book, 2012, Chapter 1.

[13] Hölzel, B. K., Carmody, J., Vangel, M., Congleton, C., Yerramsetti, S. M., Gard, T., & Lazar, S. W., "Mindfulness practice leads to increases in regional brain gray matter density" in *Psychiatry Research: Neuroimaging,* 2011, 191(1): pp. 36 – 43.

[14] For studies on the effects of sleep, see, for example, Killgore, W. D., Kahn-Greene, E. T., Lipizzi, E. L., Newman, R. A., Kamimori, G. H., & Balkin, T. J., "Sleep deprivation reduces perceived emotional intelligence and constructive thinking skills" in *Sleep Medicine,* 2008, 9(5): pp. 517 – 526. See also Yoo, S.-S., Gujar, N., Hu, P., Jolesz, F. A., & Walker, M. P., "The human emotional brain without sleep—A prefrontal amygdala disconnect" in *Current Biology,* 2007, 17(20): pp. R877 – R878.

[15] For the study with chocolate, see Van Rensburg, K. J., Taylor, A., & Hodgson, T., "The effects of acute exercise on attentional bias towards smoking-related stimuli during temporary abstinence from smoking" in *Addiction,* 2009, 104(11): pp. 1910 – 1917. For the study with smoking, see Taylor, A. H., & Oliver, A. J., "Acute effects of brisk walking on urges to eat chocolate, affect, and responses to a stressor and chocolate cue. An experimental study" in *Appetite,* 2009, 52(1): pp. 155 – 160.

[16] The two evaluation systems (in contrast to one's weaker self, the devil inside) are covered in a simple but vivid manner in: Storch, M., *Machen Sie doch, was Sie wollen! – Wie ein Strudelwurm den Weg zu Zufriedenheit und Freiheit zeigt,* Huber. e-Book, 2009a.

[17] On the theory of somatic markers, see Damasio, A., Tranel, D., & Damasio, H., "Somatic Markers and the Guidance of Behavior: Theory and Preliminary Testing" in: S. H. Levin, H. H. Eisenberg, & B. A.L. (Eds.), *Frontal Lobe Function and Dysfunction,* New York: Oxford University Press, 1991, pp. 217 – 228. See also Damasio, R., *Descartes' Irrtum: Fühlen, Denken und das menschliche Gehirn,* Ullstein eBooks, 2014.

[18] Various volition strategies, incl. the Rubicon model, can be found in Heckhausen, J., & Heckhausen, H., *Motivation und Handeln:* Springer, 2010. Action control theory is discussed, for example, in Kuhl, J., 1994, "A theory of action and state orientations" in Kuhl, & J. Beckmann (Eds.), *Volition and Personality,* Seattle: Hofgrefe & Huber, 1994, 9 – 46. The motivation-volition model is discussed, for example, in Fuchs, R., "Körperliche Aktivität" in R. Schwarzer (Ed.), *Enzyklopädie der Psychologie. Gesundheitspsychologie,* Göttingen: Hofgrefe, 2005, pp. 447 – 465.

[19] The distraction-free typewriter Freewrite https://getfreewrite.com/ (retrieved: 27 June 2016). Reviewed by Ivo Senden at https://www.youtube.com/watch?v=7p6OdqWnAWU (retrieved 29 May 2018)

[20] Kehr, H. M., *Authentisches Selbstmanagement: Übungen zur Steigerung von Motivation und Willensstärke,* Beltz, 2009.

[21] For cognitive restructuring, see, for example, Wilken, B., *Methoden der kognitiven Umstrukturierung: Ein Leitfaden für die psychotherapeutische Praxis,* Kohlhammer Verlag, 2015.

[22] For more on Prof. Waldemar Pelz and his research, visit his website http://www.wpelz.de/ (21 April 2016).

LEVERS FOR TRAINING DESIGN

It is not about learning new things,
but about learning to put useful things into practice.
After all, the true sign of a training's success is not the applause at the
end, but the real value created in our day-to-day work.

(adapted from Ingo Krawiec)

Lever 4
Clarity of Expectations

Lever 5
Content Relevance

Lever 6
Active Practice

Lever 7
Transfer Planning

In this part, you will learn:

- Why asking about expectations in a training session is a waste of time,
- Why we're indifferent to 100,000 deaths,
- How to make a memorable impact on trainees,
- Why you can get along without SMART objectives,
- And what you can do to set the levers in training design to "transfer effective."

LEVER 4 – CLARITY OF EXPECTATIONS

TWO PRACTICAL EXAMPLES

Nina and Matthias will participate in two different trainings on "Thinking and acting strategically" tomorrow. Read what went through their minds the day before. Can you work out who is more likely to have greater transfer success?

Nina, 39, team leader in a bank

> *So tomorrow – management training again – mandatory – that's just great! My desk is full, and I'm supposed to focus on strategic thinking. Which "strategy" anyway? My boss decides what to do, and – let's be honest – that changes every day. So why do I need to learn to think strategically? I'm not allowed to think for myself. And anyway, "strategic" is nothing but a buzzword – hot air – nothing tangible. I'm curious as to which highly scientific models the trainer will share with us. I just hope my boss doesn't call me again to ask where I am right now. Well, I'll just sit there and let it happen!*

Matthias, 38, head of department at an insurance company

> *Yes, I feel I'm now sufficiently prepared for the training tomorrow. To be honest, I don't think I've ever dealt with our strategy paper in such detail before. It's been really enlightening! The questions and assignments the trainer sent us in advance all made sense. The conversation with my boss was also really informative: The corporate strategy affects all departments and teams – everyone should make their own contribution and make decisions based on the overall strategic direction. The seminar description reads: "Benefits: Using strategy tools such as BSC, SWOT, and BCG as the basis for the strategic orientation of your department." – Great! These are tools I need urgently. After all, my boss expects my presentation in three weeks. I am really thankful that I was nominated for the training!*

What do you think? In your opinion, who will be more successful in transferring, Nina or Matthias? Why?

Nina is negative about training. She does not know why she should go. She sees no clear benefits to her. Matthias, on the other hand, has a clear and positive picture of what the training will involve. He knows what content is being processed in the training, and what goals should be achieved. It is completely clear to him what the practical benefits of training are, what he needs to learn for his everyday work, and how he will put it into practice. For transfer success, it is crucial that the participants have a clear picture of what to expect before, during and after a training. You need to know in advance what to expect and what is to be expected of you. The advance information is optimally positively connoted by the participants and shows them the need and urgency, and also the personal benefit that they can derive from the training. They enter the training with optimism and a willingness to learn. A high degree of clarity of expectations is a key ingredient for transfer success in practice.[1]

CLARITY OF EXPECTATIONS – MAKING GOALS TRANSPARENT

⊞	Clarity of expectations in a nutshell
Trainees say	"I know what I'm supposed to learn, and I want to learn it!"
Definition	Clarity of expectations is the extent to which trainees already know before the training what they can expect before, during, and after the training.
Guiding question	How can you make sure that trainees know what to expect before the training and what is expected from them as a result of the training?

Why we always fall for Swiss chocolate

It is a much-cited phenomenon: What we expect is usually what happens. In the past few years, many psychological studies have been published that astonish and at the same time make us smile: the same type of chocolate tastes better to test subjects when they are told that it comes from Switzerland instead of China – because they expect it to.

A completely ineffective drug can help alleviate pain if a subject has been previously assured that it will produce the desired effect (the famous placebo effect), and a more expensive energy drink will allow a person to complete more tasks than a cheaper equivalent.[2] These and a variety of other examples examined scientifically show that what we expect to happen actually does happen too regularly to be just a matter of chance. But why?

Two mechanisms are crucial: self-fulfillment (again something to smile about) and motivational fulfillment[3] (something very practical for our transfer theme). Take the above example with the chocolate from China or from Switzerland. Here, the expectation itself (Swiss chocolate tastes better than chocolate from China) is crucial to its fulfilment. The expectation influences our perception. We experience (and taste) the echo of our own idea of how it should be, and unconsciously seek even the smallest information and emotions that confirm our expectation (also known as "confirmation bias"). Through this unconscious self-deception, expectations cause their own fulfillment – as with the "Swiss" chocolate!

Do I want to tell you that you should stir up your trainees' positive expectations, so that they rate your training more positively as a result of confirmation bias? Of course not! After all, our goal for our training efforts is to bring about development and change, and not simply satisfy ourselves with a subjectively perceived change. (Though there'll certainly be no negative effect on the reputation of the HR department or repeat business for trainers!)

Fortunately, in addition to self-fulfillment, there is a much more practical mechanism that meets expectations: motivational fulfillment. Let's return to our examples: Drinking a more expensive energy drink can result in completing more work compared with drinking a low-priced drink. This measured difference cannot be explained by an influence on or distortion of perception alone. Our expectations also mean that we exert ourselves more. We expect the drink to give us a performance boost and are thus automatically more focused and actually achieve better results – expectation fulfilled! That's pretty convenient for our trainings. If our participants expect training to improve their sales performance through better closing techniques (the transfer goal of the training), then their motivation, commitment, and effort in training will increase, and the expected result will be achieved with a probability that is greater than sheer chance.

What participants expect from a training usually happens, because
(1) Expectations influence perception and how we interpret experience, and
(2) Participants subconsciously make a greater effort in order to meet their expectations.

Be sure to deliberately generate positive expectations for your training session!

How lumberjacks shape our current management

The renowned goal-setting theory of Locke and Latham has for more than 25 years been concerned with the question of what goals should be and what they should do. Their insights began with a pivotal discovery made by newly-qualified work psychologist Gary Latham at his company – the American Pulpwood Association. This company turned wood into paper and employed its own lumberjack crews to bring in the necessary raw materials. The task for Latham: find a way to increase the number of trees felled per day. With his idea, he not only made his career, he also made history. The solution sounds so simple and banal: instead of telling the loggers as before to fell as many trees as possible, Gary Latham gave them a specific number of trees to fell on a daily basis.[4] The number was based on what the best 10 % of lumberjack crews managed daily. So, it was a very challenging and very concrete goal. And therein lies the secret. It turned out that significantly more trees were felled as a result of setting this goal. And with a cost-free and surprisingly simple change! Today, more than 400 laboratory and field studies have documented the core message of the goal-setting theory. Clearly defined, challenging goals lead to higher performance than vague goals or goals of the "do your best" format.[5] In other words, clear goals increase performance. Today, working with clear goals is a well-known and generally accepted core element of successful management – without most of us realizing that this idea was developed in the logging industry!

Why does it work? Why do concrete, challenging goals increase performance? This can also be answered. In short, there are four impressive mechanisms that result in performance increases[6]: (1) Clear, challenging goals draw our attention to goal-relevant activities. (2) They energize and encourage us to exert ourselves to the fullest extent. (3) They increase the persistence with which we engage and manage. (4) They help us to use, rediscover,
and acquire knowledge and strategies that help us achieve our goals. It's really amazing. As soon as you have a goal clearly in mind, it has already started to take effect. Sales people with the goal of acquiring new customers focus their attention on this, invest their time and effort into the project, and eagerly look for ways to reach the goal. Perhaps you are thinking of setting yourself the goal of increasing the

transfer effectiveness of your trainings? Do it! Because even the act of identifying the goal starts the ball rolling. Amazing, or what? Of course, this useful effect also applies in the training context. If participants have a goal in advance – a clear picture of what they are to achieve through training – the four target mechanisms begin to work. And in some cases, even before the training has begun. It's always amazing to see what happens when transfer goals are communicated (transfer goals such as "consultants will use client-appropriate language during consultancy sessions" or "executives will operationalize and implement the corporate strategy within their departments"). It is only when goals are set and communicated (for example during a pre-training meeting) that future trainees change their behavior – even before the training on the new behavior has taken place. That's the impressive effect of clear goals!

Ensure that goals are clear and transparent!
Clear goals increase transfer success, because they
(1) Focus trainees' attention,
(2) Raise trainees' energy levels,
(3) Increase trainees' persistence in working to meet their goals, and
(4) Ensure that trainees make use of familiar and proven strategies for success.

Why placebos don't always work

So, is it enough to just tell the participants what will be better, easier, faster, and simpler after the training, and to stir up positive expectations, perhaps even positive feelings? Not really.[7] There are also a few terms and conditions necessary to bring about the effects of this grand interplay of expectations and goal fulfillment. So, let's turn to the small print.

In order for the goal-setting mechanisms to achieve their performance-enhancing effect, participants need commitment to the goal, and therefore must identify with it. They must consider it important and believe that they can achieve it. Intuitively, one may assume that this works particularly well if the trainees set their own goals. Perhaps that means there should be no pre-set goals that apply to everyone? Participants should instead come to the training with their own personal goals? (In this context, one often hears such delightful terms as "participant-oriented" or "customized" or "bespoke" or "individually tailored to each participant." In these trainings, you spend the first 30 to 60 minutes mulling over questions about your expectations.) In practice, it is difficult or rather impossible to fully satisfy 10 to 15 completely divergent goals in a training with pinpoint accuracy and depth, especially when the trainer first learns of them in the training. Not to mention that, in the organization itself, there is also a client with a vision. For this and other reasons, which will be discussed later, clearly defined transfer goals, which are to be universally applied to all trainees, are a must. But what about the performance-enhancing effect of goals that are assigned and not self-imposed? Do the goal-setting mechanisms still work if goals are set externally, by third parties? An interesting question with a surprising answer. While many studies have shown that goals set by trainers and/or the organization top-down or with trainees' participation and input are equally effective in terms of boosting performance, other studies have shown the opposite. As a result, different researchers teamed up to resolve this (supposed) contradiction. What they found was this: from a motivational point of view, it does not matter whether you set yourself a goal, whether you set it as part of a collaborative effort, or whether it is assigned, as long as the goal makes sense or is backed with reasons. When it is clear, or is explained, why a goal is important and meaningful, then, in terms of the effect, a top-down goal is in no way inferior to a goal that has been set in a participatory manner.[8] It is important that the trainee understands why the training (or the transfer goal) is important and meaningful, i.e., exactly the opposite of the "I don't really know why I'm here" mindset. It is therefore highly worthwhile to discuss goals with a supervisor in a kick-off, an information event, or a pre-training discussion and to clarify the reasons.

Another condition for the goal-setting mechanisms to work is that the participant believes that achieving the goal is possible. Goal-setting theory stipulates that goals should be challenging, but not overwhelming. If the target is set too high, participants do not believe they can achieve it, and then it has no performance-enhancing effect. Accordingly, it is advisable to specifically target trainees' self-efficacy before the training and exert a positive influence on their belief that they are able to attain the goal or goals (see Lever 2 – Self-Efficacy). Again, the pre-training discussion with the supervisor is particularly suitable for this. It also helps to arrange for upcoming trainees to receive training reports or transfer newsletters or journals in which past course graduates describe how they achieved their goals, or reports from trainers that communicate in a credible way that achieving the goals through training is definitely feasible. If participants rate the transfer goals as challenging but feasible with the help of the training, then the goals themselves will already begin to enhance performance.

Our expectations are also influenced by our experience so far and by our assessment of the credibility of the person who sets the goal. Announcements about the upcoming training and what it can and should achieve must be credible to the trainees. That's only too understandable. If you take a medicine that has not worked the last 10 times, it will not work, even if the package leaflet or your doctor insists it will – your expectation of its effect feeds on your experience. And if your doctor or the package leaflet does not seem credible, you will not even get the famous placebo effect, let alone the actual effect of the medicine. The same applies to training. Whether expectations develop a "self-fulfilling effect" depends crucially on what experiences we have had so far, and how credible we believe the person supplying the information to be. And so it is with participants in your training. If participants have so far experienced mainly ineffective trainings or training descriptions, or the HR department, the managers, or the trainers, who are enthusiastic about the benefits of the training, do not come across as credible, the desired effects of setting goals and expectations will be missing. Or they will work, but in the opposite direction. Participants think, "So far, these trainings have never been of any use to me, so how can more training change that?" It creates a negative expectation that becomes reality through the mechanisms of self- and/or motivational fulfilment.

Hence the recommendation: In addition to the content-related work that you have been doing for many years, you should aim specifically at building up the reputation of training within your organization. Use marketing methods to highlight the importance, relevance, and usefulness of your trainings. And if your future trainings will result in significantly more transfer successes through appropriate tools and methods, then highlight this distinctiveness in your advance communication for upcoming trainings (for example, by sending a short video in advance instead of a classic training description). Put the new transfer effectiveness in the spotlight! Awaken the expectation that such trainings will be different from now on, namely stronger in terms of transfer – because expectations then become reality!

> Actively market training!
> Communicate expectations and goals credibly and highlight the new focus on successful transfer!

Describe your training with the clarity and directness of a child at play

Speaking of training descriptions and clarity, let's get practical and look at how and where trainees' expectations are usually formed. Trainees' first (and often only) point of contact with a potential training program is usually the training description. In practice, this often takes the form of a pamphlet or booklet (the "Company Training Catalog"). It can be anything from a glossy brochure to a plain-vanilla Word file available for download on the training provider's website. Unfortunately, training descriptions – whether concise or wordy – are often full of buzzwords from the training industry (you may have already noticed the astonishing range of contexts in which people use words such as "holistic," "strategic," "competence-oriented," "experience-based," "practice-driven," etc.). If your PC is within reach, you can see for yourself.

Check out the website of a training provider. Carefully read a training description – one that sounds attractive to you. Now explain to your 10-year-old child what exactly will be different for you after this training, what the training will do for you personally, and what exactly you expect from it – but without the buzzwords! (Your child might say, "Tomorrow night, I'm going to build a wind-up car that goes much faster than Dad's – it'll be so good that it'll go into mass production.") Can you make a similarly concrete statement about the training you're considering? If so, you've found a great provider with an excellent description! Or do you have some difficulty in explaining what's in it for you, concretely? Then you're looking at an example that, unfortunately, pretty much reflects the standard for training descriptions. And that's a pity, because good training descriptions are THE medium to use to shape positive expectations about training – quickly and easily.

With a good training description, you can:

- Park interest in your training,
- Increase trainees' motivation to take part in the training
- (or get potential participants to sign up for the training),
- Make sure that the most suitable people attend the training,
- Shape and stimulate trainees' expectations,
- Influence trainees' perceived self-efficacy,
- Inform trainees what they can expect before, during, and after the training,
- Influence how positively or negatively trainees perceive the training and trainer, and
- Influence trainees' learning and transfer success.

It pays to invest time in designing transfer-effective training descriptions (see the checklist on page 97 to assess the strengths and improvement potential of your training description). Trainees have a right to know what to expect and what they will experience in a training. In addition, you shape expectations with it, and usually also meet them.

Adult learners deserve transparency. Avoid empty phrases and wording associated with marketing hype. Describe the training clearly and unambiguously!

Eliciting "expectations" in a training is a waste of time

When training descriptions are unclear, it is especially common for trainers to try to clarify what is about to happen once everyone is in the seminar room. An established method here is the "expectations session" at the beginning of the training. After introductions, the trainer asks the trainees what they expect. One of the most frequent answers is: "I have no specific expectations, I'll allow myself to be surprised." On the other hand, if participants get carried away with concrete statements, it can happen that a multitude of divergent expectations suddenly start to appear on the flipchart. So many that it becomes obvious that addressing all these expectations would expand beyond the, say, two-day window and into a two-week training session. Quite apart from the fact that trainees' spur-of-the-moment expectations often differ significantly from the client's. In this situation, trainers face the dilemma of choosing between two less-than-attractive options: either to work only superficially to try to meet at least a large part of the expectations (to the detriment of the depth of the training and at the expense of many practical exercises), or to exclude many of the expectations on the spot as "not part of the seminar." This set of mini-rejections is hardly conducive to motivating participants, who may feel like "jumping ship" at this point. In the final analysis, everyone has also lost at least an hour of valuable training time.

> Asking about expectations at the start of a training wastes valuable time and is potentially damaging. It is much better to clarify expectations before the training begins!

Summary

Adult learners have the right to know what to expect and what personal and organizational benefits they can hope to gain from training – in a concrete way and without meaningless verbiage. Then trainers can focus, get started immediately, and conduct their trainings to achieve the (transfer) goals they were designed to meet. Creating positive expectations and setting concrete transfer goals contribute to their realization through the four goal-setting mechanisms – focusing attention, energizing, increasing persistence, and relying on familiar/proven knowledge – as well as the mechanisms of self-fulfillment and motivational fulfillment. They increase learners' motivation, commitment, and persistence and thus encourage transfer success. It is therefore worthwhile to create clarity, communicate goals, and generate positive expectations in many different ways.

HOW TO IMPROVE THE CLARITY OF EXPECTATIONS

 At a glance:
Ideas for reflection and implementation

Make sure that training descriptions promote transfer
- Describe transfer and training goals clearly; avoid hype or fuzzy phrases
- Arouse curiosity and exert a positive influence on self-efficacy
- Use our checklist to find the strengths and improvement potential of your training description

Use kick-offs (before the training per se)
- Convey program content and its impact
- Beware of accepting pseudo-program points

Motivate through clear goals
- Send a "goals" email and generate a positive atmosphere
- Surprise with a video message, voice message, "Prezi-style" presentation, etc.

Ask about expectations *before* the training
- Free online survey tools
- Digital bulletin board

Sharpen focus with pre-training self-assessment
- Self-assessment with core messages from the training
- Self-assessment with transfer goals (also usable after implementation as transfer evaluation)

Distribute prep work and pre-readings
- Arouse curiosity and stimulate with interesting and provocative documents
- Include practical examples to familiarize trainees with task designs upfront

Make the training descriptions transfer-promoting

The training descriptions in your catalog, on your website, etc. typically provide trainees with their first impression. There is no second chance for a first impression – this is not just a popular phrase, but also borne out by scientific research. The training description is usually the basis upon which we decide whether we enroll in the training or not. And it shapes our expectations, which, as discussed, are usually self-fulfilling. The training description is the simplest and most widely used medium for creating clear expectations and thus positively influencing the motivation, attitude, perception, and transfer success in advance. Make sure that the benefits of the training (the transfer goals) and the training goals are communicated clearly and unambiguously, without nebulous phrases. Make your trainees curious about the training. And deliberately use your description to address self-efficacy by creating confidence, motivation, and anticipation.

Test your description in practice! Ask people in your target group who are interested in the training topic to read your training description. Ask them to what extent the following statements are true and why/why not. Their answers will help you find the strengths and improvement potential of your training description.

Strengths and improvement potential of your training description	Your score (1–4)
Please rate the following statements from 1: "Disagree strongly" to 4: "Agree strongly"	
(1) The training description is attention-getting and sparks curiosity This description caught my attention and made me curious about the training.	
(2) The training description shows "what's in it for me" I understand what practical benefits the training offers me personally. I know exactly what will be different in practice after the training, and how and where I will apply what I have learned.	
(3) The training description is clear and appealing I can understand the training description with a brief read-through. I don't have to read the entire text carefully to get the information I need.	
(4) The description makes the training goals clear It's clear what I will know and be able to do by the end of the training. The statements are concrete and free of clichés.	
(5) The training description creates transparency and clarity I have a clear picture of what activities the training will involve. I know what I can and will learn for myself and my day-to-day life. And I can judge whether the level is right for me, my current level of knowledge, and my experience.	

(6) The training description makes me feel confident, motivated, and eager to participate I have the feeling that this training will help me in my everyday life. I am confident that I will succeed in learning and applying the content, and am looking forward to the training.	
(7) The training description succinctly conveys all relevant information I have been able to find all the information relevant to me expressed in a way that is brief and to the point.	
(8) The training description is active and written from my perspective It does not use passive, impersonal language to describe what will happen to me or in the training; instead, it describes what I will experience and be able to co-create for myself.	
(9) The training description makes clear how I can contribute to my own success The description clearly conveys that I have to play an active role to make the training successful and sustainable for me.	
(10) For optional training: The description helps me decide whether or not to take part The training description helps me to decide whether the training is right for me.	

By the way, training descriptions don't always have to be printed on glossy paper! Why not use new media here? As a trainer, you can shape expectations and make the training announcement fresh and exciting by using videos, Prezi presentations, audio files, a small website, chats, a learning or transfer platform (see also pages 313 ff.) or a description using (virtual) objects. Creativity counts!

Use kick-offs

Kick-offs – held before the training per se – are already very common – and rightly so – especially with multi-module training programs. They are a proven and highly effective tool, not just for the expectations lever.

With kick-offs, you can ensure ...	How it works (examples)
... that stakeholders (trainees, trainers, executives, HR development, management, organizers, etc.), have a **clear image of the transfer goals** and **intended benefits** of the program	• **Management** explains why training program exists, and what exactly the organization expects in terms of benefits • **Training graduates** report on what they got out of the program. If they're not present in person, possible substitutes are videos or displays in the room showing past participants' statements and photos • **Transfer goals** are presented, including how they relate to meeting the organization's objectives
... that **open questions** relating to the program are clarified in advance (this saves a lot of discussion time in the modules)	• **Modules and accompanying elements** of the program are presented (and can be taken home as a handout) • **Requirements and criteria** for successful completion of the course are outlined (helpful: templates, checklists, samples, etc.) • **Questions are collected** in advance or during the kick-off **and clarified** in a plenary session. (The questions can be addressed to different persons (organization team, graduates, trainers, etc.))
... that **trainees get to know one another,** "size up" people attending, and make initial social connections	• **Trainers and trainees** introduce themselves (via plenary session, presentation, partner interview, introductions in the room, etc.) • Participants get better acquainted through **group work or team-building exercises**
... that the participants perceive the program as **important** and start the training program **confident, motivated, and with positive expectations**	• **Importance** is highlighted/enhanced by presence/words of organization's senior leaders and or the trainees' own senior management • **Confidence** increases due to exposure to reports by past participants and credibility of trainers • **Motivation and positive expectations** are encouraged by attractive and transparent transfer goals

In practice, the kick-off format ranges from a half-hour informational get-together in the lecture-and-discussion format to a one- or even several-day workshop in which the focus is on the trainees themselves. Done well, both formats provide clarity of expectations and thus encourage transfer success. While brief lectures spare resources, longer workshop formats have the advantage of encouraging commitment and emotional participation, making it easier to overcome resistance. In addition, a kick-off workshop can help you fine-tune the design of the training program. But beware! Do not accept or formulate pseudo-program points that come up at the kick-off. If you claim in the kick-off that you will address the participants' expectations, then you must incorporate such points into the program – genuinely. And if roles are jointly defined in the kick-off, then they should be handled as agreed. If all this is already fixed in advance, however, then spare yourself workshop-like elements at the kick-off and choose a better format for presenting and discussing information about your training.

Motivate through clear goals

Here's a little thought experiment. Put yourself in the position of a trainee. Several months ago, you signed up for a training session and made a note of the date. Everyday life continued, as fast-paced and demanding as always. One day, your calendar alerts you: Training tomorrow! You quickly get on the internet to check the venue, directions, and starting time. The next day you arrive and just manage to remember the title of the training. But who is up at the front of the room and what the goals and content are – that's all just a blurry memory. Given the pace of work these days, this is quite human and understandable, but not exactly conducive to transfer success, as we have already discussed. What can we do as trainers and HR developers to counteract all-too-human forgetfulness or, more positively, just-in-time approach? One possibility: send participants an email summarizing the goals and content shortly before the training. Many organizations and trainers now do this as a standard practice, and that's a good thing. A motivational, personalized email from the trainer brings to mind the long-forgotten training description, shows respect and appreciation, and thus generates a positive attitude and sense of anticipation before the training. Use the advance email to clearly define the training and transfer goals and introduce yourself as a trainer; encourage participants to submit their questions, suggestions, and wishes; and/or communicate preparatory tasks, documents, or interview invitations (various ideas can be found starting on page 103). Experience shows that, although there will be few direct replies to this mail, the mood and sense of familiarity at the beginning of the training are significantly brighter and warmer – not to mention the clarity of expectations, all of which encourages transfer success. Incidentally, it doesn't have to always be just written text in an email. Take advantage of other media, surprise your audience with a video, a voice message, a PowerPoint or video clip, etc. This shows the trainees in advance: this training is something special!

Ask about expectations before the training

As already discussed, it is damaging to wait until participants arrive at the training to ask about or attempt to clarify their expectations. What's the alternative? Quite simply, ask them about their expectations before the training. Online, this is quick, simple, and free of charge. Just think about how you currently cover expectations in your trainings and convert the questions to digital form. With software programs such as SurveyMonkey, LimeSurvey, or Google Forms,[10] you can create online surveys in minutes and (currently) for free. Simply include the link in the invitation mail to the trainees. Do you find surveys boring? Do you prefer to ask about expectations with the help of a flipchart? No problem. That, too, can be digitized in advance. For example, the online software "Padlet"[11] enables you to create a digital whiteboard in less than five minutes. You can send the link to the board by email to your participants, and they can post their expectations, fears, wishes etc. onto it, just like in a seminar room. Of course, most other social media with which you can organize group chats will work for this, too. With the pre-expectation questionnaire you can optimally prepare yourself, save valuable training time, respond immediately to overly divergent expectations, and also ensure that your participants begin to think about the training topic in advance.

Sharpen focus with pre- and post-training self-assessment

Participants' expectations for the training influence what happens in the training, what the trainees focus on, and how much they get involved. Trainers can use and reinforce this effect in a very targeted way. Put the goals and/or content of the training into a self-assessment form to be filled out in advance by the trainees. Let's look at this with a practical example. Imagine you are the trainer for a train-the-trainer program. Your target group consists of experienced trainers who want to further develop their existing training concepts. You want to get your participants to focus on particularly relevant points in advance. Two of the key messages of your training are: (1) Design a training so that your trainees have a sense of achievement, and (2): Ensure that trainees are active for at least 50 % of the training time. How can you bring these and other key messages into play beforehand? Quite simply: You send a self-assessment form to your trainees, which contains precisely these key messages – of course, reformulated as a self-assessment. With the help of this self-assessment form, your participants should first reflect on and evaluate their training concept.

Please indicate to what extent the statement applies to your current concept (ACTUAL value) and to what extent in your opinion the statement should apply to your future concept (TARGET value)

My participants have, during the course of my training, multiple opportunities for a personal, meaningful sense of achievement	My ACTUAL value: _____ My TARGET value: _____
The participants are active at least 50% of the training time. They practice, try, work out and/or reflect for themselves at least half of the training time	My ACTUAL value: _____ My TARGET value: _____

What effect does this have? By providing a short self-assessment, you ensure that your participants begin to deal with the core messages in advance, reflect on their own training concepts, and consider development potential and possible solutions. In parallel, they form expectations for the training. Furthermore, by prompting participants to rate the current state with an actual value and enter a desired target value, you also gently trigger thoughts on their expectations for themselves. All of this encourages transfer – and all of it is set in motion with a simple self-assessment form! Think about it. What could such a form look like to prepare the ground for your next training?

By the way, you can also re-use a self-assessment for a possible follow-up training or as a reminder email. After the initial training, re-send the self-assessment form a second time. Invite trainees to enter their new actual value and see how close they are to their intended target value. Reflect on the progress in the follow-up or allow trainees to report back by email.

A self-assessment form is an especially elegant, effective, and efficient way to sharpen the focus on the goals of training programs with several modules. Simply take the transfer goals as self-assessment items and ask trainees-to-be before the training how well they perform in terms of these success-critical behaviors. Following the training, ask again after the implementation phase. In this way, you can even use the self-evaluation as a way of evaluating transfer success (see also Lever 12 – Transfer Expectations in the Organization). After all, this second self-assessment will tell you how close or far trainees are from meeting their goals after the implementation phase, making it essentially a measurement of change in the success-critical behaviors (transfer goals) from before to after. Allow trainees to submit the completed forms anonymously!

	Before the training I was able to do it ... (0-100%)	Now, (after the implementation phase), I am able to do it ... (0-100%)	Progress before and after (0-100%)
Transfer Goal 1 e. g.: Before I go to my client meeting, I will prepare a Business Window			
Transfer Goal 2 e. g.: In the sales discussion, I talk less than my client			
Transfer Goal 3			
Transfer Goal 4			
etc.			

At this point, an important caveat. Sometimes the assessment of one's own behavior changes during the training. In our example, it might be that a participant is convinced before the training that he or she talks less than the client (they therefore give themselves 80 percent in the "before the training" column). Role playing, inputs, and feedback during the training make this participant aware that, in reality, they almost always speak more than their client (now they would only mark 20 percent in "before the training"). Of course, this change makes a big difference in the before-and-after progress column. Bring up this phenomenon in discussion with your participants. To deal with it, some trainers and human resource developers issue the self-assessment questionnaire twice: once before a training, and once at the end of or after the training. Or they may immediately involve management as transfer supporters. The self-assessment questionnaire will then be completed before and after not only by the participant, but also by, or with the assistance of, his or her supervisor. The complementary perspective makes the assessment more objective and is also an ingenious tool to foster supervisor support (see Lever 10 – Support from Supervisors).

Send prep work and pre-readings in advance

Before the training session, send your trainees documents and/or preparatory tasks to make them curious and to prepare them for the upcoming training. Exciting studies, provocative journal articles, case studies, videos, hypotheses, research tasks, an upstream e-learning series, questions for reflection, interview questions, etc. are all well-suited to introducing the content prior to the training and get participants focused. In addition, preparatory documents and assignments allow for a quicker and more direct entry into the training itself, especially if you start your training with solutions or reflection on the pre-reading and tasks. In addition, you save time in the training for what's really valuable: activities! The following table offers some practical examples for inspiration.

Designing preparatory tasks – Selected practical examples

In management training
Find an example

Instructions before the training
"Find a picture of a leader who impresses you (e.g., Gandhi, Steve Jobs, a well-known conductor, etc.) and bring this picture to the training."

Possible activities / further work in training
- Hold a discussion in which the trainees introduce not only themselves, but also the leader whom they've chosen as a role model. Let the trainees explain why they chose this particular role model.
- Or brainstorm "examples of impressive leadership" (actions) to get you started, and let the trainees describe each of the characteristics that make their chosen role model so impressive. Collect the answers on the flipchart.

In Change Management Training:
Reflect on key factors for success and failure

Instructions before the training
"Read the following case descriptions of successful and failed change management projects. Why was the first project successful? Why did the second one fail? Bring your notes to the training." (Appendix: case descriptions)

Possible activities / Further work in training
- Collect the dos & don'ts for change management in group work or a plenary session

In a Train-the-Trainer Seminar
A provocative article as a teaser

Instructions before the training
"Training is a useless waste of money; it destroys capital! This is the main claim made in a German bestseller The Training Lie. Do you agree? Why or why not? Look forward to an exciting discussion of this issue during our training ..."

Possible activities / Further work in training
Form groups and ask participants to discuss the article or attitudes towards business training in general using key questions. Or prepare the trainers for difficult customer interactions. "Imagine a potential customer confronts you with statements from *The Training Lie*. How would you react? What do you say to convince them that your training is not a waste of money?"

In Time Management Training
Interview colleagues

Instructions before the training
"What are the typical challenges in dealing with time? Ask two of your colleagues the following questions ..."

Possible activities / Further work in training
Get involved in the topic by addressing the challenges in a plenary session or in small groups. Or use the collected challenges as a transfer activity. At the end of the training, have the trainees prepare recommendations for their interviewees ("What would you advise your colleague?"). This allows you to consolidate what you have learned and ensures that colleagues are interested in the training content.

In Argumentation Training
Watch videos and reflect

Instructions before the training
"What makes a winning argument? What convinced you? How can you win? Watch the following video of a famous debate and answer the following questions ..." (Link to the video and questions about the video)

Possible activities / Further work in training
In small groups or a plenary session, lead a discussion on the video, including reflective questions. Continue to work by deriving techniques and figures for a winning argument.

Time for transfer!

Now it's your turn! How could you create clarity of expectations? How could you ensure that trainees know what to expect in advance of the training? What is the next step that you would like to implement? Use this space to write down your spontaneous ideas and thoughts.

This is how I will foster clarity of expectations:

[1] On the correlation between expectation clarity and advance information on training and transfer efficiency, see, for example, Baldwin, T., & Magjuka, R., "Organizational training and signals of importance: Linking program outcomes to pre-training expectations" in *Human Resource Development Quarterly,* 1991, 2(1): pp. 25 – 36; Karl, K. A., & Ungsrithong, D., "Effects of optimistic versus realistic previews of training programs on self-reported transfer of training" in *Human Resource Development Quarterly,* 1992, 3(4): pp. 373 – 384, or various validation studies on the Learning Transfer System Inventory (LTSI), in which the predictor quality was confirmed (in German, e.g., Kauffeld, S., Bates, R., Holton, E. F., III, & Müller, A. C., "Das deutsche Lerntransfer-System-Inventar (GLTSI): Psychometrische Überprüfung der deutschsprachigen Version" in *Zeitschrift für Personalpsychologie,* 2008, 7(2): pp. 50 – 69.

[2] These and other examples are described in *Süddeutsche Zeitung* – Herrmann, S.: "Wahrnehmung und Denken: Erwartungen verändern die inneren Zustände" in http://www.sueddeutsche.de/wissen/ wahrneh- mung-und-denken-so-leicht-lassen-wir-uns-manipulieren-1.1407348-2 [10th July 2012] (retrieved 25 July 2016).

[3] A detailed differentiation in terms of special-context learning can be found, for example, in Ludwig, P. H., *Ermutigung: Optimierung von Lernprozessen durch Zuversichtssteigerung,* Springer Verlag, 2013, pp. 57ff.

[4] On goals and logging, see Latham, G. P., & Kinne, S. B., "Improving job performance through training in goal setting" in *Journal of Applied Psychology,* 1974, 59(2): pp. 187; a specific number of trees to be felled is not mentioned in this publication. The fact that a high, challenging goal is one that can only be achieved by the best 10 % is taken from later studies. See, for example, Stajkovic, A. D., Locke, E. A., & Blair, E. S., "A first examination of the relationships between primed subconscious goals, assigned conscious goals, and task performance" in *Journal of Applied Psychology,* 91(5): p. 1172.

[5] On goal-setting theory, its evidence, and future research directions, see Locke, E. A., & Latham, G. P., "Building a Practically Useful Theory of Goal Setting and Task Motivation. A 35-Year Odyssey" in *American Psychologist,* 2002, 57(9), pp. 705-717. Or Locke, E. A., & Latham, G. P. "New directions in goal-setting theory" in *Current Directions in Psychological Science,* 2006, 15(5): pp. 265 – 268.

[6] A representation of the four mechanisms that drive performance improvements can be found, for example, in Locke, E. A., & Latham, G. P., "Building a Practically Useful Theory of Goal Setting and Task Motivation. A 35-Year Odyssey" in *American Psychologist,* 2002, 57(9), pp. 705-717.

[7] So far, findings are contradictory regarding whether optimistically framed expectations lead to better transfer results than realistic ones. See Hicks, W. D., & Klimoski, R. J., "Research Notes. Entry into training programs and its effects on training outcomes. A field experiment" in *Academy of Management Journal,* 1987, 30(3): pp. 542 – 552; Karl, K. A., & Ungsrithong, D., "Effects of optimistic versus

realistic previews of training programs on self-reported transfer of training" in *Human Resource Development Quarterly,* 1992, 3(4): pp. 373 – 384.

[8] An overview of various studies on self-imposed, participatory, and assigned goals can be found in Locke, E. A., & Latham, G. P., *New Developments in Goal Setting and Task Performance,* Routledge. 2013, pp. 220ff. or Locke, E. A., & Latham, G. P., "Building a Practically Useful Theory of Goal Setting and Task Motivation. A 35-Year Odyssey" in *American Psychologist,* 2002, 57(9), pp. 705-717.

[9] More about the placebo effect can be found, for example, in Price, D. D., Finniss, D. G., & Benedetti, F., "A comprehensive review of the placebo effect: Recent advances and current thought" in *Annual Review of Psychology,* 2008, 59 pp. 565 – 590.

[10] SurveyMonkey: https://de.surveymonkey.com, LimeSurvey: https://www.limesurvey.org/de, Google Forms: https://www.google.com/forms/about/ (retrieved 8 December 2016).

[11] Digital pinboard: www.padlet.com (retrieved 8 December 2016).

LEVER 5 – CONTENT RELEVANCE

TWO PRACTICAL EXAMPLES

Two months ago, Rudi and Hermione both attended a train-the-trainer course. Read what the two report today.

Rudi, 32, aspiring in-house trainer for production training

I thought the train-the-trainer course was okay. We discussed the role of a trainer, discussed the pros and cons and the potential uses of various media, practiced introductory sequences, and tried a few other exercises. But there was also a lot of content that I don't have any use for. It's already obvious to me that long presentations are far from ideal, but what else can I do when it comes to production training? The examples the trainer presented were mainly from the soft skills area, but I'm doing production training, which is totally different! In summary, I'd say I got some good inputs. If I develop my own training concept, I think will have a look through the training material we got.

Hermione, 41, aspiring in-house trainer in the civil service

This train-the-trainer course was awesome! It was exactly what I needed to start developing my own training concept! We sent our expectations and fears about our future trainer activities to the trainer in advance. The trainer told us many stories from her own experience, too. We also created multimedia presentations for our own training topics – it was a PowerPoint for me – and received feedback from both the trainer and the group. The trainer really did a great job. Instead of downplaying the whole general issue of "How to do a PowerPoint the right way," we discussed this in the form of tips and experiences using our own concrete examples. Everyone got involved! We were also introduced to many new exercises. But not in a passive way: "These are exercises that are out there, choose one." It was more like: "This is my content – now what's the best way to impar it with an exercise?" Without the train-the-trainer course, I would've simply introduced ten different careers in a two-hour classroom lecture on the subject of "Careers" in general. Now I let the trainees work out the careers by presenting them in form of the game "Activity". This is already written down in my training concept.

What's your impression from the two statements? What's the difference?

For Rudi, the training was "only" okay. In his view, the content had something to do with him and his training concept but does not quite meet his requirements. With Hermione, however, the training hits the bullseye. She got answers to the exact questions that were eating away at her. For Hermione, the training had a high content relevance – and that is crucial for transfer success. Generally speaking, content relevance means that what is learned in training is in line with what participants need to master in their daily work. At first glance, this seems a simple, almost banal-sounding demand. Upon closer examination, however, this demand is not so easy to meet, theoretically or practically. What we definitely know from transfer research is that the content of the training should be in line with what the participants need in their work – this is a crucial prerequisite for transfer success.[1] It is important that the trainees also see it this way! So, it's not just about choosing topics relevant to the workplace (through needs analysis). Rather, it also means presenting the selected content as "relevant" and making the relationship to the workplace reality evident to the trainees.

CONTENT RELEVANCE – LEARNING WHAT IS NEEDED

	Content relevance in a nutshell
Trainees say	"The contents are practical and relevant to me"
Definition	Content relevance is the extent to which trainees experience the training content as well-matched with the tasks and requirements of their work.
Guiding question	How do you ensure that trainees perceive the training content as relevant and important for their own day-to-day work?

How we learn to use 3D printers – the researchers' dispute

The content relevance lever brings us to one of the first theories established within transfer research. In 1901, Edward Thorndike and Robert Woodworth laid out their "theory of identical elements," which states that transfer takes place only if the elements of the learning field match the elements of the application field.[2] A little less cryptically, this means transfer takes place only when what is taught during training exactly matches what trainees need to know in their day-to-day work. That makes sense. When a trainer in an IT training works on a Mac even though trainees have a Microsoft computer in the office, the mismatch makes transfer difficult. Alignment is lacking. Once again, it turns out that transfer effectiveness requires that training is grounded in an appropriate needs analysis and clear transfer goals. These provide the basis for a content-relevant training and the resulting transfer success. So far, so good. But the devil is in the details …

A more in-depth look at the theory of identical elements reveals several requirements. In simplified terms, the training needs to teach a specific behavior (e.g., a very specific process) with exactly the right content components, methods, and steps, and to teach it under precisely the conditions that prevail in your trainees' work. This will enable your trainees to replicate the trained behavior in practice. In other words, if you train the exact work processes, with exactly the documents, tools, and materials that are available to the trainees at work, then transfer will happen. Depending on which training you are thinking about right now, all this will either continue to sound quite reasonable or has started to seem overly mechanical and somehow superficial. Implementing these requirements is straightforward enough for running a machine or a software program. But what do you do for topics where there is no one single "right process" or "application context"? For example, what is the "right process" or "application context" for leadership, for communication, or for conflict resolution? For these processes, the identical-elements approach seems too limited.

A new attempt was made by Charles H. Judd, another leading thinker in transfer research. He agreed that transfer success requires a match between the learning field and the application field. But, in his view, it is not so much the exact methods and sequences of steps that should be identical. What is really needed are generalizable (and therefore more abstract) principles to guide the successful completion of tasks in the workplace.[3] In other words, trainees should learn the abstract principles in training, not the exact procedures and methods. This idea of principle transfer was taken up and further developed by other researchers.[4] The focus is no longer a concrete process, a "correct sequence of actions." Instead, the focus is always on principles, strategies, or key competences, such as critical or conceptual thinking, cooperative approaches, problem-solving skills, etc. Applied in practice, this theory means the following (for example): Instead of training a specific format for an employee discussion, we train the principles of successful interviewing. Instead of going through the operation of a 3D printer step-by-step, we teach the functions and operation of 3D printers in general. And instead of using training to generate ideas for the further development of a product, we learn five new creativity techniques. This more abstract approach supposedly helps trainees apply what they have learned to new and different scenarios and situations. In theory, that sounds reasonable enough. Unfortunately, it does not work very well in practice. A considerable amount of academic and professional research shows that "spontaneous principle transfer is a relatively rare occurrence."[5] General, abstract knowledge cannot easily be applied to concrete situations. The trainees in the above examples may well already know the principles of successful interviewing or how a 3D printer works. But is this really enough to ensure that their next employee discussion will be successful or that the new 3D printer will actually be easy to operate? It often happens that participants have indeed acquired knowledge, but it remains inert, unapplied. The relationship between what has been learned and the application situation where what was learned is needed is hard to bridge. In the learning context (be it school, university, or training at work), we then ask ourselves: What does what I'm learning here have to do with me? Why would I need that? Why do I need creativity techniques, what do these abstract principles of conversation have to do with me, and why is this trainer explaining 70 different functions of 3D printers to me, even though I only need one of them? The perception of content relevance is missing. And this happens despite the fact that the trainer chose the contents very carefully and only wanted to make sure that what they are teaching is applicable to a variety of situations. What is well intentioned is not always well executed!

But a lack of perceived content relevance and thus a lack of transfer can also come from a completely different source. If we have acquired our knowledge and ability to act in one domain of knowledge, it is a fundamental challenge to apply this knowledge in another domain. Calculating an angle in a geometry lesson correctly – no problem. If an unknown angle suddenly pops up in a physics experiment, however, many students no longer know what to do. There's a reason for the huge amount of debate over education involving interdisciplinary teaching. In learning research, one speaks of "situated" or "context-bound" knowledge or learning.[6] The insight behind this: Knowledge is linked to the context in which we acquire it. In order for it to be applicable to other contexts, learners need to de-contextualize it – and that's not easy.

The dilemma in a nutshell: A narrow focus in the training (on a certain action or "correct course of action") supports content relevance and thus transfer. For many training topics, however, there is no "one right way" or "single application context." If we broaden the focus and become more abstract, we quickly lose contact with the application situations, the content is perceived as being of little relevance, and we have produced knowledge that is difficult to apply. Abstract or focused on the concrete subject matter – neither the one nor the other seems optimal.

If you've now had quite enough of this discussion of the theoretical extremes, I can empathize. Quite pragmatically, one could say: "Let's just take the middle ground

– not too concrete and not too abstract." Here, however, the theory does offer a practical recommendation, one that has proved its value: Learn the abstract through the concrete.

Combining concrete and abstract learning

There is a way to get content relevance and generalizability under one roof and thus bridge the gap between concrete and abstract learning: taking a case-based or problem-based learning approach. Consider the train-the-trainer seminar as an illustration. As you conduct this training, you may want to reflect on the role of the trainer, work out the meaning of the beginning and end sequences, introduce and test different methods, and discuss the training's dramaturgy. Despite a successful seminar, your participants may still find it difficult to apply the ideas when the one day come to developing their own training concept – the training was just too abstract. The more specific alternative: You could advise the trainees, based on your own experience, as to which methods and exercises are best suited for their training topic and practice these with them. Highly specific, highly relevant. However, such an approach immediately becomes difficult if your trainees have different training topics.

Next idea: You can try out a problem- or case-based approach.[7] As the name implies, the focus is on problems or cases. They should be as real, authentic, and pressing as possible. Taking a concrete, personal problem, trainees work out the theory required for the solution and then use it again to solve the specific problem.

> Problem-based learning means starting from the concrete problem, working out the general theory,- and using it to solve the specific problem.

What can this look like in practice? First, we need a suitable problem, a case that is as real and as pressing as possible. This can be a concrete problem that the trainee must solve in his work, an authentic case that the trainee is working on, or a task that the trainee must master in her job. To illustrate this, let's take another look at train-the-trainer seminars. The authentic task could be "Develop a training concept for the topic that you would like to train in the future!" It is important that the task for trainees is as relevant, current, and urgent as possible. It should spark curiosity and interest, and immediately motivate trainees to act. How could one make the task of "writing a training concept" more pressing for the trainees? This could be done, for example, by communicating that the completed training concept is a prerequisite for joining the in-house training staff, or that the training concept will be presented to a selected panel at the end of the training, etc. In our example, we would have created the basis for the problem-based approach. The trainees each have an authentic, real, pressing problem - and they have to develop their own training concept. What does the learning process look like in the problem-based approach? Quite simply, based on the trainees' very concrete, pressing task, the necessary knowledge is established and immediately implemented for that task. In training, participants learn how to analyze their target group, and they also apply this to their own training. They learn what matters when formulating transfer goals, and then define their own transfer goals for their concept. They learn what points to consider to give the training a good start and what introductory exercises are possible, and then plan the introductory module of their own training, etc. The key idea: Learn the abstract from the concrete! In this way, we generate generalizable knowledge while remaining very close to the concrete application.

> Problem-based learning combines the advantages of abstract and concrete learning. At the same time, it achieves high content relevance and high generalizability.

A tip: Make sure that the problem-solving process is as authentic as possible. This means that the problem, task, or situation should be handled just as it would be in the trainees' real-life situations. So, if new trainers in the company always train in a team and create concepts together, then do this in the training as well. Similarly, only use templates and aids in the training that are available in the workplace. Thus, for example, if there is an in-house template for training concepts, it should be used in the training, too, even if you as the trainer usually have and use your own templates. The problem-based approach combines the benefits of concrete and abstract learning while ensuring learners are aware of the relevance of the content at all times. Just think through your training with the problem-based approach in mind. What problem or problems would your trainees see as authentic, realistic, and urgent?

Here's another important point to consider: In problem-based learning, trainees will need instruction, but the level depends on their prior knowledge. At one end of the spectrum, trainees are presented with a case and the theory needed to solve it and discuss in plenary how the theory applies to the case (high degree of instruction). At the other extreme, involving limited instruction and largely self-directed work, participants bring their own cases, discuss them in small groups, and work out the necessary theory for themselves (e.g., doing their own literature research, posing concrete questions to you as the trainer). The watchword here: Limit instruction to only what is absolutely necessary. The resulting closeness to the trainees' workplace reality increases the perceived content relevance, the trainees' commitment, and thus the transfer success of the training.

Another 100,000 dead – so what?

Abstract theory and perceived content relevance are – and this may now be quite obvious to you – often strange bedfellows. Nevertheless, in training it is always useful and necessary to provide theoretical inputs (for example, when trainees have little or no previous knowledge, as explained above). To maintain the perception of high content relevance even in theoretical modules, I recommend making use of two psychological effects: (1) the self-reference effect and (2) the personification effect.

The self-reference effect describes the fact that we remember information better when it has something to do with us personally. For instance, we remember people who are similar to us or with whom we have shared some sort of personal information. When there is a link between information and our own lives, our self-image, or our interests, the content is easier for us to integrate with what we already know and therefore more relevant.

Personification is an effect the media uses to engage readers and audiences. If we hear or read that a disaster has claimed 100,000 lives, it does get our attention. But the news hits us harder when it is presented as the story of an individual victim or survivor (for example, a girl who has lost her mother, father, and little sister in the disaster). Although irrational, the power of the personification effect has been verified time and again. It also explains the popularity of novels and personal life stories. Bar charts and factual reports about female genital mutilation (FGM) in Africa remain mere statistics that can easily be ignored – the 1998 autobiography *Desert Flower* by Waris Dirie shook the world. So, if we want to move and motivate people, we should hold back on the dry facts and tell people's stories.

What does this have to do with your instruction in a training? How do the self-reference and the personification effects help us design the theoretical parts of a training so that they are also perceived as relevant? Quite simply, a connection with our own lives and personification foster concern, motivation, easier recall, and finally a perception of relevance. You probably already use these effects in your trainings, but it's worth giving them even more conscious attention and intensifying them. Here are some concrete suggestions for you: Instead of introducing a theory with a series of facts (only), present it in a personified story. Explain new theoretical content using metaphors and analogies that your trainees will be familiar with from their own lives. In training, work specifically with documents from your trainees' organization(s) or organizations they know. From time to time, be self-critical and ask yourself whether the examples you have used in past trainings are also relevant to the next group of trainees.

Make the training content relevant by
(1) Telling stories instead of enumerating abstract facts,
(2) Working with documents from your trainees' own or similar organizations,
(3) Adapting examples and explanations to fit your trainees.

Summary

Offering training in which trainees learn exactly what they need for their work may sound simple enough. But on closer examination, it is more challenging than it seems. Three steps will help you boost trainees' perception of the training as relevant: (1) Select the right content carefully. There is no substitute for analyzing trainees' needs and clarifying each training assignment. (2) Combine concrete and abstract learning modules in your training concept. Develop the content on the basis of cases and application situations that are as concrete, authentic, and urgent as possible. And (3) Communicate and frame the content of your training as relevant! Use stories, authentic documents, and examples tailored to your trainees.

HOW TO STRENGTHEN CONTENT RELEVANCE

At a glance:
Ideas for reflection and implementation

Clarify the assignment based on real, concrete challenges
- Collect critical incidents
- Identify trainers with strengths in transfer

Strengthen the perception of content relevance
- Deliver relevant content in a relevant package (with examples from practice)

Role-play individual transfer ideas in training
- From "Aha!" experiences to "What for?" results
- Ask transfer questions
- Introduce transfer questions as rituals

Clarify the assignment based on real, concrete challenges

Imagine you are a participant in a training. You go there with a very specific problem – one that you have been thinking about for a long time, one that you urgently need a solution for. Imagine, for example, that you are working on the complaint hotline of your company and you hear more and more from angry customers: "I want to talk to your supervisor right now!" However, your boss has made it very clear to you that you must not put anyone through. Of course, the customers on the other end of the line do not accept this answer, and a stalemate develops. So far, you have no solution to this issue, but only a specific, pressing problem. What would happen if this exact situation came up in the training "Mastering difficult telephone conversations"? How about if you knew exactly what to say to an angry customer the next time that this happens following the training? Would you then call the training "relevant" to your work? Would you apply what you have learned? Of course! Knowing the trainees' concrete and pressing challenges is a basic prerequisite for a transfer-effective training. It is crucial that the needs within the organization and the expectations of the stakeholders are clear and transparent. Only clarity within the organization makes it possible to define the task in collaboration with the trainer. In practice, the defined expectations, goals, and challenges are often far too abstract - too far away from the concrete, physical problems that affect the participants. And yet this is exactly what we need to know if we want to design content-relevant and thus transfer-effective training. How do we learn about the valuable everyday challenges faced by the trainees? And how do we get information about them before the training in order to also use these situations and problems when clarifying the assignment or designing the training? An ingenious and simple method is to collect "critical incidents." Send an email to the trainees similar to the following:

Collection of Critical Incidents – Sample email text

Dear Trainees,

On April 2, the moment will have arrived – we will all meet to work on the topic of "Mastering difficult telephone conversations." You can look forward to two days of working jointly on your questions and challenges, gathering inspiration and tips, sharing experiences, trying out new things, and learning how to conduct difficult calls successfully.

Maximizing the benefits for you - Working with real-life situations

I'm committed to designing and conducting the training to meet your individual needs and expectations. As optimal preparation for your questions and challenges, it will help me to have some specific information. Please therefore reply to this email with a short description of a difficult phone conversation and your issues, relating to a specific case.

Please describe a difficult situation in your everyday work

Please select a concrete and especially difficult telephone call and describe it briefly and informally, with details on questions such as:
- What was the conversation about? Who was involved? How did it proceed?
- When and how did the conversation become "difficult"? What were the "sticking points" and statements?
- How did you act? What was the outcome of the conversation?
- How did you feel after the conversation?
- What title or headline would you use to describe this conversation?

I'd suggest you choose a specific conversation for which you want to get tips, ideas, and new solutions as part of our training.

Please email me your case before Monday atjoe.bloggs@training.com.

Thank you in advance; I'm looking forward to two exciting days with you!

Best regards,

Joe Bloggs

As a trainer, you can use the critical incidents you collect to tailor your training to the trainees and their specific challenges. In addition, you can ensure that trainees already start thinking through the training topic in advance and thus facilitate Lever 4 - Clarity of Expectations. Because trainees work on their own topic in the training, you thereby ensure that they experience the training as relevant and that each trainee goes home with a solution to a current and relevant problem.

As a human resources development manager, you can use the critical incidents for clarifying the assignment and selecting trainer(s) – and/or for practical projects, which are the "big brother or sister" to the critical incidents (see also "Arrange for parallel work on practical projects" to support training and transfer, on pages 201 ff.). Be sure to have a critical incident collection on hand before the briefing meetings with the (potential) trainers, as the specific incidents will make any such clarification briefing more accessible and concrete.

Every training becomes relevant – and therefore stronger in terms of transfer – if what is learned can be used immediately to solve one's own challenges. To make this possible, trainers need to know what challenges and problems their participants face and make them the cornerstone of their training. This is a completely different paradigm in training design. The starting point is no longer the content (Model X or Theory Y); instead, the focus is on the trainees' problems and challenges. Educators would call this learner- and transfer-oriented, as opposed to content-oriented. What does that mean in concrete terms for the example just mentioned, "Mastering difficult telephone conversations"? A content-oriented trainer might start a discussion to clarify the assignment by talking about the content modules. For example, a content-oriented trainer might say, "For 'difficult phone conversations,' I typically take transactional analysis as the theoretical underpinning. Then look at the levels of communication, present various killer phrases and typical ways of responding, and go through question techniques. I've been very successful with this content. If you [HRD professional] would like to add the topics of 'Preparing for tough conversations' and 'Best practices in mental hygiene,' we would have to add another day. Do you have any further content-related requests?" In this conversation everything revolves around content, models, theories, and exercises to be covered in the training. A learner- and transfer-oriented trainer approaches the content of the assignment in a quite different manner. They would start by asking about and attempting to understand the concrete challenges and problems faced by the participants and the company's transfer goals. They ask questions such as: "What are the typical situations that trainees find difficult or challenging? What would be different after a successful training?". The more trainers are made specifically aware of these problems and challenges, the more relevant and transfer-effective the training can be. The training requirements don't first come up in a conversation between the

HR development manager and the trainer; instead, they emerge from the trainees' day-to-day work life. It is crucial that the clarification of the assignment results in a clear picture of what is to be achieved through the training and what concrete challenges the trainees face. Assignment clarification based on the concrete situations, challenges, and problems that the trainees face is the optimal starting point for a content-relevant and transfer-strong training.

By the way, HR people can quickly spot in the assignment clarification phase whether they are actually receiving a "customized and transfer-effective" training or just an "off-the-peg" program that the trainer has been able to sell elsewhere. And trainers can actively differentiate themselves from their mass-market competitors by clarifying the assignment with suitable questions and answers. One HR vice president at an international corporation revealed what she looks for in the assignment clarification interview, and how she distinguishes between transfer-oriented and merely sales-driven trainers. Her insights are summarized in the next table.

How HR developtment managers recognize transfer-oriented trainers	
Worst case	Best case
Selling/boasting The trainer sells me his/her product 'Oh, yes, for the topic you want to cover, 'Communication', I have a comprehensive program that fits all target groups and needs. Here's an overview (a glossy brochure).'	**Asking questions** The trainer tries to understand my need and its background. Asks questions such as: • What sparked your request for a 'Communication' training? Where and from whom did it come? • What exactly do you mean by 'communication'? • What should be changed specifically as a result of the training? Who wants this change? How pressing is this change? Why? / For whom? • Can you describe a concrete situation from the trainees' everyday work?

Little interest in trainees and company/companies involved

Trainer mainly wants info about the size of our order. Says things like: 'So, it's for your entire executive team. How many participants are we talking about here? And how many days should the training take each time? In our experience with other firms, it's best to plan for 3 days, etc.'

Strong interest in trainees and company/companies

Trainer wants to understand how company and potential trainees 'tick.'

Asks questions such as:
- Who are the executives who are likely to take part? Can you tell me more about their backgrounds, how they tick, what their roles are in your company (etc.)?
- How do these executives view the training in general or this training idea in particular? Do you yourself see a need for change?
- What is particularly important to the potential participants in a training? What would have to happen for them to drop out or stop the training?
- What cultural peculiarities exist in your organization? How would you describe how things here tick?

Focused on how good the course and/or tools are

Trainer explains how they do things, and how they should be done.
'So on the topic of sales discussions, I work with the five-point method and the RZZ tool. Experience shows that this always works brilliantly! Because typically the biggest challenge for the salespeople is to work out the advantages of the conversation, and that's exactly what the five-point method is especially well suited for.'

Ability to connect with trainees

Trainer wants to get to know the life worlds of the participants and understand how things work in the company

Asks questions such as:
- How do sales pitches go here? How do trainees do this at the moment?
- Which models, methods, or tools have you been working with? Can you show me a concrete example or a template?
- What works well from the trainees' point of view? What would your participants describe as the biggest challenge they face?
- What steps have been taken so far in terms of sales meetings? Which models have the participants already been introduced to?

Content-oriented	Goal-oriented
Trainer is satisfied with superficial cliches about goals. Mainly wants to discuss and agree on content with me. 'So, it seems you would like to strengthen your first-line managers' leadership capabilities. Sure! Then I'd suggest we build on the situative-leadership model. We'll make it heavily interactive and experience-oriented, with reflection!'	Trainer makes effort to elicit and listen to my concrete goals or co-define them with me. 'So, you would like to strengthen your first-line managers' leadership capabilities. What does that mean to you? What, concretely, should a line manager be able to do differently/better following the training?'
Off the peg/one-size fits all	**Made to measure**
Trainer has already finished designing the training and shows me the product sheet. 'After what you've described to me, our training "All about leadership" is exactly the right training for you.' (Shows me the finished brochure.) 'We will conduct it company internally, completely aligned with your needs.'	Trainer really does tailor training to *my* needs. 'If I've understood you correctly, then it is especially important to you that ... ... So I think that ... could be especially helpful. For instance, that could look like this ... Does that work for you?'
Transfer activities - not a topic	**Transfer as a key topic**
Trainer does not address transfer-promoting activities.	Trainer addresses transfer-promoting activities, asks questions, and brings in ideas. 'How do you encourage transfer promotion? Are there any standards in your training (such as pre- and post-training discussions, transfer planning tools, follow-ups, evaluations)?' 'If not: I would suggest that we think about a transfer project and, in any case, involve the managers by ...'

Accepts all assignments	Also turns down assignments
It is clear from the outset that the trainer can and will accept the job, regardless of how the conversation develops. The assignment clarification serves only to convince the customer.	Trainer uses the assignment clarification so that we can get to know each other. Both of us want to find out whether we can work together on this topic, and what the best framework is for an effective training.
No matter how diffuse the goals are or how unlikely the transfer success may be under the given conditions – the trainer takes the job in any case.	Clear goals let us both see whether the trainer is the right fit for the job, and whether training is the right approach to address the need. Trainer also turns down training requests with unsuitable framework conditions, as they will not lead to transfer success. Such a trainer attaches more value to effectiveness and the resulting reputational impact than to merely landing an additional assignment.

Strengthen the perception of the content relevance

The requirements are specified; the assignment is entirely clarified. Trainers and HRD managers have a clear idea of what should be different after the training. The training is tailored exactly to the challenges faced by trainees. They will receive training in exactly what they need for their daily work. In terms of content relevance, everything is perfect! Or is it? Experience teaches that choosing the right content is only half the battle. In training, it is important not only to provide the relevant content, but also to make the content's relevance crystal clear to trainees. Paradoxically, the second seems so essential that it can even drown out the former! Sometimes the packaging is actually more crucial than the content. Time and again, trainers or speakers fascinate people with their extraordinary rhetorical gifts. They manage to arouse interest or enthusiasm for topics that were not on the trainee's radar until then. Any old topic suddenly becomes their topic. A solution to any problem becomes their solution to their own problem. Occasionally, this initial personal relationship disappears after a short period following training, because it turns out in everyday life that it's just a topic, a problem, and a solution that have little to do with oneself. In terms of sustainable transfer effectiveness, therefore, rhetorical skills – beautiful packaging – are not enough by themselves. Without them, however, even the most carefully selected content will not be of use to us. So how do we make it so that trainees also perceive the content as relevant? What do trainers need to do in order for participants to say, "Yes, that's exactly my topic, exactly my problem, that you're discussing here. It is exactly what concerns me and affects my day-to-day life!"?

Let's take a look at different methods applied to a concrete example. Imagine a Kaizen training at a solar-thermal collector manufacturer. As a trainer, how would you go about strengthening the perceived content relevance? To get trainees to go from saying, "What's this got to do with me?" to saying, "That's my topic!"?

Low perceived content relevance	High perceived content relevance
Trainees say: What does that have to do with me!?	Trainees say: That is exactly my topic!
Content-oriented introduction and moderation (Key question: What are we going to deal with here?) • In this training, you will learn about the Kaizen philosophy. We will go through the topics of value-added and waste, the 5S exercise, and the kinds of waste and how you can identify them.	**Transfer-oriented introduction and moderation** (Key question: What's the benefit for me?) • With the help of this training, you and your team mates will learn how to do your work faster and more efficiently and, at the same time, your workload will be lighter, and the tasks will be easier and more fun! Sounds incredible, doesn't it? More success and easier work – is that possible? Yes! And you will experience it first hand; you will experience Kaizen for yourself.
Working on "artificial" cases, problems, and problems • Imagine a typical assembly-line job. How could you optimize it?	**Working on own cases, problems, and challenges** • For the training, bring a photograph of your own assembly-line workplace. How could you optimize it?
No room for trainee's experience • A major issue is that there's a lot of time spent walking back and forth, searching for things. People typically walk 5 km every day to find the right materials.	**Room for trainee's experience** • One major issue is the time spent walking and searching. How many kilometers do you estimate you walk every day to find the right tools or materials?
Examples that have little to do with trainees' own cases, problems, and challenges • At some well-known pharmaceutical company, Kaizen helped to reduce cycle times by 40 %!	**Examples that are similar to trainees' own cases, problems, and challenges** • At your competitor's / your supplier's, Kaizen helped to reduce cycle times by 40 %!

Cognitive facts with little or no emotional impact or color	Facts packed in stories that are gripping/move trainees emotionally
• Before the 5S, the average distance walked in the warehouse was 12 km per employee per shift.	• Jack Flash has worked in the warehouse at Logistics AG for 8 years. He saw first-hand how the company grew and grew. And so did the warehouse. It got so big that he had to walk a total of 12 km per shift. Every day. That's the distance from here to Springfield – on foot!
Remaining abstract	**Illustrating abstract topics with examples**
• In Kaizen, the key principle is process orientation as distinct from results orientation. Not only the results are decisive, but also the process for getting results.	• In Kaizen, the key principle is process orientation as distinct from results orientation. That means: Your supervisors are not standing at the end of the assembly line and complaining that there are not enough products coming down the line. No. Your supervisors are supporting you and your colleagues at your work stations. There, you all work jointly on the given problem until you find a way to make the process step simpler, more efficient, and safer or more stable.

It pays to invest time not only in selecting the right content, but also in packaging it so that it is well matched with the target group. This is the only reliable way to ensure that trainees perceive the content as relevant and thus transfer-effective.

Stimulate individual transfer ideas in training

By specifying requirements, clarifying the assignment, and providing a content-relevant framing, we make it possible for our trainees to say of the training: "Yes, what I'm learning here has something to do with me and my everyday life." Much has already been achieved, and most of the trainees are highly satisfied with this feeling. But we can and should do even more to boost content relevance and transfer success; specifically: clarify the question, "What exactly does what I am learning here have to do with me, and when?" Thinking about this question and coming up with corresponding transfer ideas is cognitive work, for which a degree of motivation and incentive is required. All too often, we settle for learning new and interesting facts – with such insights accompanied by a joyful "Aha!" and "Oh really! That's fascinating!" We don't stop to ask what these facts and "Aha!" moments can mean in concrete terms for us and our actions. With content-relevant "Aha!s," trainees often have the feeling during training that they are experiencing a very useful training, but they still don't implement much, because the concretization and transmission step was absent, (see also Lever 7 – Transfer Planning). The "Aha" knowledge remains abstract, difficult to apply or context-bound, and therefore has no impact. Trainers can easily counteract this by taking the second step – the "What for?" – with their trainees. Make it a habit, after every theoretical input, every exercise, every reflection, or even every single element in the training to ask over and again: "What does that mean for you and your daily work?" And: "How can you use this in a very concrete way in your workplace?" And: "What exactly will you do now with this model, this insight, this idea? How can you benefit from this?" Encourage trainees to capture these important ideas (say: "Be sure to write down your idea for application, or this valuable idea will be forgotten tomorrow!"). Even if the concrete application for you as a trainer seems perfectly clear and feels appropriate, with any further questions seeming like overkill, the trainees will, in the majority of cases, experience these moments completely differently. This additional reflection loop in the form of transfer questions ("What …?" questions) is helpful and can prove to be a decisive breakthrough factor for your trainees. You can pose such questions in training as impetus for individual reflection, which are then written down. You can discuss in a plenary, discuss in buzz-groups, do group work, etc. You can introduce these transfer questions as a ritual, for example, as a standard activity before or after each break, as an element every 90 minutes, or, every time you use a certain word or phrase, use a symbol (e.g., raising a "Transfer Time-Out" card) or a sound (e.g., a transfer bell or gong) to initiate the discussion. What's important is that you don't just create "Aha!s," but also cover the "Why?s" and do this for every element of your training. This increases your training's content relevance and thus the transfer effectiveness.

Time for transfer!

Now it's your turn! How will you promote content relevance? How do you ensure that the training content is perceived by the trainees as relevant and important for their own everyday lives? What is the next step that you would like to implement? Take some time to jot down your ideas and thoughts.

This is how I will promote content relevance:

¹ For the correlation between content relevance and training transfer, see, for example, Axtell, C. M., Maitlis, S., & Yearta, S. K., "Predicting immediate and longer-term transfer of training" in *Personnel Review*, 1997, 26(3): pp. 201 – 213; Bates, R. A., Holton III, E. F., Seyler, D. L., & Carvalho, M. A.; "The role of interpersonal factors in the application of computer-based training in an industrial setting" in *Human Resource Development International*, 2000, 3(1): pp. 19 – 42; Lim, D. H., "Training design factors influencing transfer of training to the workplace within an international context" in *Journal of Vocational Education and Training*, 2000, 52(2): pp. 243 – 258. Mathieu, J. E., Tannenbaum, S. I., & Salas, E., "Influences of individual and situational characteristics on measures of training effectiveness" in *Academy of Management Journal*, 1992, 35(4): pp. 828 – 847.

² Thorndike, E., & Woodworth, R. S. 1901. The influence of improvement in one mental function upon the efficiency of other functions. (I). Psychological Review, 8(3): pp.247.

³ The origins of the theory of principle transfer can be found in Judd, C. H., *Educational Psychology*. Boston, Massachusetts: Houghton Mifflin, 1939.

⁴ For the development and further elaboration of the theory of principle transfer, see, for example, Weinert, F. E., "Lernübertragung" in C. F. Graumann, H. Heckhausen, & M. Hofer (Eds.), *Pädagogische Psychologie*, Frankfurt am Main: Fischer Taschenbuch-Verlag, 1974, (Bd.2): pp. 685 – 709; and also Dieterich, R., "Transferwirksames Lernen und Lehren" in R. Dieterich (Ed.), *Psychologische Perpektiven der Erwachsenenbildung*, Bad Heilbrunnn/Obb.: Klinkhardt, 1987, pp. 23 – 38.

⁵ Mandl, H., Gräsel, C., & Prenzel, M., *Das Problem des Lerntransfers in der betrieblichen Weiterbildung*, Inst. für Empirische Pädagogik und Pädagogische Psychologie, 1991, p. 133.

⁶ For a discussion of the issue and how to deal with situational or contextual knowledge, see, for example, Mandl, H., "Wissensnutzung als verkanntes Problem. Grundannahmen und Instruktionsansätze" in *news&science. Begabtenförderung und Begabtenforschung*, ÖZBF, 2011, 27(1): pp. 4 – 5, or Mandl, H., Kopp, B., & Dvorak, S., *Aktuelle theoretische Ansätze und empirische Befunde im Bereich der Lehr-Lern-Forschung – Schwerpunkt Erwachsenenbildung*, 2004, and also Mandl, H., Gräsel, C., & Prenzel, M., *Das Problem des Lerntransfers in der betrieblichen Weiterbildung*, Institut für Empirische Pädagogik und Pädagogische Psychologie, 1991.

⁷ The spectrum of approaches to learning from authentic problems is diverse. An overview of various approaches – including problem-based learning (PBL) or case-based learning – as well as the theoretical background and mechanisms of action is given, for example, in Zumbach, J., Haider, K., & Mandl, H., *Fallbasiertes Lernen: Theoretischer Hintergrund und praktische Anwendung*, 2008; Zumbach, J., Problembasiertes Lernen. Münster: Waxmann, 2008; and also Gräsel, C., *Problemorientiertes Lernen: Strategieanwendung und Gestaltungsmöglichkeiten*, Hogrefe, Verlag für Psychologie, 1997.

LEVER 6 – ACTIVE PRACTICE

TWO PRACTICAL EXAMPLES

Helene and Henry have just attended different trainings on "Kaizen – The Japanese Philosophy for Success." On the way home, the following thoughts pass through their minds.

Helene, 31, management assistant in the cylinder construction industry

I am absolutely convinced that Kaizen works. The key idea is that everyone in the company looks for ways to improve every day and that every process leads to an increase in performance, as statistics have clearly shown. The trainer told us that we need to focus on value-adding activities and avoid the eight types of waste as much as possible. Shorten pathways, reduce stocks and buffers, avoid mistakes in the production process, among many other things. The "5S" model was also quite interesting. I feel like I know what Kaizen is, and what it's all about. The only question is: How can we implement it in our own work …?

Henry, 38, deputy production manager in the agricultural machinery industry

Kaizen is a great thing – not just in theory, but in practice. The trainer was brilliant – very different from what I'm used to. I could read the whole theory by myself, but to really try things out, that was what helped me! For example, the 5S model, which makes sure that the workplace is neat and tidy. I knew the theory: sort, set in order, shine, and so on. But now I've implemented it myself, in our production hall! In doing so, I got to know the many little things that mattered. For example, putting a red dot on things when I can't decide myself whether they can be thrown away. Or the tape that we have stuck across all the folders so that they are always in the right order. Even for the eight types of waste, we didn't just get a boring lecture. In a simulation, we experienced for ourselves the unbelievable amount of time and effort we can save just by thinking about optimization! And in the group work, we all took pictures of places where we found each kind of waste in the organization. Through the wide range of activities – both doing and watching – and giving and getting feedback, I now not only know what Kaizen is, but — what's even better I know how to implement it in our organization!

Who do you think will probably have more transfer success, Helene or Henry? On what do you base your assessment? What's the difference?

Helene knows about Kaizen after her training – but Henry is able to do Kaizen! Why? Because Helene was given the information, but Henry had to work for it. By trying it out, he practiced actively. And that makes the difference between knowledge and ability. Active practice means that trainees learn and experience the content for themselves. They interact intensely with the subject-matter and gain practical experience with it. Passive classroom-like lectures are largely replaced by active discussions, group work, case studies, presentations, reflection, and application issues. Being active enhances trainees' motivation, lays down long-term memories, and creates the foundation for transfer success. In active practice, what you have learned is not only "discussed," but also actively tried out. Second-hand experiences are replaced by first-hand experiences. For the negotiating training, this means that it is not enough for trainees just to work out negotiating techniques and then have them present them. Likewise, in an appraisal interview it is not enough simply to pin the dos & don'ts for such an interview on a bulletin board. Active practice means trying out the negotiation techniques in a situation that is as real as possible, or actually conducting an appraisal interview in the training. It is about engaging intensely with real tasks and problems and actually doing things instead of just talking about them. Feedback and reflection loops help to fine-tune. This is the only way for trainees to understand the desired new behavior, experience it in its complexity, and learn in a transfer-effective way. Transfer research recommends that, depending on the transfer goal and the difficulty of the training content, trainees should spend one-third to one-half of the training time on active practice.[1] Devoting 30 to 50 percent of the total time to really practicing a new action - that's an ambitious recommendation in view of the many other activities with slides, brainstorming with cards, and group work to discuss and present the topics though not actually try them out. But it's a rule of thumb that pays off in terms of greater transfer success.

ACTIVE PRACTICE – LEARNING BY DOING

	Active practice in a nutshell
Trainees say	"I have already experienced, practiced, and tried it during training!"
Definition	Active practice in training is the extent to which training design provides opportunities to experience and practice new behaviors that are desirable in the work context.
Guiding question	How can you ensure that the action that is aspired to in practice is experienced, tried out, and practiced as realistically as possible during training?

Leave traces in the brain

Passive knowledge transfer and "assisted reading" in the form of hours-long PowerPoint presentations are not the most effective form of learning – this is (at least theoretically) now common knowledge. Sustainable knowledge and skills are a result of active, experiential learning. Let the trainees develop, experience, and try out the content for themselves! Reflect together and create feedback options – this is the unanimous recommendation from the various research disciplines. That active learning and practice are superior to passive study is considered a fact. And it is also evidenced in transfer success.[2] But why?

As we learn, the synaptic connections between the neurons in our brains are altered. The stronger these connections, the easier it is for us to remember and recall what has been stored. The more we engage with content, the more likely it is to create long-term traces (strong connections) in our memory.

Content is processed by various areas in the brain. The more areas that do this, and the more often and the more deeply they engage with the content, the easier it is for us to retain the content in the long term.[3] So if we only read or hear a text (especially one that has little to do with us personally), our minds are less engaged – and processing remains superficial. If, on the other hand, we are asked to answer questions about the text, to present the content to others, to find counter-arguments or possible applications, etc., then our minds are more activated – the processing goes deeper. Deep processing, deep memory traces, easier memory recall. Furthermore, if a connection is then made between the text and us personally, and thus with our emotions, it increases the content's subjective importance to us. For instance, if we are asked to give our own opinion on a text we've just learned in training, to consider how we might convince our co-workers to use what we've learned, or to say how we will transfer the content into our day-to-day work, this activation will increase the learning effect yet again.

> Deep processing creates strong connections in the brain, especially when we are affected personally and emotionally. This makes it easier to recall content and retain it longer.

So, is it now sufficient for transfer success if trainers no longer present the theory themselves and, instead, let it percolate in groups, which then present and discuss? If the goal of your training is for your trainees to be able to recite facts by heart, that would be a pretty good approach. But it has little to do with transfer. Transfer means applying what you have learned, acting on it. Reeling off content alone has nothing to do with practical application.

Why the best drivers are often the worst teachers

Would you rather be operated on by the doctor who has read more than a thousand medical books but has not performed a single operation, or would you prefer the doctor who has never read a book but has operated a thousand times?[4] After training, would you prefer that one of your trainees is able to give an impressive lecture on the psychological underpinnings of the negotiating techniques and their likelihood of success, or that your trainee uses the techniques successfully in his or her day-to-day life? What is the difference? All four have undeniable knowledge (in the broadest sense), but of different types.

Literature in this area speaks of factual knowledge (declarative knowledge, "knowing that ...") and application knowledge (procedural knowledge, "knowing how"). In everyday life, we might say the well-read doctor or the trainee who delivers the perfect lecture is the one with the knowledge. The experienced surgeon or the trainee who negotiates successfully in practice is the one with ability. If you respond the way most people do, in both cases you will have chosen the experts, that is, those with the procedural knowledge. The purpose of trainings is to generate application (procedural) knowledge and thus enable trainees to succeed in practice. So how can we acquire procedural knowledge? Well, how did you learn your skills? How did you learn to walk, or ride a bike? – "Step by step, mistake by mistake" as aptly claimed by Manfred Spitzer. In other words, basically by trial and error. And in the best case, with some helpful tips from a parent running alongside the bike. How do you learn to give a lecture or to negotiate to achieve your own goals? In the same way! By trial and error, and with some support along the way.

While theoretical factual-declarative knowledge can be acquired in a variety of ways (reading a book, doing research on the internet, talking to colleagues, etc.), using procedural knowledge is more challenging. If you have only read books on cycling, lecturing, or negotiating, you probably would not call yourself a master (although some professors, consultants, and others are that self-confident!). Declarative knowledge helps, no question, but for practical success – for ability – it is usually not enough by itself.

Real experts often find it difficult to verbalize their procedural knowledge. Can you describe and explain exactly how to get out of bed in the morning, drive a car, or form the past tense of verbs in your native language? Try it! Not so easy, right? You just do it without thinking about it. The same goes for professional chess players or Olympic champions. They are world class. But after the winners are interviewed, we as a viewer are left knowing little about how, precisely, they achieved their performance. Facts are stored directly as such, and we can verbalize them. Procedural knowledge is stored procedurally in the form of multiple-branched "if-then" rules that can no longer be easily verbalized due to their complexity or are no longer consciously controlled as a result of automation. Take the example of driving a car. The facts: Some cars have a gearstick and a clutch. Depending on the speed and desired acceleration, these need to be used.

Now one of the many if-then rules when driving:
> *If* my car is in first gear and I drive
> faster than 20 km/h and
> I want to accelerate,
> *then* I put my foot on the clutch,
> pull the gear lever into second gear, slowly
> take my foot off the clutch and at the same
> time slowly step on the accelerator.

This rule is still very roughly formulated and difficult to verbalize in detail (or can you spontaneously say at how many millimeters per second you move your foot off the clutch in this case?). And the rule is actually much more complicated (it changes, for example, if you are driving uphill or behind the wheel of a sports car). You see, procedural knowledge is way too complex for us to be able to recall all of these rules explicitly (as facts) and make them verbally retrievable. And we do not need this either. The rules are automatically extracted in the "doing" of the action and implicitly memorized. We simply can, without knowing exactly how we do it!

> Learning an ability means extracting rules, and that is what our brains succeed at particularly effortlessly and automatically while we are doing something!

From knowledge to ability and back again

Does that mean that ability is acquired only by doing? Do we perhaps no longer need any knowledge? Are knowledge and knowledge transfer superfluous? Should we just learn by doing – by trial and error? A radical idea, isn't it? But let's think this through critically. Let's think back to our doctor example. A doctor – the bookworm – who has read a lot but has never operated. And the second doctor, the one who doesn't like to read but has gained a lot of practical experience. How did the second doctor get to where he or she is today? If their learning was exclusively by trial and error, it would be fair to ask a provocative question: How many patients had to die before the first successful operation? And how many would die if junior doctors only learned by trial-and-error? Too many! This example shows us that (factual-declarative) knowledge has great, even decisive, value. We need it, especially when it comes to such complex tasks as surgery. Knowledge is like a compass that shows us where we can find promising alternatives for action. Knowledge helps us find orientation among the infinite alternatives of action. Thus, knowledge becomes a decisive step in the efficient acquisition of skills (abilities), and an optimal starting point for using them. Thus, it's the combination of practical action and theoretical knowledge that brings us to mastery the fastest. Or as Masha Ibeschitz aptly puts it: "Knowledge or theory makes you smarter – practice makes you wiser – sustainble success requires both!"

> Knowledge makes us into doers faster. Instead of having to learn everything through trial and error, knowledge shows us where to find the most promising actions.

And how do we now get from the starting point of knowledge to the destination point of ability? Or, more scientifically, how do we proceduralize declarative knowledge? Anderson has addressed this topic in his much-publicized ACT (Adaptive Control of Thoughts) theory.[5] Step 1: we store knowledge in the form of facts (for example, to change the gear in the car, I have to operate the gearstick). At the same time, our brains also examine how and where this new factual knowledge can match up with existing knowledge. (Yes, I have seen such a stick in many cars; it's the thing between the driver and front passenger seats.) Step 2: proceduralizing the knowledge. We watch, try, and re-try until we get it right (watch what the instructor does – now try it yourself – engage the clutch and shift the gearstick – take your foot off the clutch and accelerate – the engine dies – aha, that was apparently too little gas – try again, but slower – now the car is shuddering – aha, that was too much ...). Gradually we extract the implicit if-then rules, at first roughly, and then more fine-tuned. We gradually do less and less conscious cognitive work and thinking. More and more it just "works" (Perhaps your driving instructor has repeatedly told you, "Engage gear and slooooowly let up the clutch – accelerate, accelerate!" And a few hours later, when driving on a flat road, you can do it naturally and without the instructor's commands. It's only when you're driving on a hill that you suddenly hear the reminder "Accelerate, accelerate!" Another subtlety of the driving if-then rules). And now for step 3 on the path to ability and mastery: Optimization! The action has become automatic, a "program" largely independent of cognitive control. We do not need to "tune in" our minds, we act instinctively, by feeling. (Today, while in the car, you will probably have hundreds of thoughts pass through your mind, talk to the passenger, or make a phone call and still drive along effortlessly, without having to say anything or even having to think about the clutch-accelerator issue.) We automate the action so much that we forget the facts behind it more and more, making it increasingly difficult to explain. (This explains the disappointment commonly felt by someone sitting in the car for the first time and wanting to learn to drive from a family member, only to hear, "Yeah, you just have to play with the clutch and accelerator until you get it right"). It's just like the professional chess players and Olympic champions who are the best in their fields but can no longer explain their actions! It is truly an art to be both an expert and a good teacher for someone who is just starting out – and this is the perfect combination for learners!

> Abilities are learned in three steps: (1) Store facts declaratively; (2) Convert factual knowledge into rules by trial and error, observation, and correction; (3) Optimize rules and make them automatic through repetition.

The transition to acting automatically is not the only reason why processes are difficult to explain. In many cases, it makes learning necessary! We have automated some actions to such an extent that we are no longer aware that they are or were counter-productive. What happens if we have been driving in our own car for years, and suddenly get into the company car, which has an automatic transmission? We reach out for the non-existent gearstick and automatically extend a foot to feel for a non-existent clutch pedal. And what do we do then? We act like we're in driving school again and talk to ourselves about the process, perhaps out loud: "Wait a sec, this is an automatic! Let go of the stick!" We deliberately have to bring the automated action – the if-then-rules – back into our consciousness, add any new facts that may be relevant, and replace the old with the new rules, until sooner or later this routine can run unconsciously again. When driving, this may not have any major consequences, and it just looks a bit odd that we again and again try to operate the non-existing gearstick. But the same applies to other, more crucial learning topics! Let's consider a manager, for example. Managers are under intensifying time pressure, because in times of stress, they tend to revert to automatically doing everything themselves, instead of delegating things. Because, back when they were ordinary employees, the rule was: if more work arrives, then work faster. The only way to stop this vicious circle of reverting to old habits is through reflection, re-evaluation of the automatic pattern of action. -Such deliberate reflection allows a manager to replace the old method with a newer, more efficient rule. So, we see, as effective and efficient as it is to store certain rules in the "automatic" procedural memory where they are no longer a burden on the conscious mind, these automatic routines can get in the way when we want to explain our actions (as mentioned for the chess player or Olympic athlete), and when rules persist that are now wrong or inefficient in the present. Then we need to recall the implicit rules and assumptions, review the supposed facts they are based on, and, on the basis of reflection and feedback, recalibrate them. Factual knowledge and procedural "know how" go hand in hand. Both are crucial, meaningful, and necessary in order to learn efficiently and sustainably.

> Learning sometimes also means being aware of and changing the unconscious rules behind automated action.

How your trainees become doers and experts

Extracting rules, combining knowledge and skills, activating deep processing levels, and committing knowledge to long-term memory – what does all this mean for our trainings? How exactly do we support our trainees on the way through knowledge to ability and mastery? All these findings, which have now been confirmed by modern brain-activity research, lead us back to a pragmatic, scientifically based, and already famous model: David A. Kolb's learning cycle. His learning cycle provides us with practical support in designing our trainings.

According to Kolb[6], learning how to do something works in four stages: Concrete experiences form the basis for reflections and observations. From these, learners can derive abstract theories and concepts, or accept them from an external source. The theories and concepts are then used to experiment and try out, before finally gaining concrete experiences in a real-life situation.

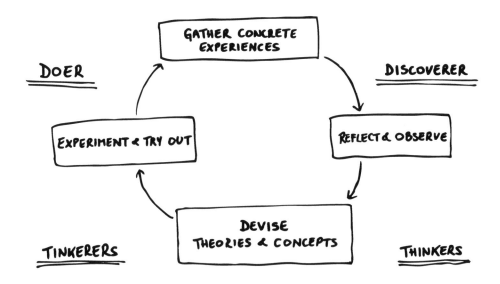

Fig. 4   Abilities can be developed in four stages - the learning cycle according to David A. Kolb

Studies show that learners have one or several preferred learning modes[7]: *Discoverers* prefer a divergent learning mode. They especially enjoy learning through feedback, reflection, and exchange of experiences. They love to share experiences and discuss different perspectives. Discoverers like to work in groups, gather information and experiences from their colleagues, observe others, and listen attentively and openly to what others have experienced and learned.

Thinkers prefer an assimilating learning mode. They know how to gather a wide range of information and compile it into a coherent, logical form. Thinkers are less interested in individual personal testimonials, but they love abstract theories and general concepts. It is less crucial to them what they can do with a theory, a concept, or a model. What counts for thinkers is that it can explain and capture phenomena in a coherent, stringent, logical, and convincing manner. It is this deep and general understanding that satisfies the thinker. In learning situations, thinkers prefer readings, lectures, discussions, and exploration of models, and they spend much of the time thinking through things by themselves and independently.

Tinkerers prefer a converging learning mode. They are experts in applying theories. They want to know the theory behind how something functions, so as to use that knowledge for their own purposes. Theories are good when they help provide solid answers to questions about practical issues, such as solving problems or making informed decisions. Tinkerers love to try out a theory, model, or idea directly and to experiment with it.

Doers prefer an accommodating learning style. They like "hands-on" learning – through trial-and-error. They try different approaches and develop a feel for what works best in practice. Empirical values and their gut feeling serve as a basis for their actions, and less analytical data and abstract theories. They love to work with others, to implement projects, to face new challenges, and to go straight to the field immediately and without many or any preliminaries.

Each person is in part a discoverer, a thinker, a tinkerer and a doer. But each of us has one or more learning preferences – one or more preferred learning modes. These can be determined by our genes and our personality type, but also by our education, our job, our chosen career path, and, yes, the culture in which we grew up and live. The fact that we prefer to learn in a certain mode does not mean that other learning modes are ineffective for us. On the contrary, unfamiliar learning modes can bring about decisive learning success. For example, managers often feel comfortable in the realm of active experimentation, where they have concrete experiences. Reflective observation, on the other hand, is a less popular and less common learning mode for them. However, when managers engage in training involving reflective learning, it often leads to substantial and highly decisive developmental steps.

Trainers and other instructors often demonstrate a preference for the thinker learning mode. They are skilled in reflecting and like theories, models, and concepts. When this is our own learning preference, it quickly leads us to filter the content of the course and to adapt it to our own preferences. So, we may employ many solid models and good theories and place a strong emphasis on reflection – just because we see this as valuable and educational. However, without noticing it, we trainers may spend too little time in training on applying the theories and putting them into practice, role-playing, and gaining experiences in realistic situations. Yet balance is crucial to the ability to motivate and teach trainees. Kolb and his research highlight the fact that we can best support our trainees by incorporating all four modes of learning – discovering, thinking, tinkering, and doing. Where we start is irrelevant. But it is recommended to start where trainees' preferences lie. This generates motivation and ensures that content and methods are perceived as relevant and compatible. Because training groups usually contain a mix of learning mode preferences, and effective learning of skills requires all four learning modes, we as trainers should design our training concepts specifically to combine reflection, theory, experimenting, testing, and giving practical experiences. Transfer research has shown that it is often the realm of experimentation and experience that gets too little attention in trainings. So, it pays to critically scrutinize your own learning preferences. Perhaps it is the reflection- and theory-loving thinker in us as trainers that whispers in our ear: "This theory/ reflection exercise is clear on its own," even though a practical exercise would be more useful for learning and transfer success! It is only through trial and practice that our trainees become knowers *and* doers!

> Learning new skills effectively usually depends on being exposed to the content via all four learning modes! So, in your training concept, combine all four: reflection, theory, experimentation/exercises, and practical experience.

Summary

When participants are to apply what they have learned, it is not enough for them to simply acquire knowledge in training. Because knowing is not the same as doing. Learning how to do something involves extracting rules from the process. Factual knowledge can help, because it shows us where to find promising alternative courses of action. Communicate such declarative knowledge (knowing that) so that the helpful facts leave deep marks in the memory and are thus easily recalled and also retained for a long time. The way to accomplish this is to have trainees work with the content themselves. So, dispense with long lectures and give preference to modules that are active, personally relevant to the trainees, and have some emotional color or content! However, laying the basis for long-term retention of facts is only the first step. In order to make factual knowledge applicable, it must be proceduralized – that is, "knowing that" must become "knowing how." And that requires learning by doing. In practical exercises and experimentation, trainees automatically extract the rules covering each step in making an action successful in all its complexity. Our brain is a pro in extracting rules. All we have to do is give it the opportunity to play around and fine-tune the rules based on practice, reflection, and experience. For effective learning in the context of mastering how to do something, it is necessary to combine all four learning modes (reflection, theory, exercises/experimentation, and practical experience). Let us not be influenced by time pressures or by our own preferences for theory-laden training, which turns our trainees into knowers, but not into doers. Let's stick to the rule of thumb for transfer-effective training: schedule at least 30 % of the training time for active practice!

At a glance:
Ideas for reflection and implementation

Doing instead of just talking about it
- From active learning to active, realistic practice
  (with examples from practice)

Learn rules based on examples, cases, demos, or errors
- Behavior modeling
- Error management approach

Give your input models more processing depth
- Accompanying quiz
- Fill-in-the-blanks and open answers
- Buzz-groups (with sample exercises)
- Accompanying tasks
- Knowledge gallery
- Myth or reality

Activate your trainees instead of "over-serving" them
- Assign tasks to trainees
- Get commitment to self-responsibility for learning and transfer success

Doing instead of just talking about it

In the field of training, active practice is often equated with active learning. When trainers glance over their own training concepts, they may be tempted to say, "My participants are very active in my trainings, probably for even more than 30 % of the training time." If trainees are active – for example, developing a theoretical model themselves, discussing what they have learned in group work, or experiencing certain phenomena themselves in exercises – we might be talking about active learning, but not active practice. These forms of active learning, in contrast to classroom-style presentation, are an effective means of developing and memorizing knowledge with a deep processing effect. But many trainings overlook the importance of active practice, i.e., learning by doing exactly the action that the training is devoted to. Let's look at the difference between active learning (being active in training) and active practice as illustrated by some practical examples:

Training topic	Example of active learning	Examples of active practice
Conducting discussions in conflict resolution	In group work, trainees reflect in tandems on what partner's "iceberg" contains under the water's surface	In role-playing, trainees themselves conduct discussions to resolve conflict
Planning projects with project management tools	In small groups, trainees consider which of the 10 stumbling blocks of project management led to the failure of their projects	Trainees plan a project in their own area of work
Leadership	Trainees collect pros and cons of certain leadership styles and discuss their suitability for specific managerial situations	Different leadership situations are simulated. In addition, small groups each receive a specific task. One trainee is designated as manager and then tries out leading the group using a specific management style
Designing training concepts	Trainees discuss the elements of a training concept (introduction, input phases, exercises, repetition, daily wrap-up, etc.)	Trainees design their own training
Successful selling at point-of-sale	Trainees collect phrases suitable for addressing customers on the the sales floor	Trainees conduct sales talks with real customers at point of sale
Telesales	Trainees create a guideline script for their next acquisition call	Trainees call a potential customer

In the optimal case, active practice means doing in training exactly what will later be required at work. It is important to design the conditions of the exercise to match those of the workplace as closely as possible. The very best active practice exercises succeed in combining the orientation to action with a very high degree of realism.

Training topic	Examples of active practice	Examples of active, realistic practice
Persuasive presentations	Trainees give a short speech on a topic pulled randomly from a hat/box (e.g., "The need for toothpaste for cats")	Trainees give a short talk that they would realistically deliver in their work context (e.g., the elevator pitch to persuade a potential investor to fund their business idea next month)
Solution-oriented coaching	In role plays, trainees practice the clarification phase in coaching discussions	Trainees conduct a complete coaching discussion with a real coaching customer
Writing a business plan	Trainees create a business plan for a business idea of their choice	Trainees create their business plan for their own planned business

In order to empower the participants and prepare them optimally for successfully accomplishing the desired action (the presentation, the coaching interview, the business plan, the acquisition phone call, the sales pitch, the training concept, the arbitration, etc.), it goes without saying that supportive theory, helpful models, tips, exchanges, and reflections are needed – without a doubt. Active learning is exactly what's needed here. However, to support trainees' in gaining real ability to do these things – and to be convinced themselves that they can do it – requires additional active practice, optimally not only active but also as realistic as possible. So, take another look at your training concept and make sure that your trainees not only learn actively (and talk about the intended action) but also practice actively and attempt their intended actions under near-realistic conditions. Follow the recommendation of the transfer researchers: design your training with active practice for at least 30 % of the training time! In addition, it is advisable for trainees to have the opportunity to try out an exercise multiple times (for example, to give a presentation twice). This allows trainees to reflect on their actions and refine and improve them on the basis of feedback and their own experiences. It also gives trainees a solidly successful experience in applying the new skill in preparation for its real use at work and thus increases their self-efficacy.

Learn rules based on examples, cases, demonstrations – and errors!

We can do things when we have understood and extracted the underlying rules. In order to facilitate skills acquisition, it is important to support trainees in learning rules. A practical way to implement this has been proposed by Ralf Besser. He recommends that the participants themselves extract such rules on the basis of a number of examples or cases.[8] How does this work in practice? Hand out practical examples to your trainees – without a prior lecture or theoretical inputs. The examples should be selected such that trainees can work out the underlying rules. The examples might consist of three case descriptions, three error descriptions, three typical assignments, etc., from which rules can be derived. Why three examples? Because a single example is clearly not enough. With only two, the underlying rule could still be a coincidence. It is only from exposure to three or more instances that the feeling of law or regularity emerges. Trainees then split into their small groups to discuss their set of examples with the assignment to answer this question: "What fundamental principle can you derive from the three examples?" This leads the trainees to actively and independently search for the rules.

Another practical approach to actively learning rules is behavior modeling. The idea comes from the US psychologist Albert Bandura, who found out that we learn very well through observation (see also pages 49 ff.). We also become accustomed to observational learning from an early age. We have learned many key things by watching our parents or others who have mastered a successful action. *Behavior modeling* makes learning by observing a core element in training. Various studies have shown that it increases a training's transfer effectiveness.[9] How does learning by observing work? How can you use its recipe for success in your own training? Specifically, behavior modeling means not only informing your trainees about content, techniques, models, stumbling blocks, etc., but also demonstrating how to perform the behavior successfully. When you practice "Negotiation Techniques," you do not show the techniques on a PowerPoint slide but experience them through role-playing with another trainee. If you train "Conflict Resolution," then you act out a conflicted conversation. And if you train "Selling by Phone," then you demonstrate how you act on the phone yourself. If you do not want to do it yourself, you can also use videos. The only thing that matters is that the participants can observe the complex action in a situation that is as realistic as possible. Through this observation – and supplementary questions to promote reflection on the action – trainees can extract the rules of successful action from the situation in question, and that is, as everyone knows, the basis for strengthening one's own ability. A tip: It is particularly effective if the participants can observe both positive and negative demonstrations or, in general, see several action alternatives in real life or near-real life (such as video clips) – as this then makes extracting the underlying rules even easier (see also pages 55 ff.).

In addition to behavior modeling – i.e., learning about action models – another approach to training has proved to be especially transfer-oriented: the *error management approach*.[10] In a nutshell, one could describe this approach as learning by making mistakes, by trial and error. It is an exploratory approach – that is, learning through trial and error and receiving feedback. The whole thing works like this: After minimal introduction to a topic, trainees immediately try to handle the learning content themselves. The feedback they receive makes the attempts more effective, efficient, and better with each attempt. Let me give you an example. Imagine you are holding a training on "Giving a Successful Speech." Now you could follow a classic training setup. First, some lecture content (e.g., what is needed to get started), next an exercise (e.g., collection of ideas for speech introductions), then another piece of lecture content, the next exercise, etc. The error management approach, in contrast, might look like this: a mini-input (for example, five points that make your speech effective) – and then every trainee holds their own complete speech! Everyone gets detailed and individualized feedback. Then the next round. Again, a complete speech from each participant. And, again, there's feedback and so on to improve the individual performance along the way. In the error management approach, it's important that you specifically point out that mistakes are inevitable. Errors are the basis of learning and critical to learning success, especially in this approach! Incidentally, this approach is used frequently and particularly successfully in software training. As you have seen, the approach also has exciting implications for other training areas. Through repeated practice, trainees gradually extract the central and important rules for their own success. In addition, this continuous self-tuning promotes self-efficacy and motivation – important determinants of transfer success.

Bring more processing depth into your lecture content

A typical element of trainings are lectures. Trainers present their lecture content via PowerPoint or flipchart – trainees sit passively in their chairs and soak up the content. The attention curve usually drops rapidly, and the danger of only communicating knowledge rather than action is high – a situation that is far from optimal for motivation, learning, and transfer effectiveness. So, how can you make lectures more active? How can you, as a trainer, make sure that what you say is heard with a high degree of processing depth, and thus sustainably memorized? Here are some ideas to inspire you:

Lectures accompanied by quiz elements. Keep your trainees active by challenging them with quiz questions parallel to your lecture!

What can this look like in practice? Divide the trainees into small groups before you start your lecture. The task of these groups: Answer quiz questions and earn points. Start your lecture with the first quiz question. In a production training session, a first question might be: "How long do you think it took to develop this product?" The groups briefly discuss this and write down their guesses. You as a trainer give the points to the group(s) that answer correctly or were closest to the correct answer. Only now do you elaborate your content (in our example: "Yes, Group 2 was pretty close with their answer of six years. Development for this product started exactly six years and three months ago today. The idea arose, as so often, over a glass of wine and written down on a napkin."). Keep your speaking time short, ideally only a few minutes at a time, and then, depending on the content, immediately ask the next quiz question (e.g., "What do you think, what is the lifespan of this new product?"). After the groups have written down their answers and given them, you provide the correct answer, as well as additional information ("This time, Group 4 was the closest. It's three years. And that's guaranteed – thanks to technology XY.") And so on. With this method, you manage to convey your content and, at the same time, to persuade your trainees to think about it and participate by answering the quiz questions. The competitive nature of the exercises further supports motivation.

Handout with blank spaces. Keep your trainees active by giving them handouts with gaps or blank spaces

Many well-known speakers work with gaps in their lecture notes. They give lecture handouts not as a complete body of text but as a text with blank spaces, which trainees fill in during the lecture. If you use PowerPoint slides during your lecture, you can easily adapt this technique. Print out the slides in advance for each trainee – but in a way that lacks some crucial terms or phrases (just place white rectangles over these before printing or photocopying). Distribute the PowerPoint presentation with the blanks before your lecture. Explain to the participants the benefit of the blanks (e.g., "We memorize things much more easily and for longer if we not only hear and see them, but also make notes on them ourselves."). You will be amazed at how committed and active the trainees are when it comes to filling in these blanks. The human brain strives to complete the incomplete – and that is what we take advantage of here.

The same principle applies to open spaces. Encourage each participant to think about what this content means for their own practice, or how they might use the content for themselves. Perhaps you will explain different principles in your training, each with its own presentation slide. Print off the sheets so that your presentation slides are on the top half of the A4 paper and there is a blank space in the bottom half with a prompt question (e.g., "What does this mean for my work in practice?" Or: "How could you use this principle yourself?"). During your lecture, take a short break after each slide so that participants can make notes.

Lectures with buzz groups. Keep your trainees active by repeatedly asking them to briefly reflect on what they have just heard or to solve a mini-task with one or more colleagues. Here are some ideas for tasks and questions for the buzz groups:

Example of tasks and questions for buzz groups[11]

- Explain the content to a layperson or someone who was not in the room
- In a few sentences, summarize the most important points from what you've just heard
- Apply the content to a practical example or in a mini role-play
- Discuss how individuals already know or have already experienced in their own practice what they've just heard
- Ask each other questions about the content just heard and answer them
- Imagine that the person sitting next to you is your boss or colleague and explain the content to him or her
- Think about what you just heard has to do with you or how you could apply what you heard to your own practical work
- etc.

Be sure to consider in advance what question or task you will assign to the buzz-groups. It should be easy to deal with in five minutes, easy to understand, and beneficial to trainees. Furthermore, it is helpful before delivery of the first piece of lecture content to inform trainees that the content and buzz discussion phases will alternate.

What should you do after the buzz discussions? Unlike regular group work, the buzz-group's discussion does not have to be tediously resolved (e.g., through a presentation, a summary, etc.). Just ask, "Is that okay?" or "Are there any questions left?" Then move on to the next 10 minutes of content.

Psychologically, the switchover from listening to content to actively processing it in the buzz-group is ideal. What trainees hear, they then immediately repeat and process in more depth. This firmly anchors the content, the goal of keeping your trainees active in input phases.

Lectures with accompanying tasks. Keep trainees active by assigning tasks in parallel with your lecture content.

There are a number of ways to keep participants active through accompanying tasks. For example, prior to your lecture, hand out a sheet of questions to which you will respond in the lecture segment. As you deliver your lecture content, participants enter their answers to the questions on this sheet. (Alternately, you can design this for trainees to do after delivery of the lecture content or by means of short breaks in your presentation.) Review the questions after the lecture content together as a group. This approach has three advantages: (1) You keep your trainees are active (remember, the brain does not like empty spaces). (2) Through the prepared questions, you can direct the focus of the participants toward the core messages. (3) You reinforce what has been learned by repeating it once again in the common resolution in the plenary. Alternately, you can give each participant only one question to focus on in the upcoming lecture. As in the above, all questions and answers are pulled together through a group discussion.

Instead of issuing questions, you can also invite your trainees to create a *knowledge gallery* together. For this purpose, you distribute cards and ask trainees to record the most important, exciting, and relevant facts and insights learned during the lecture. These cards are then presented during a group discussion and then hung on a clothesline or pinned to a board clearly visible within the room. This "group memory" keeps the important content ever-present and preserves it for immediate reference and potentially later use. Alternately, the knowledge cards can also be created subsequent to delivery of the lecture content or during short breaks.

Another exciting form of activity during delivery of your lecture content is the *myth versus reality* assignment. For this, give each participant two cards, one red and one green. During your lecture, you repeatedly make statements that may or may not be true. For example, a slide on your product presentation may say, "This product has twice the service life of the competitor's product X." The best are ones that are currently well-propagated as rumors anyway. After the claim, pause and ask participants to vote for "myth" or "reality." ("If you think this is true, please hold up the green card. If you think it's a myth, hold up the red one.") Give the solution, resolve any issues, and continue with your lecture content until the next assertion. Important: Make sure that the false information (myths!) does not become established as facts in trainees' minds. Make clear what the truth is and repeat it several times!

Activate your trainees instead of "over-serving" them

Active practice means that trainees are active themselves, not passively consuming. But that doesn't come easily to many trainers. Instead of taking a back seat and having trainees do as much as they can for themselves, many trainers "(over-)serve" their groups. Professor Bernd Weidenmann suspects that this trainer behavior is due to three needs or beliefs.[12]

- The desire for control ("If I do it myself, it will work for sure")
- The claim to be caring ("I want to deliver the best-possible work")
- The desire for likability ("If I do many things for them, they will like me")

Fashionable terms such as "infotainment" support this attitude. They signal that it is the trainers' task to entertain trainees with knowledge and to keep them happy as an entertainer might at a holiday resort. Trainees should be able to passively consume, as if sitting in front of a TV or a live show. Of course, such an attitude is anything but conducive to learning and transfer success. In addition, the three trainer needs just mentioned are probably more attributable to selfishness than true trainee orientation, says Bernd Weidenmann. Their manifestation usually leads to the opposite of what was intended. Recognition for successful training is more likely to go to trainers who assign activities to trainees and stimulate active participation. The credo for trainers is therefore: Do as little as possible yourself; shift as much action as possible to the trainees. What can this look like in practice? How can trainers keep their trainees active? Which tasks can they hand over? Here are some ideas for your next training, inspired by Bernd Weidenmann:

Assign tasks to trainees[13]

- At the beginning of the training, ask your participants what they really want to do better after the training or which questions they would like to have answered
- Distribute some roles using task cards or a task list on a flipchart:
  ◇ The timekeeper takes care of adherence to agreed timeslots
  ◇ The break reminder tells the trainer when the group needs a break
  ◇ The manager takes care of food orders, drinks, and other organizational issues
  ◇ The activator prepares the activation exercise after lunch
  ◇ The reporter sums up what has been learned at the beginning and/or end of the day
  ◇ The transfer officer keeps asking questions about how the lessons learned could be applied in practice
- If you are brainstorming in plenary, invite a trainee to record the verbal prompts on the flipchart
- When you perform a card exercise, have trainees pin their cards to the whiteboard themselves or organize them into clusters themselves
- Reduce your own speaking time in the delivery of lecture content. Check whether lectures could be replaced or shortened by using more active methods
- Let your trainees decide for themselves how much time they need for a certain group work or want to take for the next break
- Let trainees decide for themselves how to practice theoretical content or models
- Have the participants develop the roles or situations in their role-plays for themselves

- In your concept, plan on buffering times (e.g., one hour per day) in which trainees decide for themselves what they need to do and/or practice
- Leave it up to trainees to plan evening and leisure activities
- Live by the principle: "If you have a problem, you have a responsibility to solve it." For example, if a participant complains about the room, the food, or a colleague, you can be sympathetic, but leave the solution to them (e.g., "I understand that bothers you. Talk to the receptionist / the kitchen / your colleague.").
- Have the participants plan their own transfer intentions (see Lever 7 – Transfer Planning).

The message of all these mini-interventions: this training is YOUR training. YOU – together with me – are responsible for the success or failure of this event. And YOU bear the responsibility for your learning and transfer success! Because this is adult-appropriate learning "at eye level" (see also Lever 1 - Transfer Motivation).

Time for transfer!

Now it's your turn! How do you enable active practice in training? How can you ensure that the action that you aspire to in practice is experienced, tried, and practiced as realistically as possible during training? What is the next step that you would like to implement? Spontaneously write down your ideas and thoughts.

This is how I will promote content relevance:

1 Depending on the scope and difficulty of the objectives, up to 50 % of the training time should be devoted to active practice: Day, E. A., Blair, C., Daniels, S., Kligyte, V., & Mumford, M. D., "Linking instructional objectives to the design of instructional environments: The Integrative Training Design Matrix" in *Human Resource Management Review,* 2006, 16(3): pp. 376 – 395.

2 That active training methods are superior to passive ones for knowledge acquisition and transfer results was demonstrated by the meta-study detailed in Burke, M. J., Sarpy, S. A., Smith-Crowe, K., Chan-Serafin, S., Salvador, R. O., & Islam, G., "Relative effectiveness of worker safety and health training methods" in *Journal Information,* 2006, 96(2).

3 These and other interesting facts about learning and the brain can be found in the highly readable work of Spitzer, M., *Lernen: Gehirnforschung und die Schule des Lebens,* Spektrum Akademischer Verlag, 2002.

4 The example with the doctors comes from the entertaining and readable book by Dobelli, who dedicated a chapter to the topic of knowledge, skills, and active practice in his best-selling book: Dobelli, R., *Die Kunst des klugen Handelns. 52 Irrwege, die Sie besser anderen überlassen.* (3rd Edition). Munich: dtv Verlagsgesellschaft. 2014, p. 141.

5 On ACT Theory, see, for example, Anderson, J. R., "ACT: A simple theory of complex cognition" in *American Psychologist,* 1996, 51(4): pp. 355-365.

6 A current overview of the learning cycle and types of learning according to Kolb can be found in: Kolb, A. Y., & Kolb, D. A., "Experiential Learning Theory: A Dynamic, Holistic Approach to Management Learning, Education, and Development" in S. J. Armstrong, & C. Fukami (Eds.), *Handbook of Management Learning, Education, and Development,* SAGE Publishing, 2011, pp. 42 – 68.

7 A good overview and references to various studies on the learning cycle can be found in Kolb, A. Y., & Kolb, D. A., "Experiential Learning Theory: A Dynamic, Holistic Approach to Management Learning, Education, and Development" in S. J. Armstrong, & C. Fukami (Eds.), *Handbook of Management Learning, Education, and Development,* SAGE Publishing, 2011, pp. 42 – 68.

8 A short, practical article on learning rules: Besser, R., "Konsequenzen aus der Hirnforschung: Regel- vor Faktenlernen" in *Trainer Kontakt Brief,* 2009, 7/09, Nr. 67.

9 On the effectiveness of behavioral modeling, see, for example, Burke, L. A., & Hutchins, H. M., "Training Transfer: An Integrative Literature Review" in *Human Resource Development Review,* 2007, 6(3): pp. 263 – 296; Burke, M. J., & Day, R. R., "A Cumulative Study of the Effectiveness of Managerial Training" in *Journal of Applied Psychology,* 1986, 71(2): pp.232 – 245; Latham, G. P., "Behavioral approaches to the training and learning process" in I. L. Goldstein (Ed.), *Training and Development in Organizations,* San Francisco: Jossey-Bass, 1989, pp. 256 – 259., Robertson, I. T.,

"Behaviour modelling: Its record and potential in training and development" in *British Journal of Management,* 1990, 1(2): pp.117 – 125.

[10] For a description and meta-analysis of the effectiveness of the error management approach in training, see Keith, N., & Frese, M., "Effectiveness of error management training: A meta-analysis" in *Journal of Applied Psychology,* 2008, 93(1): p. 59.

[11] These and other ideas and suggestions for buzz-groups and other exciting alternatives to classical lecture-based teaching can be found in the highly readable book by Weidenmann, B., *Handbuch Active Training: Die besten Methoden für lebendige Seminare.* (3rd Edition). Weinheim and Basel: Beltz Verlag. 2015, pp. 25ff.

[12] For the three needs behind the trainer service, see Weidenmann, B., *Handbuch Active Training: Die besten Methoden für lebendige Seminare.* (3rd Edition). Weinheim and Basel: Beltz Verlag, 2015, pp. 20ff.

[13] Some of the above-mentioned and many more suggestions and tips for trainee activation can be found in Weidenmann, B., *Handbuch Active Training: Die besten Methoden für lebendige Seminare.* (3rd Edition). Weinheim and Basel: Beltz Verlag, 2015, pp. 21ff.

LEVER 7 – TRANSFER PLANNING

TWO PRACTICAL EXAMPLES

It's Thursday afternoon. Armin and Axel have attended a training entitled "Healthy eating at the workplace – possible or not?" Read what the two think while driving home afterwards.

Armin, 32, graphic designer

It was a surprisingly enriching training. I can't believe how much I've weakened my performance with my poor eating habits. The many small tips we got were great: having "emergency snacks" in the drawer, setting the breakfast table the night before, taking a thermo box to work, and so on. I will definitely implement some of these things. Next week, I'm going to take some time and read through all of the information once again, thoroughly.

Axel, 29, technical illustrator

Great training! Straightforward facts, hands-on tips – just what I needed. I'll be getting more efficient, save time, and have fun, too. I'll do the very first step right now at the supermarket: I'll buy two packs of nuts with cranberries and a bulk pack of those cereal bars for my "emergency snack drawer." I already ordered a thermo box online during training. Also, from now on, I'll follow two strict rules: (1) When I drink my morning coffee, I'll eat a cereal bar with it. (2) When I cook dinner in the evening, one serving goes into my thermo box. During the first 30 days, my memory stickers will help me keep to my rules, both at work and at home. Yes, it feels good to be more efficient!

Which of the two do, do you reckon, is more likely to achieve good transfer results? Why? Where is the difference?

Armin has some more-or-less specific ideas of what he could implement from his training. He doesn't have a concrete plan, though. He'll need to dedicate some more time and effort to "going through the documents thoroughly," to decide for himself what he will implement, how, and when. It will be interesting to see whether Armin will actually do that, when he gets to the office on Monday and sees all the work that's been piling up while he was away. Axel, on the other hand, already has a plan worked out. He knows exactly what he's going to do, step by step, based on his transfer plan. And it is this transfer plan that makes the difference. For transfer success, it is crucial that trainees have a clear plan of how they will put into practice and use what they have learned. The more concrete the plan and the stronger people's commitment to their goal and their intentions, the easier it will be for them to achieve good transfer results in practice, and the higher the probability of success. Transfer planning is a process that requires time and cognitive effort – a process that trainees (can) rarely spend time on when they return to their workplace. It is important to make time during training to ensure that this crucial planning process can happen, supported by appropriate methods. Transfer planning is an elementary standard sequence in transfer-promoting training designs.[1]

TRANSFER PLANNING – STEP BY STEP TO IMPLEMENTATION SUCCESS

	Transfer planning in a nutshell
Trainees say	"I know what I am going to do, step by step, after training!"
Definition	Transfer planning describes the extent to which the transfer is prepared in training.
Guiding question	How can you ensure that trainees prepare in detail while still in training to implement what they learn?

What we can learn from Caesar

By setting up a transfer plan or defining an individual transfer objective (we speak of a transfer intention), trainees make a decision: They decide what they will apply.

"The die is cast." This decision has far-reaching and strongly transfer-promoting psychological consequences, as illustrated by a dramatic historical event that took place in ancient Rome.

The Rubicon: a small river in the north of Italy with a big history. In antiquity, it separated Gaul from Italy, and no Roman general was allowed to cross it with troops. At this little river, none other than Julius Caesar made a momentous decision. The Senate had ordered him to dissolve his army in Gaul. So, he had to return to Rome quickly – and with his army – as his power in Rome was hanging in the balance. On 10th January 49 BC, he stood on the Gaul-side bank of the Rubicon, deliberating. "Up to here, we can still go back. But once we cross this little bridge, we face an armed struggle." The decision he made there and then became famous: *"Alea iacta est* – The die is cast." Caesar and his army crossed the Rubicon. This decision led to war and Caesar won, making him the sole ruler of the Roman Empire.

This event lent its name to the Rubicon Model, a motivation- and volition-focused psychological model created by two German psychologists, Heinz Heckhausen and Peter Gollwitzer. The model describes how individuals select and implement their intentions to act. In a nutshell, the model has three parts: "Desire – Plan – Act." A deliberate course of action begins with a phase of consideration to determine what I really want: Should or shouldn't I? Should I do this or that? Which of the many options should I choose? It was the same flurry of questions for Caesar (Should or shouldn't we cross this river?). And that is how things often are for us (Should I clear out the garage or not? Should I ask my boss for a raise? Should I stay with the company or look for another job? Etc.). We weigh up different wishes and related goals against each other. Our criteria are desirability (the value of the action's result) and feasibility (the expectation that the action will produce the desired result). Of course, you could clear out the garage, but reading the newspaper in the garden might be even better. A higher salary would be great, but how will my boss respond if I ask her? This job is so-so, but who knows whether the next one will be better and whether they'll hire me? Inner dialogs like these and conversations with others about the topics in question can draw out the process – sometimes to the point where there is no decision at all, and thus no action. In cases like these, lots of thoughts start piling up in the back of our minds: "I really should …" or "I would actually like to …" Sooner or later they are replaced by newer thoughts of the same kind. Usually, what remains is a dull feeling of constantly wanting or having to do things instead of really taking action. In an ideal case, however, these inner dialogs result in a decision to act. Once this decision is made, the consideration process comes to an end. The Rubicon is crossed, our goal intention becomes binding. We feel committed to realizing it. (The extent of this commitment, in turn, depends on the desirability and feasibility of the goal, as discussed earlier.)

Newly developed goals cannot always be tackled immediately. In a salary negotiation, for example, it is necessary to be well prepared and to wait for a good opportunity. Then we plan according to the Rubicon model: We specify when, where, and how to approach and reach the goal – until an opportunity turns up.

Why does the Rubicon Model so strongly emphasize this crossing of the Rubicon – the transition from choosing to planning? Simply put, the answer is: because we think differently in these two phases, as extensive research by Gollwitzer and Bayer (1999) has shown.

In the first phase, in which we weigh our options, we are in a deliberating state of mind. We assess the positive and negative consequences of our goals, the likelihood of achieving them, and our influence on this likelihood very objectively and realistically. Our attention is spread across a wide range of factors. New information is processed openly – both information that supports and information that inhibits goal achievement. At this stage, we also tend to be distracted by information that is irrelevant for the realization of our goals. This state of mind is very useful for the purpose of this phase – after all, we want to make a "good" decision. Once we have made it and crossed the Rubicon, we shift into a state that supports goal achievement (known as planning state of mind). Our self-esteem increases. We are more optimistic about achieving our goal. Our attention focuses on goal attainment and achievement. Any information useful for goal achievement is increasingly picked up and processed, while other information is suppressed. Our stamina in implementing our intentions increases. As you can see, the planning state of mind is very handy when it comes to realizing our goals. Here is a summary of the fantastic effects.[2]

Deliberating state of mind	Planning state of mind
Impact on self-concept	
• We rate our self-esteem as low • We feel highly vulnerable to various risks • We assess our positive qualities (e.g., intelligence, creativity) as being somewhat better than those of comparable other people	• We rate our self-esteem as high • We feel less vulnerable to the various risks • We assess our positive qualities (e.g., intelligence, creativity) as being significantly better than those of comparable other people

Impact on informational processing	
• Openness to all sorts of information • Thoughts revolve around weighing up • We remember other people's deliberations when making choices • Wide-ranging attention	• We give preference to processing information that supports the implementation of our intention • Our thoughts revolve around planning • We remember other's planning activities • Centered attention
Impact on optimism / pessimism	
• Our sense of control over uncontrollable events is less pronounced • We assess our future performance realistically	• Our sense of control over uncontrollable events is strong, even illusionary • We assess our future performance optimistically
Effect on our powers of endurance	
• Our endurance in implementing the intention is poor	• Our endurance in implementing our intention is high

To sum up: By forming an intention (the decision to do something specific), we cross the Rubicon. The phase of weighing options ("Should I?") ends here, our thinking shifts towards implementation.

What can we infer from this with regard to our trainees' transfer success? The motto is: Let's accompany our participants on their way across the Rubicon. Why? Because even if we've taught, practiced, and repeatedly demonstrated transfer possibilities during training, it takes a lot of cognitive work for people to re-assess what they've learned and choose from the many options, ideas, and wishes what they will actually tackle (consideration phase). If we send participants back to work without a transfer intention, it is easy to see how the perceived urgency of their (everyday) tasks can get in the way of the cognitive tasks of revisiting and selecting. Trainees may have had many implementation ideas during training, written them down diligently, and had a great training experience. But back in their turbulent workplace, ideas are forgotten and the folder with their notes from the training ends up in the file cabinet. Transfer success: nil. So, let's provide trainees with the opportunity and the setting, during training, to shape their transfer intentions. At the training, we – the trainers – are available to answer any open questions (which is often necessary for them to generate an intention). Once participants have crossed their Rubicon, the shift into the planning state of mind helps make it much easier for them to master implementation: through focused attention, increased optimism, the processing of information that supports implementation, enhanced self-esteem, and much more.

> When trainees generate transfer intentions,
> (1) these intentions become binding for them,
> (2) their questions about "should I" and "do I really want to" come to an end,
> (3) trainees switch into a planning state of mind.
> So, help your trainees cross the Rubicon!

How you actually learn to eat healthier

As we have seen, developing intentions is a good way to enhance transfer success. But what should such an intention look like? What should be considered? How and why does it work, and – more to the point – does it even always work? Again, I would like to offer you some exciting new scientific insights and recommendations that we can use for transfer effectiveness.

"I'm going to eat healthier" – a decision that many of us have made before. It's an intention – but is it always realized? Unfortunately, no. Intentions like these are often referred to as "goal intentions" by intention researchers (in everyday life, we often just say "goals").[3] While they have a demonstrably positive effect on achievement, when considered alone, they are insufficient. Intention researchers have discovered that often, implementation can take place only after we've developed both a goal and a concrete plan for achieving it. Planning means we set out to achieve our goal by defining concrete actions. A kind of "short plan" is what we refer to as an "implementation intention". Goals (or, more precisely, goal intentions) define target states we have not yet achieved, but which seem desirable and important. Their format is "I want (to achieve) X!". Implementation intentions (or realization intentions) serve these goals. They are "if-then plans" that support goal realization. Their format: "If situation/condition X occurs, then I will do Y." In our earlier nutritional example, the goal is: "I want to eat healthier!" The corresponding intent could be: "When I go out to eat, I will make sure to order less fried food and more vegetables!"

Isn't that bean counting? you may wonder. Does it really make a difference? Well, according to research, it does. Gollwitzer and Brandstätter, for example, asked students to state what they wanted to do before the end of the winter break holidays (e.g., write an end-of-term paper, find a new room, etc.). While some students merely named the goal, others had already specified when and where they wanted to get started with their project (so what they had voiced was more of an implementation intention). After the break, the students were asked if they had actually carried out their projects. Of those who only had a goal, 23% had achieved it – of those who had formulated an implementation intention, 62% had carried it out. Bayer and

Gollwitzer also showed that high-school students performed better in math tests when, in addition to setting goals, they also formulated implementation intentions that promoted their self-efficacy. And even with all-time classics such as quitting smoking, exercising, and losing weight, the probability of success increases when people formulate concrete implementation intentions or formulate plans. These and other results prove that concrete plans and implementation intentions can drastically enhance implementation success, compared with goals alone.[4]

Intentions can be highly effective in a variety of ways. They have a demonstrable effect when you want to initiate and execute certain actions (such as your annual medical check-up). They work when you want to keep up recurring activities (such as regular exercise after physiotherapy or regular use of medication), suppress unwanted thoughts, feelings, and actions (such as age or gender stereotypes), or replace unwanted behavior with another (such as smoking or alcohol consumption).[5]

> Along with choosing a goal, formulating an implementation intention (or a concrete plan) increases the potential for implementation success.

Why does intent work so well? As we have learned, intentions (both goal and implementation intentions) conclude the consideration phase and get us into a realization-friendly state of mind. Intentions are additionally associated with a high level of mental activation. When we think carefully about where, how, and when to do something specific (planning) connections and pathways are created in our brain. It is therefore easy for us to remember our intention, both the situation/condition (the "if" part) and the intended action (the "then" part). Studies have further shown that we more easily (and sometimes automatically) recognize the situation/condition in which we have planned to act, without having to make an effort to remember it. The intention, "If I go to dinner, then I'll order a vegetarian option" can therefore result in this intention popping up in our minds as soon as we enter the restaurant. We don't have to ask ourselves, "What was it that I had intended to do?" – the intention is simply there. Moreover, it firmly links the situation/condition to the action (i.e., the "if" part to the "then" part), so the action is triggered automatically. If we walked into the restaurant with only the goal in mind ("I want to eat healthier"), we would have to start thinking again about how exactly we want to realize this. Faced with lots of greasy temptations, that takes a lot of cognitive capacity. By contrast, carrying out an implementation intention in an if-then format requires little to no additional cognitive performance – a result that even the scientists found surprising.[6] Intentions can work like auto-pilots or habits we don't consciously think about, just follow, so they can make us order our veggies automatically, without having to convince or motivate ourselves again. Just as you brush your teeth in the morning without ever asking yourself whether you should really do it or not.

Are implementation intentions the new panacea for achieving one's goals? Research shows that their impact is impressive[7] – much greater than one would expect. Nevertheless, there are situations in which such intentions do not lead to the desired result. This may be the case, for example, if the intended behavior is not within your control (i.e., if you go to a place that does not offer vegetable dishes) or if you choose situations/conditions that hardly ever happen, if at all, which means your implementation intention cannot really take effect (i.e., you hardly ever go out to dinner).

Especially for transfer purposes, the format "If X happens, then I will do Y" may be too tight a planning frame. It may take several steps to implement complex training content, in which case it might be impossible to squeeze the plan into this format. Since the impact of if-then plans is closely linked to the effort invested in considering and choosing the path to realize your goal, another option would be to set up action plans. In such plans, which can be more or less complex, participants will address questions such as "What will I try out and why?" or "Who will support me?" and "Where will I encounter resistance, and how can I overcome it?" and "What will be my first, second, third … step?" (etc.). Let me emphasize my point once again: It is important for trainees to work intensely on the realization of their individual transfer intentions right there in the training. This effort lays down the corresponding links and pathways in their brains and induces the goal-supporting planning state of mind.

For intentions in the if-then format, and for plans in general, the key is in people's commitment to the desired goal. If someone is not really interested in healthier eating habits, the best intention and the most sophisticated plan won't help. Intentions and plans do not have the power to get people to do something they don't want to do (thank goodness!). Nevertheless, it is important for our transfer topic to know how we can assist trainees in enhancing their probability of implementation success.

Implementation intentions enhance implementation success because

(1) Trainees easily remember intentions (pathways in the brain),
(2) The situation specified in the intention almost automatically triggers the action,
(3) With implementation intentions, trainees need to make little to no additional cognitive effort when a situation conducive to the intended action arises.

SMART goals can be a pain

Intentions and plans work because, by planning precisely, we lay out paths in our minds. Easy recall and the automatic triggering of action by the situation or condition are the mechanisms that make intentions and plans so effective. But all of this only works if we have a strong commitment to our goal and feel positive about it. We need to cross the Rubicon with firm, energetic, and motivated steps, as otherwise even the best intentions will come to nothing. The way to achieve this positive motivation and determination is by setting the right goals. So, what are the "right" goals?

You've probably come across the acronym SMART. It is considered the gold standard of the "goals scene." Incidentally, it originated from the lumberjacks, as discussed in Lever 4 – Clarity of Expectations (see pages 90 ff.). Now, if you're tempted to skip this section because you know enough about SMART, please don't. I won't bother you with yet another plea for the Specific-Measurable-Achievable-Relevant-Time-bound concept. On the contrary, we'll take a critical look at the SMART hype, and I'll point out why SMART is not always optimal.

If you've ever defined a strictly SMART goal yourself, you've surely noticed that it requires a lot of mental work. It takes quite a bit of thinking to make a vague vision specific, measurable, and time-bound. At the same time, this is an advantage of SMART goals: As in conceiving and formulating intentions, we deal intensely with our goal and the implementation path. An intense effort, in turn, generates pathways in our brain, which means easier recollection, less reconsideration, etc. We've discussed this.

But what about your motivation when you have the neatly-crafted SMART goal right in front of you? Think back to our "healthier diet" example. Before the SMART era, you might have had a radiant and dazzling image in your mind's eye: sitting in a sunny garden, in top shape, summer hat, chic, light linen clothing, stylish sunglasses, bright sunshine. An attractive waiter serves a large white plate with a crisp salad, arranged in award-worthy fashion. A delight to the eye and taste buds. A big smile on your face. What a fantastic feeling to eat healthy!

Now consider how SMART transforms the goal: "Starting today, I will only eat vegetarian food for six months." What a dry, technical way of putting it. The dazzling image is gone. And the same might be true for the warm and pleasant feelings inside. In psychology, this feeling is referred to as an "affective attitude." While the SMART goal is quite attractive in a rational sense (it makes sense to eat healthy; it's reasonable and desirable), it is not necessarily associated with positive gut feelings (see also pages 67 ff.). And let's be honest, just because something's reasonable, meaningful, and rationally desirable, that doesn't mean we're actually going to do it. If that were the case, there would be no more smokers, no extreme sports, no couch potatoes, and no fast-food aficionados. For us to actually do something, we need that positive gut feeling that carries us to our goal. And it is precisely that positive gut feeling – the positive affective attitude – that can quickly get lost in the translation into a SMART goal. As a result, we never cross our Rubicon. Our gut says, very determinedly, "I don't want to" and overwhelms our mind – unless our mind is really careful not to let that happen (see also pages 64 ff.).

So, what can we do to ensure our goal will not only convince our mind but also appeal to our gut feelings? Under Lever 3 - Transfer Volition, we've already discussed several volition strategies that could help us here (see page 68 ff.). Another option to satisfy our gut is by setting the right goals. Maja Storch, the creator of the Zurich Resource Model,[8] has dealt with this subject in great depth. Her insider tip is to define "motto goals" – goals that are phrased as slogans to stimulate enthusiasm, intrinsic motivation, and positive emotions ("affects") – in sum, a good gut feeling. That is the focus of these goals. It doesn't matter so much whether they are concrete or abstract. The point of motto goals is to develop a very individual, positive – and possibly also abstract – image of the target state at an attitude level. To get there, you keep trying out various versions until the positive gut feeling (the positive impact) materializes. For example, with some people the goal "I'll eat a vegetarian *diet*" might trigger negative feelings (such as images of a half-empty plate with two peas on it). "I eat *healthy*" may feel better for that person, yet still trigger the notion of "very green" –which might not have a positive connotation for some. So, in the end that person might end up with something like "I savor (or 'heart') veggies and light meals" or "I enjoy delicious vegetarian dishes" – goals that conjure up colorful, motivating notions and images. What constitutes a "good" goal is highly individual. The only thing that matters is that it triggers positive feelings in the person that sets the goals, as these support the high level of commitment we need in order to achieve our goals.

"Oh, but that's all rather vague," you might think now. And you're right. But still, the concept works. Maja Storch has reported on a study that compared the impacts of SMART goals and motto goals. And lo and behold, participants who had defined their goals as motto goals achieved them more often than those with SMART goals.[9]

But what about the insight that concrete, challenging goals increase performance (pages 90 ff.)? It still applies. A concrete and challenging idea is conducive to transfer success. An optimal way to achieve goals is to combine motto goals with concrete implementation intentions or plans. Goals with a positive "affect balance" (even if unconcrete) promote people's commitment to a goal. It is then concretized by defining implementation intentions or plans. At this point, SMART-plagued trainers can breathe a sigh of relief: You don't need to put your participants to the tedious task of fiddling with their goals until they fit into the SMART corset. It's much quicker and easier if you let them freely phrase goals that convey strength and energy (e.g., as motto goals or "visions"). Concreteness is less important than a positive gut feeling. Then, leveraging this powerful, positive, and motivating feeling, ask trainees to shape their concrete intentions or plans. You will find that proceeding this way will lead to completion of the task of developing goals and plans with much greater ease, fun, and motivation.

> Although SMART goals are specific, they are often associated with negative feelings (have a negative "affect balance"). Make sure your participants have a positive feeling when thinking about their goal, and, at the same time, also come up with a concrete plan.

Transfer intentions – no, thanks

Up to this point we've discussed how intentions (goals and plans) and actions are interrelated and how these intentions should be designed in order for them to have an effect on actions. What we haven't covered so far is what determines whether we form intentions at all. Here, too, we can find information that is valuable for transfer planning in training.

Answers to this question are provided by a theory (and the associated empirical evidence) that has become quite famous in the psychologist community: the Theory of Planned Behavior or TPB, created by the Polish psychology professor Icek Ajzen.[10]

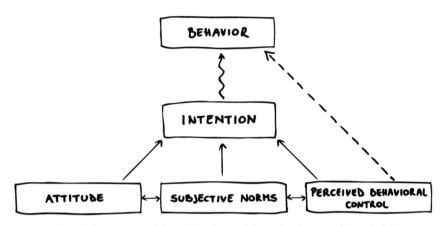

Fig. 5:   How (transfer) intentions originate. The theory of planned action according to Icek Ajzen

This theory says that intentions are determined by three factors: (1) the attitude toward the action, (2) the subjective norms, and (3) the perceived behavioral control.

(1) Our *attitude* towards the action is, casually put, the gut feeling we have about it, or what we intuitively think of it. (Do I find this action good or bad, exciting or boring, pleasing or unpleasant, worthless or valuable, desirable or undesirable? etc.) A positive attitude towards an action is a factor in the realization of the intention, and thus of the action itself. As trainers, we influence attitudes toward the possible (transfer) action throughout the entire training. Based on the contents, exercises, case examples, and perceived practical relevance, participants decide, step by step, what is good, exciting, valuable, desirable, etc. for them to apply. It is one of the trainers' tasks to design the contents and transfer suggestions in a way that makes it easy for participants to opt for applying what they have learned, and thus for transfer (see also Levers 1, 5, and 6 – Transfer Motivation, Content Relevance, and Active Practice). When, towards the end of the training, the time has come to formulate intentions, trainers are well advised to emphasize once more the benefits, value, and desirability of application and thus to promote trainees' positive attitude towards transfer. This makes it easier for the trainees to define their transfer intentions and ultimately carry out transfer actions successfully.

(2) The second crucial factor in formulating intentions, according to the Theory of Planned Behavior, is the *subjective norm*. It is about the question of what others think of our intended action. (Do people that matter to me think I should really do it?). Once again, we see what influence our social environment has. What others might think of our (planned) action affects whether we decide to act and form an intention. Applied to the training context, this is where we find the theoretical foundation for

the questions mentioned in the action plan: "Who in the company will support me in implementing my transfer intentions?" and "Where will I encounter resistance?" Asking questions such as these and devising corresponding strategies of persuasion helps participants devise intentions that lead to actions, as it is incredibly important how others perceive the transfer intentions (see also Levers 10 and 11 – Support from Supervisors and Support from Peers). In the training itself, we can use this factor deliberately by having the group discuss their transfer intentions and get encouragement (for example, using the transfer powerwalk, see page 276). Through encouragement, applause, or verbal support/recognition for their transfer intentions, we strengthen their power and impact. In addition, exercises like these activate trainees' drive for consistency – the drive to carry out what one has announced (see pages 260 ff.). If your trainees voice their intentions in front of others, they will feel even more committed to implementing them. After all, who wants to be seen as someone who doesn't keep their promises?!

(3) Finally, according to the Theory of Planned Behavior, our intention is determined by *perceived action control* – the question of whether we perceive action X as simple or difficult, possible or impossible, controllable or uncontrollable. If we ourselves believe it would be impossible or too difficult to execute an action (see also Lever 2 – Self-Efficacy), we will not formulate an intention. If we have formed an intention, then realize that the action could turn out to be more difficult than expected, we will not act. With particularly motivated participants and/or particularly good trainings, this is where we encounter a phenomenon known as "planning fallacy," which we will discuss in more detail when we get to Lever 9 – Personal Transfer Capacity (see pages 209 ff.). In a nutshell, most people underestimate the time and resources required to implement transfer intentions. In training, their over-motivation and confidence encourage them to take on far too many intentions, then back at the workplace they realize that for some reason things are not going according to plan. So, to ensure that participants keep experiencing progress implementing their intentions in their daily work, it makes sense to ensure that they don't take on too much and that they keep in mind the resources needed for implementation. It also makes sense to start with simple and manageable subtasks and gradually move on to the more difficult tasks and situations. Success experiences can boost self-efficacy.

Whether your trainees form transfer intentions depends on
(1) their attitude towards the planned action (what does their gut feeling say?),
(2) the subjective norm (what do others think of the planned action?), and
(3) their perceived action control (how easy or difficult is it to carry out the action?).

Summary

Transfer planning means accompanying participants on their way across the Rubicon. It's important to provide them with the time and setting to prepare their transfer intentions properly. Get them into the planning state of mind, as it is extremely valuable for implementation: increased optimism, self-esteem, and the more implementation-focused processing of information all make it easier to implement intentions in everyday work. As far as transfer intentions are concerned, make sure participants set goals that also have an emotional appeal (speaking to their guts, not only their minds) – even if those goals are initially not that specific. They don't always have to be SMART goals – in the beginning, a positive gut feeling and attitude towards the intended action are more important. Then, in the next step, you should get more concrete. Encourage participants to develop implementation intentions (e.g., if-then plans) or action plans to support their implementation goals. To aid them in this, prompt them by ask questions or give them templates to fill in. Be sure to point out that the actions to be planned should be within their own sphere of influence. You may also want to have participants develop their plans in smaller, more manageable steps to ensure that perceived action control is in place and a positive gut feeling will materialize, supported by a series of achievements. Also, pay attention to the "social norm" factor in the transfer planning module. What others think of the transfer intention is crucial for your trainees. In the action plan, ask questions about who will support or resist their plans, and have them develop appropriate strategies. Encouragement, applause, and affirmation for each transfer intention from the group will further promote trainees' commitment and implementation.

HOW TO SUPPORT TRANSFER PLANNING

At a glance:
Ideas for reflection and implementation

Standardize the transfer planning module
- As a rule of thumb, reserve 10% of the training time for transfer planning
- Pause before the module and give trainees a short teaser preview of it
- Clarify the usefulness and meaning of the transfer module
- Summarize what trainees have learned, what it's good for, and how it can be applied
- Have trainees perform transfer exercise(s)

Use tools and exercises for individual transfer planning
- Prompting questions or unfinished sentences
- "Letter to myself" (can also be e-mails or voice messages)
- Transfer intentions on sticky notes
- Transfer intentions as objects
- Transfer plans on blue-carbon-paper
- Desk pad
- Transfer cards
- Transfer box
- Standardized transfer planning tools
- Transfer book

Use exercises to build social and emotional support for transfer intentions
- Transfer powerwalk
- Future interview
- Transfer visions and contributions
- Mirror exercises

Make the "transfer planning" module standard

At the beginning of a training there are introductory rounds; after-lunch drowsiness can be helped with an activating exercise, and at the end there is usually a feedback round or the company's internal evaluation form to fill out. All this is standard in training programs. All of these are agenda items trainees are familiar with, standard elements they've come to expect. What is far less common is a transfer planning module at the end of the training. If anything, feedback sessions include questions like "What was most important to you?" Or "What are you going to do with what you've learned?" Formulating concrete transfer intentions, however, or setting aside a time slot for trainees to plan their own transfer – those are notable exceptions. So, this is where we should start. Let us make transfer planning a standard element in training, thus enhancing participants' transfer success.

So, what do you need to consider when designing transfer planning modules?

Time: The optimal timing depends on the individual situation – the topic, the group, the extent to which you have discussed the subject of transfer in the previous sessions, and so on. As a general rule of thumb, you should dedicate around 10% of the training time for the transfer planning module. So, if you have a two-day training totaling 16 hours, you should set aside around 1-2 hours for a transfer planning module.

Pause and teaser: Depending on the overall duration of the training, it might make sense to take a short break before you start the transfer planning module. Before that break, you can kindle everyone's curiosity by giving them a "sneak preview" of what's coming up. You might say, "Let's take a short break before tackling the most important part of the training: implementation planning. I've prepared a fun exercise, so there's something to look forward to …"

Intro highlighting value: Initiate the transfer planning module by emphasizing how important and useful this module is for trainees' personal transfer success. This introduction can consist of just a couple of sentences (e.g., "We are getting to the most important part of the training now: the part where you will decide on whether our time together has been a good investment …"). If time allows, it's a good idea to explain why you are working on transfer planning now, based on a model (such as Rubicon) and why it has such crucial importance for trainees (see also pages 80 ff.).

Summary: Wrapping up at the end is a very common feature of training programs. The optimal time for this is right before the transfer planning module. Make sure your participants are aware of the full range of what they have learned before starting on their transfer plan. This wrap-up of the entire training content allows them to draw on their full resources.

Transfer exercise(s): In the actual exercise(s), it is advisable to combine individual transfer planning, in which participants define their own goals and plans, with social and emotional reinforcement.

Use tools and exercises for individual transfer planning

The core element of all tools and exercises for transfer planning is translating the insights from the training into individual transfer intentions (preferably in writing). To support your trainees in this, you can use prompting questions or unfinished sentences to guide their individual exercises (e.g., "An element particularly important to me was …" or "This is what I will definitely implement: …") and, if appropriate, have them present excerpts of this to the group in the final round. During these steps, make sure the general euphoria remains within reasonable limits. With highly motivated participants or a very inspirational training, there is a certain tendency for trainees either to take on too much or include intentions that have little to do with the actual needs at their workplace. To prevent this, make them connect with the goals, issues, or challenges that made them attend your training in the first place (e.g., "Take some time to revisit the questions that brought you to this training. What answers do you have today? Exactly what will you implement?"). Of course, this approach requires that trainees had clear expectations at the outset (see also Lever 4 – Clarity of Expectations). Also, remind trainees to consider the resources they will need to succeed. Lead them to select and prioritize carefully, so their transfer intentions won't turn out to be a flash in the pan. Also make sure that goals are inspiring and intentions and plans concrete – otherwise they won't be effective.

In addition to the individual work using prompting questions, there are countless other ways and methods to tackle individual transfer planning. A time-tested classic is the *letter to myself.* In these times of digital information channels such as email, Twitter, WhatsApp, etc., a handwritten letter on classy stationery, delivered to people's real-life mailboxes, and bearing a stamp can be something unique. Alternative, more modern options include the *voice message or e-mail to myself, the calendar reminder, the Evernote or OneNote reminder,* and so on. Allow trainees to choose their own form, as the logic is always the same. Alternatively, you can have trainees write their intentions on *sticky notes* (virtually or on paper), which they then pin to a suitable place at their desk. Have them look for (or take pictures of) *objects* they can take home as a *reminder* or use as a wallpaper for their mobile phone or as a screen saver for their computer. Or have them take pictures of their written intentions – or record voice memos or video clips – and send them to you, so you can return them to the trainees later, with or without comments, or give them back to for them to review them once again at the follow-up session. A charmingly vintage option is to have trainees write their plans on *carbon paper* and hand the copy to you. If you are dealing with the generation that remembers these blue or black sheets from school, they will trigger delightful nostalgia. (Should you not be familiar with them, just google them or ask your (grand)mother.)

Other tools that have proved effective are those that work as a concise summary, a transfer planner, and a reminder – all in one. A simple, quickly available, and affordable version is the paper blotter *desk pad*. Placed on each trainee's desk at the beginning, it offers enough space to take notes throughout the entire training (especially if it takes only a day or two). During the transfer planning module, you invite trainees to condense their notes and put them down on the desk pad, together with their transfer intentions. If trainees then have that desk pad on their own desk back at the office for several weeks, the contents and transfer intentions will remain in their line of vision. (This only works, of course, if they have desks and fixed workstations – otherwise a digital version is recommendable.)

The *transfer card* is another simple tool that combines a summary with transfer planning: Key training content is pre-printed on it and can be checked at a glance; one field is left free for transfer planning. The *transfer box* with a mirror combines summary and transfer planning. Have trainees collect their key insights and notes on small cards and place them in their transfer box. In the transfer planning module at the end of the training, participants each spread out their notes (their "treasures") before themselves and sort them out. Only the most important notes make it back into the transfer box. Now, only after having selected the insights they value most, trainees write their transfer intentions on differently colored cards that will also go into the box. At this point you come up with another surprise, which emphasizes people's self-responsibility in implementing their transfer intentions. To top it all off, each participant receives a gift for their transfer box – an envelope containing the "secret to transfer success," or "the magic ingredient," or "the key resource that guarantees each participant success in implementation." Make sure you set the scene carefully and give out the gifts ceremonially! Participants then open their envelopes to find a small mirror in which they see themselves … I guess the message is clear enough. Glued into the transfer box, the mirror reminds trainees, each time they open it, of this surprise effect and the fact that their success depends on themselves.

As you can see, there are no limits to the possibilities you have, and to your creativity, when it comes to transfer planning. Whether you prefer modern or retro, playful or straight and simple, doesn't matter. The main thing is that participants leave your seminar room with as concrete transfer intentions as possible!

Popular and widely used are *standardized transfer planning tools* – forms, folders, and booklets, which you can use as a standard element for transfer planning within all your training. As a human resources developer, you can use this folder in all your in-house training sessions to ensure transfer planning really takes place in every training session. Give this transfer tool to your trainers by default, along with your organization's internal feedback form, ask them to use this tool at the end of the training. This way, all employees who attend a training within the organization will get accustomed to it: They'll know that their training will conclude not only with an evaluation but also with transfer planning.

As a trainer, you will find that a standardized transfer tool has important advantages for you, too. Bring it to your sales pitch to show potential clients that transfer effectiveness is not just a buzzword for you – instead you even use dedicated methods to promote it, one of them being your transfer planning folder. This way, you position yourself as a transfer-effective trainer, which gives you a competitive edge, and demonstrably promote your trainees' transfer success. In addition, experience has shown participants to consult their transfer planning folder several times in the weeks and months after training. Plus, with your logo or details on the outside your transfer planning folder becomes an additional, elegantly presented advertising space.

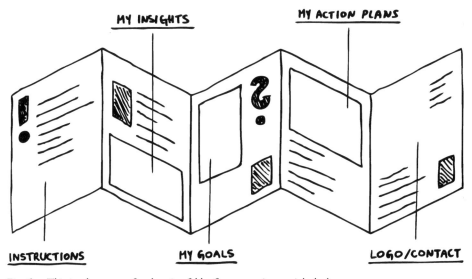

Fig. 6:   This is what a transfer planning folder for your trainees might look

For longer training programs consisting of several modules, it makes sense to standardize the transfer planning part. After all, if each of the trainers used their own transfer planning tool participants would probably end up with too many transfer intentions. So, it's best to use one consistent tool in each module – such as, for instance, a *transfer book* which accompanies each trainee through the program. You are free to be creative in choosing its design, format, and structure. The transfer book might be a high-quality, completely blank notebook which, at the trainer's instructions, participants repeatedly use to record useful information and, above all, to plan their transfer intentions. It could contain a motivational message from a board member, a managing director, or a regional manager, emphasizing the importance of the program or academy to the company. Your transfer book could also be a clearly structured step-by-step guide for each phase and assignment before, during, and after training. In that case, it could contain a preface by a recognized leader, an overview of the program, a guide, a guide for conducting pre-training discussions (see pages 242 ff. for examples), each module's objectives and content, and one or several pages to note insights and eventually plan the transfer, an area for prioritizing transfer plans, explanations, guides, and tips for the successful implementation of the trainee's own intentions (e.g., the Rubicon model), a guide and template for reporting, and so on. This way, the entire transfer process is covered, including many levers besides transfer planning. Again, new technologies offer countless possibilities: Instead of a paper book, this can also be a virtual document; or the entire content can be mapped using a transfer software (see page 313).

Use exercises to build social and emotional support for transfer intentions

Expressing our intentions in front of others strengthens our volition – that is, the will, persistence, and commitment for engaging with and implementing our transfer plans. After all, we human beings strive to fulfill what we've announced and promised (see also pages 260 ff.). The following transfer exercises take advantage of this mechanism.

In the *transfer powerwalk* exercise, participants get motivational, emotional, and social affirmation by reading out their transfer intentions to the group, then walking through a line of clapping and cheering peers – ideally to the sound of some invigorating music (depending on the group, choices include the theme songs from films such as *Indiana Jones, Pirates of the Caribbean, Mission Impossible, Chariots of Fire, …*).

In the *future interview,* participants are transported to a time when they have already implemented their intentions and achieved their goals. They interview each other for a TV report or magazine article (e.g., "The winner of the Trainer Award 2020 talks about the secrets to his/her success," or "Useful tips from a sales professional," etc.). Mentally taking them to a successful future, so to speak, strengthens their transfer motivation. As an additional boost for their volition, you may decide to send them the reports or videos with some delay as a nice little reminder.

Developing *transfer visions and contributions* promotes motivation, commitment, and responsibility by visualizing a (joint) vision of the future to which everyone is willing to make a contribution. To this end, have each of the participants formulate their own succinct and precise vision. (For example, in a training for trainers dealing with transfer effectiveness, a possible vision might be "Transfer effectiveness is my USP. It enhances my reputation, strengthens my customers' loyalty and increases my financial success.") As a next step, participants each state what contribution or concrete plans they have to achieve this vision (e.g., "Every time I write a training proposal, I'll include a module on transfer"). Both the visions and related transfer intentions are then presented to the plenary (or the trainee's small group) and received with encouraging feedback and applause. This exercise is particularly useful for teams that are working towards a joint vision pursuing a range of individual intentions (e.g., a vision such as "transfer effectiveness as a USP for our training institute" or "increasing employee satisfaction"). As before, the transfer exercise also provides the basis for a later reminder: To effectively strengthen trainees' volition, send out the vision and messages sometime after the training.

Exercises and surprise effects with *mirrors* – such as the transfer box I mentioned earlier – are great tools to provide emotional support for trainees' transfer intentions and, in particular, to address of their self-responsibility during implementation. After participants have defined their transfer plans, you can hand out a specially designed or decorated envelope indicating that it holds "the secret to successful implementation." Trainees open their envelope simultaneously and see themselves in a small mirror – an emotionally anchored message to remind them that they are the ones that determine implementation success. Or you can place trainees (in teams) in front of a mirror, where they each loudly announce their transfer intentions. As you can see, mirrors and transfer planning are a great combination and can be used in various ways. Who knows – perhaps you'll develop your very own transfer planning exercise the next time you brush your teeth …

Time for transfer!

Your turn. How do you intend to tackle transfer planning? How can you ensure participants will leave your training with inspiring goals and a clear plan that specifies, step by step, what they intend to do? What is *your* next step? Write down the ideas and thoughts that spontaneously come to mind.

This is how I will assist my trainees in their transfer planning:

[1] The connection between transfer intentions and transfer success has been demonstrated, for example, in Gegenfurtner, A., Vauras, M., Gruber, H., & Festner, D., "Motivation to transfer revisited," Paper presented and included in the Proceedings of the 9th International Conference of the Learning Sciences, 2010, -Volume 1; also Gegenfurtner, A., "Dimensions of motivation to transfer: A longitudinal analysis of their influence on retention, transfer, and attitude change" in *Vocations and Learning,* 2013, 6(2): pp. 187 – 205.

[2] The juxtaposition between the balancing and planning states of consciousness has been adapted from Heckhausen, J., & Heckhausen, H., *Motivation und Handeln,* Heidelberg, Springer, 2010, p.322.

[3] An overview is provided by, among others, Achtziger, A., & Gollwitzer, P. M., "Motivation und Volition im Handlungsverlauf" in J. Heckhausen, & H. Heckhausen (Eds.), *Motivation und Handeln,* Heidelberg, Springer, 2006, pp. 277 – 302.

[4] For an overview, see Gollwitzer, P. M., & Malzacher, J. T., "Absichten und Vorsätze" in *Enzyklopädie der Psychologie* (Teilband C/IV/4), *Motivation, Volition und Handlung,* Göttingen, Hofgrefe, 1995, pp.427 – 468. For the study on New Year's resolutions, see Gollwitzer, P., & Brandstätter, M., "Do initiation intentions prevent procrastination?" Paper presented at the 8th General Meeting of the European Association of Experimental Social Psychology, Budapest, 1990. For studies on performance enhancement through self-efficacy endeavors, see Bayer, U. C., & Gollwitzer, P. M., "Boosting scholastic test scores by willpower: The role of implementation intentions" in *Self and Identity,* 2007, 6(1): pp. 1 – 19. An overview of various studies in health behavior (smoking, losing weight, exercising) is given in Renner, B., & Schwarzer, R., "Gesundheit: Selbstschädigendes Handeln trotz Wissen" in H. Mandl & J. Gerstenmaier (Eds.), *Die Kluft zwischen Wissen und Handeln: Empirische und theoretische Lösungsansätze,* Göttingen, Hofgrefe, 2000, pp. 25-50.

[5] For an overview, see Achtziger, A., & Gollwitzer, P. M., "Motivation und Volition im Handlungs-verlauf" in J. Heckhausen, & H. Heckhausen (Eds.), Motivation und Handeln, Heidelberg, Springer, 2006, pp. 277 – 302.

[6] For cognitive performance in the undertaking of if-then plans, see, for example, Brandstätter, V., Lengfelder, A., & Gollwitzer, P. M., "Implementation intentions and efficient action initiation" in *Journal of personality and social psychology,* 2001, 81(5): pp. 946-960.

[7] A meta-analysis of the connection between intent and execution with 94 studies and a total of 8461 subjects resulted in an effect size of d=0.65. See Gollwitzer, P. M., & Sheeran, P., "Implementation intentions and goal achievement: A meta-analysis of effects and processes" in *Advances in experimental social psychology,* 2006, 38: pp.69 – 119.

[8] A detailed description of Maja Storch's Zurich Resource Model can be found in, among others, Storch, M., & Krause, F., *Selbstmanagement ressourcenorientiert. Grundlagen und Trainingsmanual für die Arbeit mit dem Züricher Ressourcen Modell* (ZRM), Bern, Hofgrefe, 2007 (4th Edition), or specifically on the topic of Goals in Storch, M., "Motto-Ziele, SMART-Ziele und Motivation" in B. Birgmeier (Ed.), *Coachingwissen. Denn sie wissen nicht, was sie tun?,* Wiesbaden: VS Verlag für Sozialwissenschaften / GWV Fachverlage GmbH, 2009b, pp. 2–24.

[9] More about the difference between motto goals and SMARTgoals can be found in, for example, Storch, M., "Motto-Ziele, SMART-Ziele und Motivation" in B. Birgmeier (Ed.), *Coachingwissen. Denn sie wissen nicht, was sie tun?,* Wiesbaden: VS Verlag für Sozialwissenschaften / GWV Fachverlage GmbH, 2009b, pp. 2 – 24. For a study on the effects of different goal forms, see Bruggmann, N. 2003. *Persönliche Ziele: ihre Funktion im psychischen System und ihre Rolle beim Einleiten von Veränderungsprozessen.* http://www.zrm.ch/images/stories/download/pdf/wissenschftl_arbeiten/ seminararbeiten/seminararbeit_bruggmann_20090904.pdf (retrieved 8 December 2006).

[10] On the Theory of Planned Behavior, see Ajzen, I., *Attitudes, personality, and behavior,* McGraw-Hill Education (UK), 2005.

LEVERS FOR THE ORGANIZATION

> The workplace can untrain people far more efficiently than even the best training department can train people
>
> *(Brinkerhoff & Gill, 1994)*

Lever 8
Opportunities for Application

Lever 9
Personal Transfer Capacity

Lever 10
Support from Supervisors

Lever 11
Support from Peers

Lever 12
Transfer Expectations in the Organization

In this section, you will learn
- Why immediate applications are crucial and how you can provide occasions for immediate application even in programs for high-potentials,
- How to best deal with transfer excuse number one: "We didn't have the time"
- How you win over supervisors as transfer supporters,
- What Alcoholics Anonymous can teach us about transfer promotion,
- Whether your organization (unintentionally) signals that your transfer is completely irrelevant, and
- What you can do to set the levers of the organization to "transfer effective."

LEVER 8 – OPPORTUNITIES FOR APPLICATION

TWO PRACTICAL EXAMPLES

Six months ago, Manuel and Katharina attended a training entitled "Persuasive Presentations." Read what they have to say.

Manuel, 29, bank clerk

The "Persuasive Presentations" training has made an incredible difference for me. During the training, I had lots of ideas for surprising intros, for devising a dramaturgy with turning points, highlights, and just the right touch of emotion. The theory and the group's real-life experiences really fueled my creative powers. And the exercises and video analyses helped me to stop shifting my weight from one leg to the other during presentations, so I now make a much more confident impression. I really am comfortable with my presentations now and enjoy sharing my expertise with clients.

Katharina, 28, bank clerk

The "Persuasive Presentations" training was really great. I can still remember that it is very important to convey not only convincing facts but also emotions. I had great ideas for surprising introductions, and I also practiced developing a presentation dramaturgy using a concrete example. We gave several presentations at the training and received feedback. In the end, I really managed to speak more slowly, which made me appear more confident and knowledgeable. Unfortunately, I haven't done any more presentations since the training. That's still Manuel's job, and I'm a bit jealous of that – but, oh well. I know we've practiced really great stuff, but of course I've forgotten a lot. If I had to give a presentation now, I'd probably wind up talking too fast, like before. But if I ever get to be responsible for presentations at the bank, I'd definitely attend such a training again.

What do you think of the responses? Is there anything you find absurd?

Both Manuel and Katharina have succeeded in learning new things at the presentation training. Both acquired new skills but, six months later, only one of them still has a mastery of those skills. In Manuel's daily work, there is a regular need and plenty of opportunities for him to apply what he has learned. For Katharina, there are no such opportunities; so, after not having practiced her new skills for six months, she feels she's forgotten a lot.

If we want transfer success – if we want trainees to apply their newly learned skills at work – they need to have opportunities for application. Trivial as this may sound, several studies have shown a lack of application opportunities to be the number-one transfer barrier.[1] Trainees report things like, "The training was awesome, but I wasn't able to put things into practice because I'm not the person in charge of those things / because we don't have the equipment / the money / the technology required / because I'd need tools that aren't available at our company / because I can't get sufficient information of the type I need / because the situations where I actually need to use what I've learned at the training are an exception rather than the rule." In short, a variety of obstacles prevents people from applying what they have learned and practiced and, what's more, leads to demotivation among previously highly committed trainees.

So, to make transfer possible it is essential to provide the necessary resources (such as the budget, material, technology, tools, information, responsibility, application settings, and so on). Executives play a key role here. Granted, creating application opportunities is not easy, sometimes even impossible. But if that is the case, it calls for critical scrutiny. Does the given training really make sense for these people at this particular time? The question is necessary not only for the sake of transfer effectiveness, but also and in particular because trainees deserve to have their learning commitment rewarded with success experiences gained in practical application.

OPPORTUNITIES FOR APPLICATION – EVERYDAY WORK IS FULL OF POSSIBILITIES

	Opportunities for application in a nutshell
Trainees say	"It's possible for me to apply what I've learned to situations in my day-to-day work."
Definition	Opportunities for application is the extent to which the necessary situations and resources for application are available in the workplace.
Guiding question	How can you ensure that participants have the opportunity, permission, or assignment and the necessary resources to apply what they have learned?

Thank goodness, no transfer

No possibility to apply new skills – no transfer. Sounds logical, almost trivial, doesn't it? Actually, it's not that simple in practice, as it's seldom a matter of opportunities being either "available" or "not available." One example is junior leadership programs, where application opportunities are likely to exist but are not available immediately. Or think of pilots training for emergency situations – those are application scenarios we all hope will never materialize. Or consider a comprehensive training for new employees. Often, they will be introduced to lots of business processes they will never need in their daily work, or at least not in depth – which means that application opportunities exist, but not at the level of complexity people have learned and practiced in training. As these examples show, the possibilities for applying training content in practice have different dimensions: (1) time (ranging from immediately to much later), (2) frequency (ranging from constantly to very rarely or never), and (3) complexity (from superficial to full applicability of the content).[2]

The opportunities to apply new skills have three dimensions: time, frequency, and complexity.

The reasoning behind providing training even when the application possibilities are limited is fairly obvious: It is a matter of security, of being "ready" for the (potential) challenges of the future. We create a pool of skills and abilities, which we can access immediately as needed (such as capable young leaders ready to take the helm, or airline pilots who can manage an emergency landing). Transfer success comes with the situation – that's the idea. But does it really work that way?

A pocket compendium of catchwords for HR developers and trainers

"Your HR development measures are merely reactive. All you do is fill qualification gaps." That's a kick in the gut for any HR developer. What everyone wants, of course, is (pro)active, strategic, future-oriented HR development. Not just overcoming past shortcomings but also preparing and equipping the organization to be more competitive in meeting future challenges. So far, so good. On the other hand, we hear and read disdainful comments about how inefficient it is to "stockpile knowledge" and how important to ensure that staff training programs are "demand-oriented" – also referred to as "learning on demand" or "just-in-time learning." Having people learn exactly what they need right there and then in the workplace – it certainly sounds logical. But somehow, a faint sense of contradiction sets in. OK, off-the-shelf and reactive are no-nos. Instead, development work is supposedly all about being just-in-time, strategic, future-oriented, and on-demand. The truth is, there are too many nice-sounding buzzwords (empty phrases?) out there, each of them making its particular perspective or school of thought seem superior. So, what are we really talking about here? Let's get more specific and take a closer look at some of the phenomena and facts.

You never forget how to ride a bike

Forgetting is a phenomenon we are all familiar with. Even if we've acquired and actually mastered a skill, it's possible we somehow "lose" it. What exactly happens in our brain when we forget has yet to be fully investigated.[3] One attempt at an explanation is that "memory trails" gradually fade and eventually disappear when not in use (the "trace decay" theory) – almost like a hiking trail that becomes overgrown over the years when nobody uses it. Another approach assumes that we forget because new or more recent impressions overlay the old ones (the "interference" theory). However, there are some other empirically well-substantiated facts about forgetting that I don't want to keep from you. Initially, forgetting happens very fast. Harry Bahrick, a professor at Ohio Wesleyan University, looked into the subject: He studied students' Spanish language skills and constructed a "forgetting curve" that spanned 50 years. As it turned out, those who had attended the course three years before remembered much less (40 %) than those who had finished the course just recently. After three years, however, the curve settled to an almost constant level. Fifty years after completion of the course, people would remember more than 30 % of the vocabulary.[4] As this experiment revealed, forgetting happens much faster at the beginning (in the first few weeks, months, and years), then slows down.

> In the beginning, trainees forget quickly, later the forgetting process slows down.

Does what we have learned make a difference in forgetting? Do we forget certain things faster than others? Not surprisingly, the answer is yes. Studies show, we forget 78 % of meaningless syllables within five days, and 80 % after thirty days. Things look slightly better with prose: We forget 53 % within five days, and about 60 % in thirty days. With principles and rules, it's a whole different story: After five days, we've forgotten only 1 %, after around 30 days, about 5 %. So, essential content obviously lasts longer.[5]

But what about the famous saying "You never forget how to ride a bike"? Are there things we never forget? Again, the answer is yes. Things that are stored in our procedural memory (i.e., knowing how to do something, such as riding a bike, swimming, etc.) seem to remain engrained in our memory particularly well. Most of us can still cycle even if we haven't done it for years. Another example for the permanence of procedural knowledge is the training in a flight simulator: In an experiment, very specific procedures were practiced over and over again there, and lo and behold, nine and even twenty-four months later, respectively, participants were still able to repeat the steps – there was hardly a dip in performance, almost nothing had been forgotten.[6]

> Participants forget declarative knowledge faster than procedural knowledge.

Does this apply to all action-focused trainings? Does it mean that we simply have to practice a lot in training to prevent forgetting? Well, it certainly helps. But it does not prevent forgetting. After all, most skills do not involve the same steps or processes over and over again, as cycling does (so-called "closed skills"). Instead, it often takes a mixture of procedural and declarative knowledge to be able to execute an action in a manner adapted to the specific situation (so-called "open skills") and, unfortunately, a lot of forgetting happens here. A study by McKenna and Glendon (1985) demonstrated this for the field of first aid. Immediately after a training, participants would successfully revive all their patients. One year after training, only 15 % of all resuscitation attempts were successful.[7] Which goes to show that, even with abilities like these, if we cannot use them, we will forget them and have to relearn them!

> What trainees do not apply will be forgotten quickly.

There is a piece of good news, too: Relearning is much faster and easier than learning something new. The metaphoric "hiking trail" in our brain may be overgrown, but after some more "treading," it can be used again. So, forgetting does not necessarily mean losing completely – just having to make another effort.

Why recent MBA graduates leave the organization

As we have seen so far, we are better at retaining content, if it is important and meaningful to us and if we have dealt with the topic before. However, stockpiling knowledge has an effect not only on the retention or forgetting of knowledge, but also on our motivation. Our introductory example illustrates this very well. You remember Manuel and Katharina and their presentation training? Put yourself in Katharina's position. You've never given a presentation before, and you know it won't happen anytime soon. What kind of motivation will you bring to the training: Let's see what this is all about? Maybe there is something in it for me? A nice change from sitting at my desk? Why should I go there at all? As a trainer or HR developer, you're probably familiar with statements like these. After all, we hear them from some of the participants at the beginning of nearly every training. Level of learning motivation: so-so. Often, trainers need a lot of animation talent and effort in their seminars to make up for the lack of urgency or feasibility in the organization. If, on the other hand, trainees feel they will actually need the training content right afterwards in the workplace, their motivation and transfer success increase.[8]

What if we don't know anything about the existence or non-existence of application opportunities before the training? Let's play this through using our example: What if Katharina isn't aware beforehand that Manuel will continue to give all the presentations? A high level of commitment during training, good learning success, great transfer motivation afterwards – in sum, really good conditions. Back in her workplace, however, Katharina will experience a sobering surprise: Having learned a lot and practiced intensely, she'll realize there are no opportunities to apply what she's learned and to experience success in practice. Katharina will be angry, and she'll have every right to be. There's a lack of appreciation for her learning effort and her ability to implement her skills in the organization. This demotivation can have severe consequences: A survey among recent MBA graduates revealed that 41 % were thinking of changing jobs within the next 12 months. Of those leaving their employer, 43 % did so for salary reasons – closely followed by reasons associated with a lack of application opportunities (e.g., no promotion prospects – 32 %, job not being challenging enough – 26 %).[9] Let's hope that Katharina won't immediately begin to think of quitting. However, it is easy to imagine how a lack of opportunities to apply what people have learned will affect the general attitude towards training at her organization.

The lack of possibilities for application thus affects motivation in two ways: If it is clear beforehand that it will (probably) be impossible to apply the new skills, or if there is no pressing reason to apply them, people's learning motivation and learning success decrease. If people find out only after training that they can't apply what they've learned, this can – quite understandably – cause dissatisfaction and, in addition, have a negative impact on attitudes towards training in the organization, not to mention the lack of transfer success.

> The opportunity to apply what has been learned fosters motivation and a positive attitude towards training. A lack of application opportunities is demotivating and, in the long run, harms the reputation of your training programs.

Is the solution always training, no matter what the problem is?

As we have seen, it is not as self-evident to have application opportunities at one's fingertips after a training as one might think. Yet, we are surprised when participants don't apply what they've learned and seek explanations. A common and banal reason is that there simply are no application opportunities within the organization.

So why does this happen? Why hold training programs when things can't be applied in the organization? The answer, which might seem perplexing, is: because trainings are increasingly considered a cure-all (or pseudo-solution) for all kinds of problems. Let me give you some examples. Problem: According to the latest survey, employees are dissatisfied with their managers. Solution: a leadership training. Problem: an increasing number of burn-out cases. Solution: a stress management training. Problem: a decrease in sales. Solution: a sales training. Mind you, all these trainings might work and produce the desired results – but it is just as likely that they have no effect whatsoever.

So, training is used as a universal solution (or pseudo-solution) for all sorts of business problems and challenges, simply because training is a well-established, well-known intervention, which, compared to other kinds of interventions (such as organizational development projects, restructuring, cultural development projects, and the like), is less likely to meet with resistance. In fact, the popularity of training has reached a level that reverses the demand-supply sequence. At many companies, it is no longer "We have a specific need – we'll organize a training," but rather "We should offer more training – what additional needs could we cover, what topic(s) would be exciting, what would appeal to employees?" (see also Lever 12 – Transfer Expectations of the Organization). In modern organizations, training courses are part of business. It is simply expected that organizations of a certain size will offer a selection of training events. As a result, they've often become a routine and a habit, and thus their use inflationary.[10] In cases like these, people in HR development need to show courage. Let's liberate ourselves from the quantity dogma and, instead, focus on quality, on transfer-effective HR development! The first step is to challenge the supposed need for training. Not every idea for further education that comes up in discussions with employees has to immediately turn into a new training offer – nor do demands such as "Why don't you do something with management / quality assurance / procurement / etc., they really need some training" or "When will our department get to go to a training? It's always the others" or "Company XY offers seminars on YZ, so we should be doing the same." Also, remember that your company doesn't necessarily have to follow every new training trend. Often these are nothing but short-term fads that help individual trainers or institutes make good money. And contrary to a widespread view, the scope of a company's internal training program isn't a criterion for the quality and success of HR development. If we want to be effective, we should have the courage to use training as an intervention deliberately and see it for what it really is: one option out of a large range of HR interventions.

So, when are training sessions a correct and appropriate intervention? you may wonder. A well-known and very catchy model from the renowned organizational and business psychologist Professor Lutz von Rosenstiel helps us find the answer. He studied the question of what employee behavior in organizations depends on – including the behavior we want to change through training. Rosenstiel identified four conditions: (1) individual desire (i.e., employees' goals, needs, motivation & volition), (2) individual skill (employees' knowledge, skills, and abilities), (3) empowerment and obligation (the norms and values that shape social acceptability in the organization) and (4) situational enabling (favorable and inhibiting external circumstances).[11]

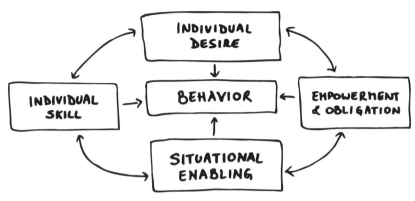

Fig. 7   The conditions of behavior according to Lutz von Rosenstiel

If we look at these four conditions, what is training aimed at? Quite obviously, at individual skills. Training can help to build knowledge, skills, and capabilities. However, to achieve genuine and sustainable behavioral change, there are three other crucial conditions: Trainees must want to change their behavior, and the new behaviors must be both socially acceptable and feasible in the given situation. To illustrate this, let's look at our previous examples again. First, the company that is suffering a sales decline: They send their sales team to a training course to learn new sales techniques – that is, improve their individual skills. But – who knows? – perhaps the team will never be able to use those new techniques. Why? For instance, because a competitor has entered the market with a better technology, which our company's products can't compete with. In that case, even the best sales techniques and the best training won't help, as the reason the sales team's efforts are no longer successful is not a lack of individual skill but inhibiting external circumstances (i.e., adverse situational conditions).

The next example was stress prevention training to reduce the increasing burn-out rate. Does this make sense? It depends on whether the problem is really related to individual skill. Let us imagine that in the stress prevention training, trainees learn to take regular breaks, switch off their phones on weekends, and stop working overtime – no doubt, all sensible and effective new behaviors. But perhaps this new behavior conflicts with the organization's values and standards – which means that our participants will get funny looks from their colleagues if they have an apple break at 10 a.m., their supervisors will point to their all-in work contracts if they leave at 5 p.m. sharp, and all in all, they will rightly fear being accused of slacking off and a lack of commitment. If that happens, they won't stick to the new behavioral routines. Burn-out, in this company, is not a question of individual skill and routines but of empowerment and obligation.

What about our third example, the poor feedback results for managers? Can a training help here? Again, the question is whether we are dealing with a lack of skill or very different reasons – such as, for instance, a leadership team demanding that supervisors impose overly ambitious targets on their staff, or a general salary decrease. And if managers do learn to replace their authoritarian leadership style with a more participative one, would this "new" style even be permitted and wanted in their organization?

If you want to find out whether a certain training makes sense, use the Rosenstiel framework. And to decide whether training is the right kind of intervention, we ask the skill question: "Does the problem exist because the individuals concerned lack a certain skill?"

> Is training the right solution? Ask the skill question.

If your answer is no, training is not the right problem-solving intervention. If your answer is yes and you have clearly defined the target behavior – that is, the transfer goals, then use critical questions to check the other three conditions: individual desire, empowerment and obligation, and situational enabling. It is only when all four conditions are met that there will be opportunities for application, and the training can be transfer-effective.

Summary

From a transfer perspective, there is a straightforward ground rule: Transfer-effective training requires opportunities for application. Ideally, these should exist immediately and frequently after the training, and allow trainees to put into practice what they have learned at about the same level of depth. This ensures learning and transfer motivation, prevents forgetting, and boosts the reputation of the training in the organization.

To facilitate transfer, learning on demand is definitely better than stockpiling knowledge. We learn particularly well and sustainably when we work on concrete real-life examples involving pressing needs. If opportunities for application are missing or insufficient (in terms of time, frequency, complexity, as well as empowerment and obligation, and situational enabling), this can demotivate trainees, cause them to forget, and even damage the reputation of the training in the long run. In exceptional cases, it may be necessary and important to conduct training courses with limited opportunities for application (e.g., emergency pilot training). In general, however, we should be acutely aware of the disadvantages of limited application opportunities and strive to prevent training programs from turning into an across-the-board or even would-be solution for just about any kind of organizational issue (such as using stress prevention training as a would-be solution to burn-out when it really the corporate culture that is to blame).

It is the responsibility of HR development to ensure that training is used as an intervention only when the root cause of a problem is a lack of skill. It is also the responsibility of HR development to ensure that application opportunities will be available and supported by social and organizational empowerment, and to do this well in advance, ideally stressing the significance and urgency. (This obviously requires the active involvement of management and other organizational stakeholders – a point we'll discuss when we get to the other organizational levers.) Last but not least, it is a question of transfer aspirations, perhaps even of professionalism, for trainers to decline engagements that are doomed to fail from the outset due to a lack of application opportunities – or, at the very least, suggest that such opportunities be created.

HOW TO ENSURE APPLICATION OPPORTUNITIES ARE AVAILABLE

**At a glance:
Ideas for reflection and implementation**

Challenge, clarify, and sharpen needs and expectations
- Insist on clarity of needs and expectations with the requester / client
- Ask condition-related questions and reality check them: Is training the right intervention for the problem/opportunity?
- Conduct a workshop on transfer goals

Fill pipeline with concrete application opportunities
- In advance, have supervisors and trainees themselves define urgent and important situations and challenges that they are going to tackle after the training
- Make sure application tasks meet three criteria – concrete, important and urgent, and "DIY"

Arrange for parallel work on practical projects
- Ensure that, in the course of the training/transfer phases, all trainees take part in implementing a project set up by senior management with clear-cut benefits for the company

Also devise application opportunities for "high-potential" programs
- Sharpen focus and goal of high-potential programs
- Help trainees preserve what they've learned over a longer horizon

Challenge, clarify, and sharpen needs and expectations

If we want to achieve transfer effectiveness, we need to work with clear needs and expectations. What sounds very plausible on the face of it may not be that easy in practice. Often, the requirements stated by departments, executives, management, etc., are anything but clear ("Why don't you do something with our managers?" "We need a training to improve our communication"). Ask the departments, executives, and supervisors in charge to specify their needs and expectations and assist them in doing so. How is HR development supposed to deliver "the right thing" if they don't have a very clear idea of the purpose and expected outcome? By accepting vague "rush orders" such as "we need a training in XY," both HR developers and trainers are bound to lose out. They won't even have a chance to do effective work and be perceived as a strong partner delivering tangible results. Only when needs and expectations are clear and transfer goals phrased clearly, can we design and implement effective training architectures. Demand this clarity from your clients!

As an HR developer reading these lines, you may have legitimate objections now, based on past experiences: "This is not possible in our company," "Our managers / departments / top executives communicate unclear needs, yet expect me to act!" Quite a challenge indeed. But an opportunity, too: a chance for your function, HR development, to shift from the operational role of "training supplier and organizer" into that of a strategic business partner, an in-house HR development expert. Mind you, of course we can't expect people to suddenly start communicating their training needs to us as clear transfer goals, but we can work towards this clarity together with our (internal) clients step by step: by asking questions, by paraphrasing, by joint reflection. Let's make sure we always ask about conditions before we hastily hire someone for an ineffective training program – or, as trainers, before we accept such a project and eventually are held responsible for it. Let's slip into the role of a sparring partner or coach and, little by little, jointly lay open the organization's actual needs. Experience has shown that this questioning process often reveals needs completely different from what had originally been requested, and the people involved are often quite grateful for having realized this. This way, the process strengthens your position as an expert and competent (internal) consultant for development issues. Experience has also shown that, once the topic of transfer has spread across the company (for instance, because people have experienced the meaning and value as well as the logic of the wording in a joint transfer goals workshop), sooner or later your telephone will ring and the manager on the other end will be very straightforward with his or her training request: "We need a training. The transfer goals are: first ..., second ..., and third ..." This way, HR development makes even more sense than before.

Checkpoint 1: Is training an appropriate tool at all?

Ask the skill question:
"Does the problem that we want to address with the training exist because the target group lacks a skill or skills?"

Yes. The problem would be solved if the target group only knew how to handle it!	**No or not primarily.** The problem also has other causes (structural, responsibility assignments, culture, micropolitics, lack of motivation, conflicts, market conditions, etc.)
GO! Training could be the right tool. Define the transfer goals and then proceed to Checkpoint 2.	**STOP!** Training is not (yet) the right tool. Look for a more suitable intervention to eradicate the cause(s) of the problem.

Checkpoint 2: Are the transfer goals achievable?

Review the transfer goals that you fully formulated for Checkpoint 1 and ask yourself the four condition questions for each transfer goal:

1. Individual skill. "Is it realistic for the target group to learn everything necessary to achieve the behavior in the transfer goal(s) within the time frame and scope of a training?"
2. Individual desire. "Is the target group intrinsically motivated to achieve this transfer goal for its own reasons (or will members resist in terms of behavior)?"
3. Social norms (empowerment and obligation). "Does the target group have permission / empowerment to implement the behavior implied by the transfer goal within the organization (or is it prohibited from doing so by written or unwritten rules or norms within the organization)?"
4. Situational enabling. "Is the behavior defined in the transfer goal realistically implementable (or are there external circumstances and barriers that could block, limit, or hinder it)?"

Four times yes. All conditions are fulfilled.	**Less than four times yes.** Not all conditions are fulfilled.
GO! The transfer goals are achievable. The training to reach the defined transfer goals has good prospects of success. Proceed to Checkpoint 3.	**STOP!** The transfer goals may not be achievable. Reconsider the transfer goals! What wording do they have to have to elicit a "yes" to all four conditions?

Checkpoint 3: Are the transfer goals complete?

Ask the cross-check question:
"If the transfer goals are fully met, does that solve the problem?"

Yes. If the transfer goals are met, we will have solved our problem.	**No.** If the transfer goals are met, the problem will not yet be solved.
GO! The training with the transfer goals you have defined is the right intervention. Go ahead and start designing!	**STOP!** The training with the transfer goals defined so far will not (yet) solve the initial problem. Is the problem really a matter of ability (knowing how to do something), or does it have other causes (see Checkpoint 1)? What additional transfer goals would have to be met in order to solve the problem? Add these transfer goals!

What if the training need involves more than one internal client? What can we do when it is more comprehensive, if it involves different people's expectations, such as a large multi-module internal leadership or sales program? In cases like these, it is helpful to conduct a transfer goals workshop. Here, stakeholders and trainers jointly define exactly what the need is and what the training program is expected to achieve. From there, the group jointly derives transfer goals, which describe clearly and very specifically how things should be in practice after the program (in the "target state"). The key is to involve the potential trainees' supervisors. This ensures that they commit to the defined goals and actively promote and support the transfer from the training program (see also Lever 10 - Support from Supervisors). A transfer goals workshop is suitable both when a training program is redesigned and when, after a program has been conducted several times, it is time to refine the goals and sharpen the focus on transfer effectiveness. Typically, some or all of the following stakeholders participate in a transfer goal workshop: potential trainees, the trainees' supervisors, HR developers, management / decision-makers, and the trainers. Results of the workshop are clear transfer goals, strong commitment to the goals and the program, and everyone's willingness to work towards transfer effectiveness in their respective roles.

Fill pipeline with concrete application opportunities

If what is learned is needed quickly for everyday work – ideally with some urgency, of which participants are aware – their motivation and transfer effectiveness increase. To create this kind of setting, ask the trainees to bring concrete real-life assignments to the training. Depending on the subject matter, supervisors are probably ideal sources for these assignments. For instance, in a preparatory meeting prior to a training entitled "More Efficient Meetings," a supervisor could tell a participant something like this: "I expect you to bring back hands-on ideas for how we can make our meetings more efficient. Why don't we block Monday morning, 9 a.m., to discuss your suggestions?" Ooh – somebody's serious here! Or else the supervisor might say, "What a lucky coincidence that you're going to the PowerPoint training next week. I'd like you to prepare the presentation for next month's board meeting". Specific application assignments like these make very clear that the supervisor expects results from the training (see also Lever 10 – Support from Supervisors). They also focus people's perspective while in training, enhance motivation, and get trainees to shift from an attitude of passive consumption to active learning. Depending on the training topic, application assignments may also be determined by the trainees themselves: Before the start of actual training, ask each trainee to briefly describe a situation or task they would like to be able to master with the help of the training. This can be a part of the letter of motivation with which people apply for the training, or a preparatory task posed by the trainer (see pages 103 ff.), or a critical incident that has been identified in a recent survey or questionnaire (see pages 119 ff.). For example, an application assignment formulated by a trainee might sound like this: "I want to develop a clear concept of how to resolve the current conflict in my team" or "I want to give an inspiring product presentation next month and get ready for it."

Three points are crucial in formulating and creating application opportunities that are transfer effective:

(1) The application opportunity is *concrete* – the trainees have a specific situation in mind. (For instance, "I want to improve my conflict-resolution skills" would create a rather vague mental image, in contrast to "I want to come up with a concept for solving a real conflict that the team is currently experiencing").

(2) The application opportunity is perceived as both *urgent* and *important* ("Two years from now, I'd like to give a product presentation for which I need to gather some ideas" generates less drive than a presentation that will definitely have to be given within the next few weeks/months).

(3) The application opportunity is a *"do-it-yourself"* activity: it must be performed by the trainee, not the trainer (i.e., not: "I want a concept from the trainer on how to resolve my team's conflict," but rather "I want to develop a concept..." Likewise, it is also not the trainer who will prepare the product presentation for me – I will do it myself).

It is advisable to emphasize these points and have the trainees write down their assignments (in the preparatory meeting with their supervisors, in the letter of motivation, etc.) and to keep reminding trainees to focus on their assignments again and again ("Now think of the assignment you brought to the training. How might this model help you?" – see also pages 127 ff.). The fact that the application assignments for the training all meet these three main criteria, and the fact that trainees take responsibility to work on these practical tasks during training both make one thing very clear: learners have opportunities to apply their new or more advanced skills to important and urgent tasks – which increases transfer effectiveness.

Arrange for parallel work on practical projects

Another transfer-promoting measure is to include accompanying practical projects (sometimes also referred to as project assignments) – these are the "big brothers and sisters" of application assignments, so to speak. They are particularly common for multi-module training programs and, ideally, sponsored by senior management. Not only do these projects help trainees stay on the ball, they also make an additional contribution to the organization, often a key optimization factor that has an impact on the organization's financial results. For example, suppose you are planning a training program for your sales managers, the objective being to put your company's growth strategy on a solid footing and develop new markets for your products. Less transfer-oriented programs would likely include module after module, in which experienced experts and trainers introduce participating managers to various potential analyses, sales strategies, customer segmentations, and a process for developing a marketing plan. Whether and how participants will then use what they've learned remains an open question (for the time being). It is therefore a much more promising approach to assign trainees to the project of developing an entire sales strategy for their product in the new markets. Then, during the training, they learn by working on their own project. Ideally, these practical projects are defined directly by top management, clearly communicating what outcome is expected, what conditions must be observed (e.g., markets), and what resources are available (e.g., budget). This clarity of expectation, in itself, has a positive impact on transfer success (see Lever 4 – Clarity of Expectations).

In practical projects, trainers act not only as conveyors of theoretical knowledge and skills but also as project advisors during training (and beyond). For example, they can accompany such projects as coaches or sparring partners outside the seminar room, virtually or face to face. As a complement for the training course, it can be nice to have a representative of top management or an executive in charge stop by for informal "fireside chats" in the evening to answer participants' questions and set the course for the development process. Arranging for various presentations on implementation plans and progress, and ensuring that they take place in suitable settings, will help give the projects the recognition they deserve.

To sum up, the objective is to produce fully implemented practical projects that visibly add value for the company. With a training design like this, it will be easy for trainees to muster the drive and transfer volition to stay on the ball until transfer success materializes. And for the developers of the training program, it will be easy to get approval of the budget for the next round, as the practical projects alone typically prove that the program has paid off many times over for the organization.

Also devise application opportunities for "high-potential" programs

A lack of immediate application opportunities isn't conducive to transfer success – that much is clear. But what if you design a training or program for high-potentials? I am talking about junior people who will sooner or later be placed in certain positions – but these positions won't always be available right after training, in some cases never, so trainees won't be able to apply what they've learned. Is this a knock-out criterion for transfer successes? Does it mean we should forget about high-potential programs, or other training with a longer-range horizon? If not, how can we create application opportunities for these programs as well? How can we bridge the time between the training and the real-life application situation? This is a challenge, but surmountable. If there are no immediate application opportunities, we can (1) sharpen the focus and goal of the high-potential program, or (2) "preserve" the knowledge and skills as well as possible, so trainees can access what they learned when the application opportunity eventually occurs. This requires building in some features that will made trainees aware of the content time and again in the period between the training and the application situation.

(1) Sharpen the focus and goal of the high-potential program. What applies to training in general seems more and more relevant for high-potential programs, too. Many modern organizations have them, the primary goal being to develop future managers – it has almost become standard. There is basically nothing wrong with this; it only becomes questionable and problematic in terms of transfer when lots of prospective managers attend the program, then most of them never get to put their new skills into practice because they'll never actually become managers, or only much later.

My first suggestion is: Ask yourself once again, very critically, what the program is actually meant to accomplish. Many high-potential programs are essentially selection programs, in which participants' performance and behavior are monitored closely and analyzed thoroughly, in order to filter out those with particular potential and who might make good candidates for a particular position. Nothing against that.

The problem only begins when this is not openly communicated. Instead, trainees are told something else to keep up their interest ("This program prepares you for the management position you'll get"). Experience shows that this may work for quite some time, even years – but then there is disillusionment, demotivation, and dissatisfaction, justifiably so, and this can also harm the reputation of the training itself. So, why all the hide-and-seek, why disguise the selection process as a training program? If your purpose or mission is to pick the best candidate for a position, communicate it!

In many cases, the question, "What exactly do you want to achieve with your high-potential program?" will produce a different answer – such as "Basically, we want to show our employees different development perspectives in the company and help them choose a specific career path." Wonderful! Then this will become your transfer goal – and one with immediate application opportunities. Design the program around this very goal and communicate it accordingly. Perhaps, your high-potential program will then contain not only modules such as "Using Management Tools Successfully" or "Change Management for Executives," but also "Identifying My Strengths and Potential" or "Leadership and Expert Career-Paths – Which Suits Me Better?" This could be combined with an individual assessment of each trainee's current position, or a comparison of the potential analyzed with the job profiles of corresponding positions. Or you could have fireside chats and mentoring events with people from the company who have made a management or expert career, etc. When transfer goals are sharpened, a very management-focused high-potential program can emerge, nearly a completely new program with immediate applications for the training content.

(2) Help trainees preserve what they've learned. It's always possible that sharpening the transfer goal and focus doesn't get you any further. Your high-potential or other program still involves the specific problem that application opportunities are likely to materialize much later. It is therefore important for trainees to "preserve" what they've learned, so they can access it in the application situation. This means we need to pay special attention and allocate more time to everyone's lessons learned and transfer plans. A good approach here is to have people develop their own personal implementation concepts. In a high-potential program for future managers, this could be a personal management concept. It will be their personal career companion, a concise compendium, and a highly personalized success program for the time prior to and upon their taking a leadership position. This concept might include one or more of the following elements:
- Me as a manager – how I want to be perceived as a leader (e.g., a "back-to-the-future" laudatio)
- My vision of me as a leader
- My leadership models – A thorough analysis of why these people inspire me and

which of their approaches I will adopt for myself

- What truly matters to me; what is important to me?
- What will my challenges be, and how can I master them?
- What will my first week look like?
- My lessons learned in a nutshell
- My top 10 secrets of leadership
- My personal development plan to become a successful manager:
  - What leadership strengths / resources do I already have?
  - What skills do I still want to develop?
  - How exactly will I do that (what will I read, who will I talk to, what will I observe in myself and others)?

The personal leadership concept is a compact and highly personal reference work. It should help trainees quickly recall the quintessence of what they individually have learned and apply it as soon as the application opportunity arrives.

Time for transfer!

Your turn: How can you make sure trainees have opportunities for application in real life? How might you help participants find an opportunity to apply what they have learned? What is the next step you will take? Write down your spontaneous ideas and thoughts.

This is how I will ensure application opportunities:

[1] On a lack of applications as a central transfer barrier, see, for example, Clarke, N., "Job/Work Environment Factors Influencing Training Transfer Within a Human Service Agency: Some Indicative Support for Baldwin and Ford's Transfer Climate Construct" in *International Journal of Training and Development,* 2002, 6: pp. 146 – 162, or Lim, D. H., & Johnson, S. D., "Trainee perceptions of factors that influence learning transfer" in *International Journal of Training & Development,* 2002, 6(1): p. 36.

[2] These three dimensions are described in Ford, J. K., Quiñones, M. A., Sego, D. J., & Sorra, J. S., "Factors affecting the opportunity to perform trained tasks on the job" in *Personnel psychology,* 1992, 45(3): pp. 511 – 527.

[3] For an overview of research and theory relating to forgetting, see, for example, Myers, D. G., Wahl, S., Hoppe-Graff, S., & Keller, B., *Psychologie,* Heidelberg: Springer, 2008 (2nd Edition), pp. 379 – 428, or Zimbardo, P.G., *Psychologie,* Heidelberg, Springer Verlag, 2013 (6th Edition), pp. 302 – 343; Baddeley, A., *Essentials of Human Memory* (Classic Edition): Taylor & Francis, 2013.

[4] The study with the Spanish vocabulary was conducted by Bahrick, H. P., "Semantic memory content in permastore: Fifty years of memory for Spanish learned in school" in *Journal of Experimental Psychology,* General, 1984, 113(1): 1.

[5] Studies on retention time are described in Michel, C., & Novak, F., *Kleines psychologisches Wörterbuch,* Freiburg: Herder Taschenbuch Verlag., 1990.

[6] For the study with flight simulators, see Fleishman, E. A., & Parker Jr, J. F., "Factors in the retention and relearning of perceptual-motor skill" in *Journal of Experimental Psychology,* 1962, 64(3): p. 215.

[7] The study on performing successful resuscitation following a first-aid course can be found in McKenna, S. P., & Glendon, A. I., "Occupational first-aid training: Decay in cardiopulmonary resuscitation (CPR) skills" in *Journal of Occupational Psychology,* 1985, 58(2): pp. 109 – 117.

[8] For the relationship between application possibilities and transfer see, for example, Lim, D. H., & Morris, M. L., "Influence of Trainee Characteristics, Instructional Satisfaction, and Organizational Climate on Perceived Learning and Training Transfer" in *Human Resource Development Quarterly,* 2006, 17(1): pp. 85 – 115. Gaudine, A. P., & Saks, A. M., "A longitudinal quasi-experiment on the effects of posttraining transfer interventions" in *Human Resource Development Quarterly,* 2004, 15(1): pp. 57 – 76, or Brinkerhoff, R. O., & Montesino, M., "Partnerships for Training Transfer: Lessons from a Corporate Study" in *Human Resource Development Quarterly,* 1995, 6(3): pp. 263 – 274.

[9] The study with MBA graduates can be found in Leach, L., *Alumni Perspective Survey: Survey Report 2012:* Graduate Management Admission Council (GMAC), 2014.

[10] More on the topic of training as a routine, habit, and expectation of modern organizations can be found in Weinbauer-Heidel, I., *Transferförderung in der betrieblichen Weiterbildungspraxis: Warum transferfördernde Maßnahmen (nicht) implementiert werden,* Wiesbaden: Springer Gabler Verlag, 2016.

[11] A compact and practical description of the model can be found in Rosenstiel, L. v., *Motivation im Betrieb. Mit Fallstudien aus der Praxis,* Springer Gabler Verlag, 2015 (11th Edition), pp. 38ff., and in Rosenstiel, L. v., *Grundlagen der Organisationspsychologie,* Stuttgart: Schäffer-Poeschel, 2015 (6th Edition), p. 56f.

LEVER 9 –
PERSONAL TRANSFER CAPACITY

TWO PRACTICAL EXAMPLES

Keyla and Alexa attended training on Prezi presentation software four months ago. Read what the two report today.

Keyla, 32, project manager for farming equipment

The presentation software Prezi is a really great innovation. I had experienced the program myself at a conference and was really excited about it. While the other speakers came along with typical PowerPoints, this speaker constantly zoomed in and out on his Prezi presentation. Connections became much clearer, and the audience really sat up and took notice with rapt attention. I wanted to learn how to do this, too. I did not just want to show our customers individualized solutions with glossy brochures and PowerPoints, but also to bring the product into the room and bring it alive with the presentation. My boss thought the idea was great. The training lasted for a day and a half, and it was really not very complicated. We created different presentations ourselves, for example, about our upcoming holidays. It was brilliantly explained! Great training! Unfortunately, I haven't been able to use it yet with customers. Back at work, I had to deal with our new CRM system, and when the next presentation appointment was due, I went back to PowerPoint – it was just too short notice. But let's see, maybe it will happen ..."

Alexa, 34, key account manager for a machinery manufacturer

I love Prezi – and my customers do, too! Zooming in and out directly on the product makes the presentations come alive, so our products are much more tangible. The Prezi training lasts four months. I had previously talked to my boss about how we wanted this software to benefit us. And we decided together to put off the training into the summer, when customer demands are a bit lighter. After covering a few basics, the training went straight into letting me work on my project. The first slides were ready at the end of the training, and two weeks later we presented our first finished Prezis to each other in the group. We were already given the deadline in the training, and I'm really happy about how it's all worked out – who knows if I would otherwise have really stuck to it. The first project was still relatively small – just to familiarize yourself. Meanwhile, my Prezis are becoming more and more comprehensive and better, and I'm building them faster and faster. Yes, Prezi is an integral part of my life today!

What do you think of these stories? What is the main difference?

Keyla had a classic capacity problem. Another pressing project – the new CRM system – caused her to postpone the transfer project and, if that happens repeatedly, she'll soon set it aside completely. Transfer success? Not a chance. Alexa, on the other hand, has managed to implement her transfer project in her everyday working life. She was able to find and apply the necessary personal transfer capacity.

Personal transfer capacity describes the extent to which individuals can muster the time, energy, and "headspace" in their working lives to incorporate what they have learned into their daily work routine. So, the question is whether workload, time pressure. and energy level leave enough room for transfer. Low personal transfer capacities, such as stress, pressure, congestion, and little "headroom" for new things, act as a key barrier to transfer success.[1] Personal transfer capacity is often one of the biggest barriers to transfer, especially in leadership and management training.[2] Transfer successes require time and headroom to try, make mistakes, gain experience, and become better or more experienced. This information is all fine and well meant, you may say, but isn't a high workload today (unfortunately) the standard, in all honesty? Yes, you are probably right. And yet, through a transfer-promoting, realistic understanding of learning, through time planning and conception of the training process, and the correct transfer planning in training, we can help to promote personal transfer capacity.

PERSONAL TRANSFER CAPACITY – WE (DON'T) HAVE THE TIME!

	Personal transfer capacity in a nutshell
Trainees say	"My working day allows me to take time to apply what I learned."
Definition	Personal transfer capacity is the extent to which trainees have the capacity – in terms of time and workload – to successfully apply newly learned skills.
Guiding question	How can you help ensure that trainees have enough time and capacity to apply what they have learned to their daily work?

Time. The bottleneck resource of the modern age. Acceleration, increasing workload, doing more in less time – these are all challenges that we know only too well. Time is probably the "fairest" resource in the world, because everyone has the same amount of it; 24 hours a day. The demand for "faster and more" does not stop at personal development when it comes to learning. Here, too, the mantra: more skills (acquired) in less time. Especially without any waste of (working) time. Learning that is easy, fast, and with little (time) expenditure – this is what companies and trainees alike want. But (how) does it work? Let's take a closer look.

Why is there always too much on our to-do lists?

Why is there never enough time for us monochrome people? No matter how many new technologies we use and how efficiently we work, somehow, time and time again, there is never enough. How can that be? Science says: We have less of a time problem, and more of a planning problem!

Time problems are often planning problems.

Do you work with to-do lists? How often do you go to work with a completely scatterbrained list of tasks? Every day? Once a week? On average, people only manage to fully organize themselves every 20th day. Only every 20th day can they fully achieve everything they want to do.[3] We take on too much, too often! That would be understandable if we could say we were planning for the very first time. But in the majority of cases, we have many years of experience with to-do lists and also with many of the tasks jotted down on them. One might therefore assume that we would have learned from our experiences to plan more realistically. The fact is we haven't learned. Again and again, we plan too optimistically. Again and again, people and organizations underestimate the capacities and resources needed for a task. Nobel Prize for Economics laureate Daniel Kahneman and his colleague Aman Tversky called this phenomenon the "Planning Fallacy"[4] How does the phenomenon come about? Why do we so consistently underestimate the time and resources we need to complete a task? According to Kahneman and Tversky, that happens because we do not take our experiences into account. We only think about the task itself and plan as if there were nothing else around. No other projects, no bad days, no phases in which we simply run out of discipline, no illnesses, no bosses, colleagues or customers who put obstacles in the way. We actually plan as if there were only the task at hand and optimal conditions to do it. We ignore experiences from which we could have learned while planning. No wonder we rarely meet the resulting schedules! The problem of improper planning is reinforced by wishful thinking: we believe that we can cope with our tasks and projects faster and easier, because we want so much for this to be true.[5] High motivation makes us even more vulnerable to faulty planning.

What can we do to counteract this? How can we protect ourselves from the Planning Fallacy? Plans become more realistic when we determine exactly when and where we will do the work.[6] We should definitely consider our experiences with these or similar tasks.[7] So the question is not how long you think you will need, but rather: "How long did I need last time?" Furthermore, research shows that worst-case estimates are often still too optimistic. It is important to consciously incorporate barriers, obstacles, and the unexpected. It also helps to get feedback from others, because they usually appraise time for our own tasks more realistically than we do ourselves.[8]

> Plans become more realistic if we (1) build on our previous experience, (2) plan for barriers, obstacles, and the unexpected, and (3) receive feedback from others on our plan.

Realistic planning is a challenge for people in general, and therefore also for our trainees in training. Once again, this shows us that orderly and assisted transfer planning at the end of a training is a decisive and important step, in which we should not leave our trainees unguided – we already covered this with the transfer planning lever. The more precisely trainees plan, the better the predictive power of the lists. The higher the motivation, the more likely it is that obstacles will be considered. And the more feedback and exchange opportunities our trainees receive for their transfer plans, the more realistic the planning becomes. It's worth it to support trainees in order to prevent them from falling into the Planning Fallacy trap and becoming overwhelmed by reality. Good and realistic planning equips trainees and their transfer projects to deal with practical realities and ensures that a lack of capacity does not, yet again, undermine everything.

> Support trainees in order to prevent them from falling into the Planning Fallacy trap. Realistic planning promotes personal transfer capacity, and thus transfer success.

That's enough for the psychological side. Now let's focus on the business end. In the context of learning and transfer, the capacity problem goes much deeper. Because, for learning, our society believes in, and lives, in a world full of myths.

Learning as "refueling" is a time waster

Time is short, and demands upon it are increasing. Therefore, the mantra is: More skills (acquired) in less time. In human resource development this translates into more trainings of shorter duration. That's exactly what the trend is. More and more employees are attending trainings. And these trainings are becoming shorter and shorter. But can employees really do more with less time? Will they really become more competent faster and faster? And does this actually reduce the cumulative (time) expenditure? The understanding of learning that underlies this logic is aptly described by Professor Axel Koch, who used the following metaphor: Trainees arrive at a (short) seminar like a car at a filling station.[9] You "refuel" – fill the mental fuel tank – and leave the station refueled, your errand completed. And immediately you can go about your daily work once again full of fuel. That this is an illusion is pretty clear. Each of us knows, in principle, that learning takes time and energy: we need to absorb content, repeat, try out, practice, reflect, practice again, and more. Yet wishful thinking is widespread – "fill up fast with little effort" – as if learning takes little or no time and requires little or no follow-up.

In practice, learning is thus often perceived as an event. A one-time event that is as short as possible. Oh, it's no problem at all to quickly modify communication habits that you've practiced for thirty, forty, or fifty years. Half a day? Sure! Go to training, refuel quickly, drive back to work, and you're done. Event completed. Unsurprisingly, this leads to success in only the rare and exceptional case. So, have the failures led to a rethinking of the myths of learning-as-refueling and learning-as-event training design? Are learning settings in companies now more realistic? Not in the majority of cases! A related metaphor also comes to mind: "Slow and steady wins the race." (In German, it's known as the "water on stone" or "steady drip" effect.) In the training context, the emphasis is on the recurrent effort. Communication training is carried out over and over again. If it didn't work the first time, then the next training will, or the one after that on the same topic. Go forth, refuel, drive home. And perhaps (though it's rather unlikely) the repetition will eventually lead to skills acquisition.

Cumulatively speaking, many trainings without corresponding transfer measures actually cost companies, trainees, and HR departments endless amounts of time. What we really wanted was to save time and effort with shorter training sessions without much preparation or follow-up. What we achieve with this approach is usually exactly the opposite. Again and again, we see largely ineffective trainings, which when added together are real time-sinks. The "time-saving" learning-as-refueling becomes an expensive eater of resources: time, cost, energy, and motivation. No wonder nobody here has time for transfer.

> It is not transfer-promoting activities that are time-consuming. The real time and resource eaters are the trainings that are designed as an event not a process.

What "I don't have the time" really means

The goal of acquiring more skills in less time is thus not attainable by means of more/shorter training. What is required is fewer but more sustainable trainings. An important step in this direction is to break away from the illusion of learning as refueling and replace it with realistic expectations of sustainable learning and transfer success. We need to be aware that sustainable (and therefore time-saving) training requires investing time and effort in the initial phase – as paradoxical as it sounds. Sustainable and time-saving learning is not an event, but instead a process, with different steps before, during, and after the training.

"But I have no time to prepare, follow up, and apply," you may already hear the trainees and executives exclaiming. However, this often means nothing other than

"I was not aware of how much time it will take" or "It doesn't have enough priority in my everyday work" or "I didn't plan the time (because I wasn't aware of the need or didn't think it was important enough)." Creating personal transfer capacities is therefore usually a matter of expectation, prioritization, and planning. And for this there are different starting points.

As our introductory example showed, it makes little sense to set up trainings at times when competing projects tie up capacities: the introduction of a CRM system, a change project, a restructuring, a new product launch. All of these are projects that are usually given high priority. A communication training, a leadership training, a presentation training, etc. will (when uncontrolled) have little chance of eliciting the necessary follow-up and thus transfer success when delivered alongside such projects. It is also necessary to pluck up the courage to say no to a training if the necessary capacities of the trainees are otherwise tied up.

Incidentally, it is usually neither capacity-saving nor useful to carry out long training sessions. Several studies have shown that long sessions – "massed training" or "massed practice" – are less effective than targeted and shorter training (spaced practice or spaced training).[10] Dividing the learning content into smaller portions therefore makes perfect sense from a learning and transfer perspective. Less content is learned in one go and can be stored more effectively, also making it possible to immediately work on the practical experience and emerging questions in the next short training. In addition, this "spaced practice" is usually much easier to integrate into the daily working routine. Shorter training units prevent oversized piles of paperwork and tasks from diverting all attention away from transfer when returning from training. But beware: spaced practice does not mean putting the same content into shorter training sessions (the refueling myth rears its head again!). Spaced training means serving content in smaller, wholesome portions and giving trainees the time and space to digest before serving up the next course.

In addition, with a suitable transfer architecture, we can ensure that transfer space is planned and made available for trainees. Elements that are already planned and announced in advance – such as transfer partnerships, follow-ups, ongoing work on projects started in training (as in the introductory example), informal exchanges in a weekly coffee meeting, and much more – have a positive effect not only on many other levers of transfer effectiveness, but also on the personal transfer capacity lever that we're considering here. They support the trainees in planning and using these transfer times.

So, let's assume that training time and duration are carefully selected, and thinking is no longer driven by myths. What else needs to be considered in terms of transfer capacities?

Let's devote ourselves to the topic of time anticipation. After all, this also has a decisive influence as to whether our trainees get into trouble with time planning. So far, we have seen that we are not very adept at time management when it comes to company-based training. Do you remember the last time you looked for a suitable training for yourself? Imagine that you want to continue your learning in the field of coaching and are looking for a suitable training on the topic of "systemic coaching." You find a great offer in the training brochure of your favorite provider. Systemic coaching for HRD professionals. Duration: 2.5 days; Wednesday, Thursday, and Friday morning. Do you consciously plan application and practice times for yourself? Will you perhaps take the next Monday off, to deepen what you have learned? If you are like most people, you will feel like you are able to walk out of the seminar room at Friday lunchtime with concentrated additional coaching skills, and head straight into a relaxing weekend with your family. On Monday, coaching will start! Yes, we are all heavily infected by the deceptive "learning-as-refueling" myth. After all, that's what the description says: 2.5 days. Who starts out thinking that this time in attendance at the training is only the beginning of the learning and transfer success process? This type of time specification hinders our view and ensures that we don't start to think about the important issue of transfer times! And this is without regard for the planning fallacy, to which we are all subject! Instead of thinking only in terms of "presence time" (i.e., periods of physical presence in the teaching environment), we should calculate and communicate learning times. Incidentally, this thinking is already well established in certain contexts, namely at universities. Students do not plan (only) for semester credit hours (in terms of attendance hours) but also for ECTS (European Credit Transfer System) credits.[11] The ECTS points are derived from all the learning activities of a course (including attendance hours, exam preparation, thesis, internship times, or self-study periods). While some courses may have few semester hours per week, ECTS points clearly show that they are very time-consuming. Students already think in terms of effort and no longer just plan in relation to presence time. This promotes realistic expectations and feasible planning. So, should we introduce an ECTS-style scheme into organizational training? It may be worth thinking about the idea! In any case, we should refrain from misleading statements such as "Duration: 2.5 days" and at least provide advice or guidelines regarding preparation, follow-up, transfer projects, transfer partnerships, etc.

"I don't have the time" equates to "I didn't allocate the time because I didn't realize the need, or didn't think it was important enough."

Summary

Planning is not necessarily easy for us humans, in and of itself. More generally, we should avoid the Planning Fallacy by helping our trainees plan their learning and transfer processes in a realistic way. In addition, it is time to finally put aside old myths. Fast learning-as-refueling is an illusion. And a merely repetitive "slow and steady" training mentality is a waste of valuable time. Learning is not an event, but a process. It is better to have less training, but have it be realistic, sustainable, and planned as a process. Effective training not only requires "presence time" but also embedding in a transfer architecture that creates transfer room, considers transfer capacities, and fosters realistic expectations and feasible planning among trainees. Training that appears more complex at first glance pays off not only in terms of transfer effectiveness for companies and trainees, but also in terms of overall time savings.

HOW TO STRENGTHEN PERSONAL TRANSFER CAPACITY

At a glance:
Ideas for reflection and implementation

Choose the right time for training
- Consider the agendas of the trainees

Design processes instead of events
- State that training days are only one step in the learning and transfer process
- Stay connected and take small steps toward transfer promotion
- Create process-oriented rather than event-oriented training descriptions
- Think about credit systems (development credits, learning points, etc.)

Spaced training – opt for several short training units
- Split content into bite-size pieces
- Make use of e-learning technologies
- Bring in external theory

Discuss understandings of, and myths related to, learning in training
- Convey the idea that training is just preparation for the practice
- Prepare trainees for the need for successful behavioral change (e.g., the Rubicon model, behavior modification stages)
- Protect trainees from the "refueling" illusion and convey a realistic picture of the transfer process

Choose the right time for training

The HR developer: "When would be the earliest date for you to hold the next two-day seminar with us?" The trainer: "In February, I'm pretty booked up. I could manage 21-22 March." HR: "Yes, that'd be great." – In practice, this is often how dates are scheduled for a training. The question revolves around the trainer. Where do attendance days fit into the trainer's calendar? The actual main actors – the trainees and their everyday lives – often receive less attention. It pays to take the trainees' perspective and ask how well-timed a well-designed learning and transfer process is for them. If possible, such a training should not be scheduled in the most work-intensive periods. It's a good idea to consider such times and the company's major projects, or to make use of their urgency. For example, it makes little sense to arrange a sales training for a bookstore during the Christmas period, because the workload is hectic, and training is the last thing on employees' minds. However, the time immediately preceding the Christmas rush could be particularly fruitful in this respect. Especially if the salespeople have certain Christmas targets and goals. This makes training automatically more pressing and more relevant.

Design processes instead of events

When we design learning as an event, we should not be surprised if it also becomes an event – a unique, time-limited experience that does not bring any lasting effect or change in and of itself. The finish line, however, is not the completed seminar, but the changed behavior, the achievement of the transfer and business goals (which we will come back to in Lever 12 – Transfer Planning). The one or two days of training is only one part of the learning and transfer process. And that is exactly what you have to consider in its conception.[12] It's only when HR developers and trainers start to plan in terms of processes, not events, that we can expect our trainees to likewise plan and have the time and capacity they need for transfer.

Does that mean that we have to make a half-year process out of a day-long Excel training? How can we get clients, trainees, and executives to accept such a thing? An acceptance of this is (unfortunately still) absent from many organizations. However, transfer promotion only works if it is compatible with and supported by the organization. So, it's about only going as far as the organization will accept – just a few steps along the process. Be inspired by the input example. Would a pre-training discussion with the supervisor be conceivable as a transfer-promoting measure? Perhaps as a first step, an informal recommendation can be included in the invitation mail ("Discuss the following questions with your manager")? (For more examples of supervisor involvement, see pages 242 ff.). Perhaps it will be possible to work on a small project during the training that the trainees need for their real-life work? (For more about practical projects, see page 201 ff.) It is not necessary to create additional work in the form of fictitious example projects! Already working on real projects and the transfer plans while in the training is much more time-saving and also transfer-promoting. Perhaps a short follow-up or reflection period can also be identified in advance – a Skype conversation or coffee meeting in the company cafeteria, where progress and questions are shared. And then maybe there can be an evaluation of the achievement of the transfer goal. It's not about "inflating" a mini-training, nor about developing a huge, unattainable process for each day-long training. It's about thinking in terms of processes and interweaving this thinking in the conception to an extent that the organization is willing to accept. Include small, single steps; individual transfer-promoting measures that the organization currently tolerates, within the current training.

If it is possible to think and design in processes rather than in events, it is important to communicate this to the trainees, too. A training description with "Duration: 2 days" written down sends the wrong signals. If you have an educational program, it is recommended that you employ consistent and process-oriented wording. For each training: preparation, classroom-based training, implementation/application. Or training and practice phases or learning and implementation phases. Describe in brief keywords which elements are used in each phase of this training process. Avoid communicating in a "learning as an event" logic, in which post-processing indicates that the main "event" (the training) is already over. It is exactly the opposite: the training is much more the preparation for the main "process" (the implementation)!

If you design multi-module training programs, graphics can be helpful. Do not simply describe the contents of each module, but also visualize all elements. This shows the trainees that the program is more than a collage of individual modules.

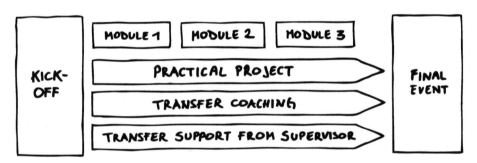

Fig. 8:   Visualize your training program and the transfer-promoting measures as a process

Also, the introduction of a credit system is a good way to signal to the trainees that this is not merely about physical presence in the training event. According to the model of ECTS points in the university system, there could also be development credits (DCs) or learning points for different tasks and sub-steps in your academy or course, which reflect the respective required effort outlay. Pre-training discussion with the supervisor: 3 DCs, doing the preparatory task: 6 DCs, classroom training: 12 DCs, transfer project: 36 DCs, etc. Instantly show the trainees that this program is more than simply sitting in the classroom!

Spaced training - opt for several short training units

Training content is better stored and more successfully utilized when it is acquired in bite-size portions (spaced training) rather than in the form of a single large serving (massed training). In practical terms, this means splitting a two-day training into four or five half-days, or even smaller units. Each half-day module has a core theme or focus topic, preferably a single key message and a matching application task. At the next half-day module, content can be reviewed immediately (this promotes long-term storage) and application experiences exchanged and discussed (this promotes transfer volition and self-efficacy). At the same time, learning is transformed, so that it is no longer a single event, but, as intended, a process.

On the one hand, such spaced trainings can be integrated particularly well into everyday working life. It is often easier to get 12 trainees together for a few hours than several days at a time. On the other hand, there are the possible increased travel times and costs, which inhibit the uptake of spaced training. Here innumerable new technical possibilities could act as an optimal remedy: in the e-learning area, there is so-called micro-learning, which virtually connects the parties to the spaced training in digital form and has been firmly established. This does not mean we should replace classroom training with digital "knowledge nuggets." It is instead to be considered a useful addition. So why not outsource the theory into the e-learning world in the form of small learning units, and use the time in classroom training for something that e-learning can never offer: space for practical exercises and experimentation in a safe environment, with valuable feedback from colleagues and the trainer? The success of concepts such as the "inverted classroom" (also called flipped classroom or inverted teaching) has shown that this works. It's worth Googling it!

Discuss understandings of, and myths related to, learning in training

The myth of fast learning-as-refueling is deeply rooted in our society (see pages 213 ff.). We cannot – and should not – assume that our trainees are aware of how crucial the main phase of learning is – namely applying, trying out, practicing and undertaking in their workplace. But this very awareness is crucial for trainees to plan and carry out their personal transfer capacities. As a trainer, always point out during a training that the training itself is just the preparation for the practice. Whether the training is successful or was a waste of time is determined in the application phase. This phase is crucial for efficacy. The time present in training is just a tool on the way there. Also, prepare the trainees for the time it takes to achieve transfer success, and to develop new, and change habitual, behaviors: Time for practice, time for reflection, time for making mistakes. Guide them away from the illusion that they have been "refueling" for the moment they leave the training room, and that the application of what they have learned works perfectly. Show the trainees one of the many models of behavioral change as evidence of this. The Rubicon model (see pages 158 ff.) or the stages of behavioral change from the transtheoretical model[13] are just two examples of such models. Also, in the reminder mail (see pages 76 ff.), clarification regarding the transfer process and the required resources can again be discussed. It is important that we protect trainees from the illusion of learning-as-refueling and give them a realistic picture of the transfer process and a good plan for undertaking it.

Time for transfer!

Now it's your turn! How do you support personal transfer capacity? How could you help trainees find opportunities to apply what they have learned? What is the next step that you would like to implement? Spontaneously write down your ideas and thoughts.

This is how I will support personal transfer capacity:

[1] On missing transfer capacities acting as a significant barrier to transfer success, see, for example, Awoniyi, E. A., Griego, O. V., & Morgan, G. A., "Person-environment fit and transfer of training" in *International Journal of Training & Development,* 2002, 6(1): pp. 25 – 35, or Holton, E. F., Chen, H.-C., & Naquin, S. S. "An examination of learning transfer system characteristics across organizational settings" in *Human Resource Development Quarterly,* 2003, 14(4): pp. 459 – 482, or Holton III, E. F., Bates, R. A., Seyler, D. L., & Carvalho, M. B., "Toward construct validation of a transfer climate instrument" in *Human Resource Development Quarterly,* 1997. 8(2): pp. 95 – 113.

[2] The issue of lack of time in Leadership Development Programs is discussed in Cromwell, S. E., & Kolb, J. A., "An examination of work-environment support factors affecting transfer of supervisory skills training to the workplace" *Human Resource Development Quarterly,* 2004, 15(4): pp. 449 – 471, Huczynski, A., & Lewis, J. W., "An empirical study into the learning transfer process in management training" in *Journal of Management Studies,* 2004, 17(2): pp. 227 – 240.

[3] This example, alongside a short-but-entertaining outline of the Planning Fallacy, can be found in: Dobelli, R., *Die Kunst des klugen Handelns. 52 Irrwege, die Sie besser anderen überlassen,* Munich: dtv Verlagsgesellschaft, 2014 (3rd Edition) p. 177.

[4] For the term Planning Fallacy, see Kahneman, D., & Tversky, A., "Intuitive prediction: Biases and corrective procedures" in *TIMS Studies in Management Science,* 1979, 12: pp. 313 – 327. A good overview of various findings and studies can be found, for example, in Bühler, R., Griffin, D., & Peetz, J., "The planning fallacy: Cognitive, motivational, and social origins" in M. Zanna (Ed.), *Advances in experimental social psychology,* Burlington, Academic Press, 2010, Vol. 43: pp. 1 – 62, or Pezzo, M. V., Litman, J. A., & Pezzo, S. P., On the distinction between yuppies and hippies: "Individual differences in prediction biases for planning future tasks" in *Personality and individual differences,* 2006, 41(7): pp. 1359 – 1371.

[5] On wishful thinking as a co-cause of the Planning Fallacy, see Bühler, R., Griffin, D., & MacDonald, H., "The role of motivated reasoning in optimistic time predictions" in *Personality and social psychology bulletin,* 1997, 23(3): pp. 238 – 247.

[6] On the idea that implementation intentions promote realistic planning, see, for example, Koole, S., & van't Spijker, M., "Overcoming the planning fallacy through willpower: Effects of implementation intentions on actual and predicted task-completion times" in *European Journal of Social Psychology,* 2000, 30(6): pp. 873 – 888.

[7] The notion that plans become more realistic when we include past experiences is described in Bühler, R., Griffin, D., & Ross, M., "Exploring the 'planning fallacy': Why people underestimate their task completion times" in *Journal of personality and social psychology,* 1994, 67(3): p. 366.

⁸ Feedback as a method for realistic planning is described, for example, in Roy, M. M., Mitten, S. T., & Christenfeld, N. J., "Correcting memory improves accuracy of predicted task duration" in *Journal of Experimental Psychology: Applied,* 2008, 14(3): p. 266.

⁹ Further information about Prof. Axel Koch, his research, and the Transfer Strengthening Methods he has developed can be found at www.transferstaerke.de.

¹⁰ Various studies on massed practice compared to spaced practice are cited in, for example, Kauffeld, S., *Nachhaltige Weiterbildung. Betriebliche Seminare und Trainings entwickeln, Erfolge messen, Transfer sichern:* Springer, 2010, pp. 79ff.

¹¹ ECTS stands for European Credit Transfer System. This is the European system for transferring and accumulating academic credentials with the aim of making higher education comparable across the EU and also enabling students to move between study programs across borders.

¹² For a more in-depth look and feel for learning as an event and learning as a process paradigm, see the highly readable book: Pollock, R. V. H., Jefferson, A., & Wick, C. W., *The six disciplines of breakthrough learning: How to turn training and development into business results,* Wiley, 2015.

¹³ The Transtheoretical Model of Behavioral Change was developed by James C. Prochaska, Carlo Di Clemente, and John Norcross, who combined and used various psychotherapeutic theories to explain and make controllable intentional human behavioral change. A good and accessible overview of the model can be found in Prochabska, J. O., Norcross, J. C., & DiClemente, C. C., *Changing for good: The revolutionary program that explains the six stages of change and teaches you how to free yourself from bad habits,* New York: W. Morrow, 1994.

LEVER 10 – SUPPORT FROM SUPERVISORS

TWO PRACTICAL EXAMPLES

Two months ago, Manfred and Margit attended a "Designing Meetings More Efficiently" training. Read how the two are today.

Manfred, 47, deputy head in the energy sector

And, once again, I lost two hours in a meeting that I'll never get back again. A lot was talked about, but without result. I can hardly stand it any longer. It wouldn't be that hard to make our meetings more efficient. Because I was so annoyed, I even attended a seminar two months ago. My boss just said, "Well, if you want to, why not!?" In the seminar, I learned a lot. Not only about what matters – things like being on time, the agenda, the right people, strict time-keeping, and open discussion – but also how to implement these solutions in a very concrete way. Back at work, I immediately went to my boss, totally motivated to discuss with him how we could use all the ideas for more efficient meetings. His response: "Ah, yes, you went to that seminar. Sure, we can talk about it. But, right now, I need the latest customer statistics. ASAP!" Of course, the conversation about meetings never happened. And then, when I took the intiative to set up a digital agenda, so everyone could enter their topics before the next meeting and we could plunge right into discussion, what happens? The boss comes into my office and is like: "Well, now, that's a bit over-bureaucratic! We've never done this before!" Meetings were and remain a waste of our time – and I'm seriously considering whether I should bother attending any more trainings.

Margit, 38, team assistant in software development

When I suggested to my boss that I could attend the "Designing Meetings More Efficiently" course, she was very interested. At the next lunch we had together, we both looked over the seminar description. We liked what we saw and jointly agreed on what our future meetings should be like: shorter and more to-the-point – that was the goal. And we also agreed that she and I would plan the next meeting together after the seminar. In the seminar, I was able to ask lots of specific questions and got some really great ideas. As soon as I returned to work, my boss waved me into her office, and we discussed the takeaways I'd brought back from the seminar. Today, we hold our regular meetings correctly, always starting with the most important point, leaving a small space for the unscheduled, and not holding a meeting without a predetermined agenda. In the beginning, I was quite worried when preparing an agenda because I did not want to annoy anyone with my constant demands. But my boss helped me, always supported me, and gave me feedback on the emails. Today I can say that we have achieved our goal: our meetings are shorter and more to-the-point – the seminar has really paid off!

What do you think of these reports? What is the difference?

Margit has her supervisor's backing. The boss herself is interested in Margit returning with ideas for more efficient meetings and supports their implementation in many ways. Manfred's boss, however, shows no interest, either before or after the training. Support? Missing in action. Sorry about that. And transfer success never happened.

Support from supervisors describes the extent to which a trainee's supervisor actively requests, supports, and reinforces the transfer of training. Supervisors can consciously or unconsciously block the application of what trainees have learned. (The "killer phrase" – which Manfred also heard – is essentially: "This is the way we've always done things around here!"). Supervisors can leave the transfer success to the trainee's luck or own initiative by simply ignoring the training and its (possible) goals and outcomes. Even this indifference can have a highly negative effect on transfer success. After all, supervisors, in keeping with their role, assign work, define priorities, and, through praise, feedback, and their own actions as role models, control how, with what, and with what level of commitment, their employees work. However, supervisors can also use these channels to provide targeted support for training transfer. They can clarify expectations and goals in advance with their employees, provide time for preparatory tasks, enable undisturbed learning in training, show interest in the training and learning, discuss individual transfer goals or action plans after training, confirm and prioritize them, create application opportunities and situations, praise employees for the application of what they have learned, give them feedback and tips, act as role models themselves, and so on. Numerous studies have shown that support from supervisors is a decisive factor in transfer success.[1]

SUPPORT FROM SUPERVISORS – THE BOSS AND TRANSFER SUCCESS

	Support from supervisors in a nutshell
Trainees say	"My supervisor demands and encourages implementation."
Definition	Supervisor support is the extent to which trainees' supervisors actively demand, monitor, support and reinforce transfer.
Guiding question	How can you ensure that supervisors support, promote, and demand the application of what trainees have learned?

When it comes to facilitating and supporting trainees' transfer success, supervisors and HR development are equally responsible and equally important partners on the organization side. In most cases, transfer cannot work without supervisors' support, as HR development has no direct impact on work assignments, application situations, priority setting, or transfer promotion – here, in the sense of praise and feedback. At the same time, supervisors need the time, expertise, and resources of HR in order to arrange for effective training for their direct reports. HR and supervisors are in the same boat. If only one rows – no matter how hard and enthusiastically – the boat will only move in a circle, never arriving at a destination. However, if the training is successful and thus transfer-effective, both win!

> HR and supervisors sit in the same boat when it comes to transfer. For transfer success to occur both must row. If the transfer succeeds, both win!

Although research – and our common sense – tell us in no uncertain terms how important supervisors' support is for the successful transfer of training, implementation in practice typically falls short. In Austria (where I live), only 9 % of companies have implemented pre-training activities as their standard operating procedure (e.g., discussions between supervisor and trainee-to-be to go over the content and benefits of the training or to define common goals). The same applies to transfer support following the training. In only 9 % of Austrian companies is it standard practice for supervisors to provide targeted application options or support transfer by praising or expressing appreciation for trainees who apply what they have learned.[2] Another study reported that 60 % of supervisors had no idea after a week-long US$2,500 program what goals their employees were pursuing after completing the training.[3] As these examples indicate, in practice, supervisors who specifically support the transfer goals of their employees are the exception not the rule.

Why supervisors (don't) support transfer

The support from supervisors is essential for trainees' transfer success. So why is this support so often absent? Here are some of the crucial and surprising reasons.[4]

Why supervisors DO NOT support transfer

- **Lack of knowledge**
  Supervisors do not know the transfer problem or the importance of their role in transfer success

- **Lack of responsibility**
  Supervisors do not feel responsible for transfer or training ("That's the job of HR development")
  Supervisors expect trainees to return from training "developed" without any particular contribution by the supervisor

- **Lack of urgency**
  Other tasks have a higher priority than transfer support; it is not one of the supervisor's "official tasks" and is thus not measured or assessed

- **Goals lacking or unclear**
  Employees' development needs and/or the transfer goals of the training are not clear enough for the supervisors

- **Fear and resistance**
  Because supervisors fear additional bureaucracy and because they themselves know too little about the training and about the contents and models discussed there.
  In order not to "lose face" in front of their employees, they avoid talking about the training or the transfer of what trainees have learned, because they fear that their own freedom of action regarding decision-making may be restricted.

When supervisors do not actively engage in transfer promotion, it is often because transfer of training isn't even on their radar. Transfer as a concept and problem may be unknown to them. There is a lack of knowledge about the crucial role that supervisors play in the transfer success of their direct reports and what they might do to help in concrete terms. In addition, a sense of responsibility may be lacking. Training – and HR agendas, in general – are considered to be the responsibility of HR development or trainers. The expectation is that employees go to training and return two days later "developed" – the widespread myth of learning-as-refueling (see pages 213 ff.). Often, a sense of urgency is missing. Compared with other managerial agendas and tasks (running day-to-day business operations, problem solving, decision making, phone calls with customers, meeting preparation, etc.), transfer support (e.g., pre- and post-training discussions) has little priority. This sometimes has to do with the fact that transfer support is not usually considered part of performance appraisals or evaluations. Only rarely are figures collected and tracked on employees' transfer success or the quality of supervisors' transfer support, although this is the norm for employee satisfaction or financial parameters (see also pages 282 ff.). In addition, transfer support from the organization or HR development is often not actively and emphatically demanded, although this is standard for discussions with employees (e.g., on performance). Poorly defined goals are another reason for supervisors' lack of support for transfer. If supervisors do not have a clear picture of what should be different or better after the training (transfer goal), it is only understandable that they can hardly support their employees in achieving these unclear or absent goals. Of course, the same applies if employees' development needs have been only vaguely defined. Finally, the study showed that there are also fears at play. Transfer support is often absent due to the fact that supervisors shy away from the (supposed) bureaucracy and paperwork involved. Essentially, the train of thought is: "We already have a form for employee appraisal and one for supervisor appraisal. Now we've got transfer meeting forms coming along, too. I'm not putting up with this!" Furthermore, some supervisors feel some anxiety about discussing the content, outcomes, and benefits of the training with their employees because they are unfamiliar with the training content itself. Imagine the employee comes back from training and reports on how impressive and effective systemic questioning techniques are. The supervisor unfortunately has no idea what this is about, let alone when, where, and why you might need these techniques. For fear of being deemed incompetent or losing face, the issue is just not talked about. Transfer support? Little or none.

As you can see, there are a number of issues that prevent supervisors from actively facilitating transfer support. Some of these reasons can be talked about openly, while others are real enough but rarely directly named or identified. How can one succeed in winning over supervisors as transfer supporters despite these obstacles? What makes (some) supervisors play their crucial role in transfer success? Here are the results of the research:

- **Sense of responsibility and self-image**
  Supervisors who do support transfer see themselves as developers of human resources and consider the development of their employees as their job

- **Self-interest and benefits**
  The supervisor wants and expects the time invested in training to be worthwhile and lead to clear results and positive changes
  The supervisor has a personal stake in seeing his or her employees achieve the desired transfer goal, i.e., the specific success-critical behavior

- **Involvement/sense of "ownership"**
  Supervisors are involved in setting goals, designing, and/or implementing the training or program

Supervisors are actively involved as transfer supporters when they see themselves as human resource developers. They see developing and promoting their employees as part and parcel of their role. Supervisors also support transfer whenever they themselves have an interest in the change that is sought through the training. (You remember Margit's boss in our introductory example. For her, it was important for meetings to be shorter and more efficient.) But more generally, when supervisors realize that training without transfer support is simply a waste of time, they are unwilling to accept the loss. The logic here is, "If I have to do without my employees for two whole days for the sake of training, then that training had better make a positive difference! To make sure that happens, I'm going to actively support transfer success!" And, finally, supervisors often engage in transfer if they care about the training or the training program. This is usually the case when they themselves are involved in coming up with the concept or setting the objectives. The training (program) is their own "baby" as a result of active involvement, and they therefore automatically have a very close bond, and want it to be successful.

It is very helpful to know the issues that cause supervisors to (not) support transfer. Their motivations and concerns help us to introduce engaging and viable transfer interventions, to argue convincingly, and to empower supervisors as committed partners for transfer success. But what exactly should they do now? What exactly are transfer-supporting actions? Let's take a closer look.

What transfer-supporting supervisors do

How can supervisors perform their role as transfer supporters? What exactly do supervisors do when they promote and support transfer? The transfer researchers Natalie Govaerts and Filip Dochy have compiled this information in an elaborate meta-analysis.[5] Here's a summary of the behaviors and settings of transfer-supporting supervisors:

This is how transfer-supporting supervisors act
Fundamental attitudes and actions
• **Clarify goals.** Transfer-supporting supervisors help their employees set, clarify, and refine realistic training and transfer goals
• **Give emotional support.** Transfer-supporting supervisors repeatedly show that they believe that their employees can and will successfully complete the training
• **Encourage and promote.** Transfer-supporting supervisors continually encourage employees to apply what they've learned in their day-to-day work
• **Coach.** Transfer-supporting supervisors take a coaching approach to assisting their employees in applying what they have learned
• **Serve as a role model.** Transfer-supporting supervisors embody what their employees learn in training
Before the training
• **Help with training selection.** Transfer-supporting supervisors actively participate in discussing needs and training that meets these needs
• **Are informed.** Transfer-supporting supervisors familiarize themselves with and/or participate in the creation of the content and objectives of the training
• **Give reasons for taking part.** Transfer-supporting supervisors explain to their employees why they have been selected for training, or explain why they agreed that the employees should attend the training
• **Assist in preparation.** Transfer-supporting supervisors help their employees to prepare for training (provide time, complete preparation tasks, reduce the workload, provide information, etc.)
• **Clarify value / benefits / goals and expectations.** Transfer-supporting supervisors clarify with their employees what they expect from participation, what value and practical benefits the training should have, and what goals it aims to achieve
• **Show and promote positive attitudes.** Transfer-supporting supervisors show their employee that they consider it good, meaningful, and valuable to be involved in training. In this way, they encourage employees to go to training with positive expectations and attitudes

During the training

- **Support behind-the-scenes.** Transfer-supporting supervisors ensure that trainees are not distracted by day-to-day work during training (e.g., calls, mails, urgent requests, distribution of incoming work, etc.).

After the training

- **Show interest in the training.** Transfer-supporting supervisors show an interest in what the trainee learned during training
- **Are open to change.** Transfer-supporting supervisors are open to ideas and that their employees bring back from a training
- **Discuss application opportunities.** Transfer-supporting supervisors talk with trainees about opportunities to practice and apply what they have learned
- **Create opportunities to practice and apply.** Transfer-supporting supervisors ensure that trainees get frequent and near-real-time chances to practice and apply what they have learned
- **Tolerate mistakes.** Transfer-supporting supervisors are forgiving of mistakes that initially happen as a result of an employee's practice and application
- **Give informal encouragement.** Transfer-supporting supervisors openly show appreciation when employees apply what they have learned
- **Reward.** Transfer-supporting supervisors reward trainees for applying what they've learned to their work
- **Promote sharing.** Transfer-supporting supervisors encourage employees to share what they have learned in training with other colleagues
- **Give feedback.** Transfer-supporting supervisors provide feedback to trainees on their application attempts and successes, and on their performance in the workplace
- **Provide practical support.** Transfer-supporting supervisors help their employees to acquire the resources they need (time, budget, materials)
- **Monitor applications.** Transfer-supporting supervisors make sure that their employees work on implementation and attempt to apply what they have learned
- **Promote support and deepening of implementation.** Transfer-supporting supervisors approve and support additional transfer-promoting activities (such as participation in follow-ups, transfer coaching, peer exchanges, etc.)

Now you might think, "That sounds like a huge amount of effort! Our supervisors would never agree to that!" You will be pleasantly surprised how much impact can be achieved in a short time.

Transfer support – elaborate bureaucracy?

We have seen what kinds of supervisor activities have a transfer-supporting effect. But how does all this affirmation, information, appreciation, praise, etc. look in practice? Maybe you are thinking of long meetings, comprehensive forms, detailed questionnaires, and standardized operating procedures and process descriptions. All this sounds like a lot of effort, a lot of bureaucracy and – as important as it may be – the source of a lot of resistance on the part of the supervisors, who are, after all, more than busy with their own work. Having or giving someone additional tasks sounds negative. However, I can reassure you – it doesn't have to be that way!

What if you could prove to supervisors that two 15-minute discussions would significantly increase their employees' transfer success? And without any complicated bureaucracy? Would that meet with supervisors' interest? Yes? Then here comes the scientific evidence:

Brinkerhoff and Montesino (1995) carried out a study on behalf of a training center. The training center's purpose in this study was to show executives the importance of their role in their employees' transfer success, thereby capturing the supervisors' interest and commitment. A total of 95 trainees from one company participated in a variety of training sessions (including "Effective Collaboration Techniques," "Effective Time Management," and "Managing Meetings and Groups Effectively"). A group of 37 randomly selected trainees were assigned to the experimental group, the others to a control group. The control group attended the training without information or intervention. The members of the experimental group attended the exact same trainings. In the experimental group, however, the supervisors of the trainees were also tasked with conducting short discussions with their employees in the week before the training, and another one in the week after the training. They were told that each conversation should last approximately 15 minutes and were given a simple list of topics to discuss in these meetings.

Transfer conversations in 15 minutes	
Topics for the meeting BEFORE the training	Topics for the meeting AFTER the training
(1) Discuss what the training is all about (2) Discuss how the training is important to the work of your employee (3) Define one or more specific expectations as to how the lessons learned can be applied in their role (4) Encourage your employee to implement what they have learned in the workplace	(1) Find out what skills your employee has acquired during the training (2) Discuss together what obstacles and barriers your employee is concerned about relating to application (3) Define together a concrete opportunity or situation in the near future for the employee to usefully practice/apply what they have learned (4) Assure your employee that they will receive support or coaching for the implementation, if they wish (5) Underline that you clearly expect your employee to apply what they have learned to their real work

You see – the whole thing was really quite simple. Can such informal 15-minute talks really make such a difference? The answer is clear: Yes! The study shows that the trainees in the experimental group were able to record significantly higher transfer success rates, without any burdensome bureaucracy. Trainees in the experimental group felt encouraged in their learning, considered themselves more responsible for transfer, and had significantly more application possibilities than the control group. In addition, they experienced fewer transfer-inhibiting factors (only 27 compared with 41 in the control group) and more transfer-promoting factors (123 to 83 in the control group).

This study shows by way of example that even short, simple, and less structured conversations – i.e., very simple and small interventions – can significantly increase transfer success. It can be especially useful to start with such small, unbureaucratic interventions if the specific supervisor has not shown interest in the issue of transfer and transfer support. Instead of forcing the issue by means of "official" forms, it is advisable to use tips and simple lists of topics as support for the discussions, depending on the corporate culture and the standing of the HR development function. That means, no additional "enforced bureaucracy," but rather "offers of support." This reduces resistance and gradually wins supervisors over regarding more comprehensive transfer interventions.

> Keep supervisors' transfer support simple and unbureaucratic. All journeys begin with a first step!

The fine print of support from supervisors

Support from supervisors is essential for transfer success – that's for sure. However, not every intervention fits into every organization and every training group. For example, a post-training discussion in one case can significantly increase transfer success. In another case, however, it may have no significant effect. Why? And what does the effect depend on?

Transfer researchers have two main answers to these questions: autonomy and conviction. Autonomy deals with the question of how much freedom, independence, and room for maneuver trainees have in their everyday work. Imagine, for example, the type of job people have who are directors of an institute at a university. They are accustomed to setting goals for themselves, assigning work to staff members completely at their own discretion, and organizing their own resources, as needed. We can further assume that people in such positions seldom get to see their supervisors as part of their day-to-day work. When they talk about work, it is mostly with colleagues. When these institute directors (and others like them) attend a training course, they have the opportunity to create their own application opportunities without their supervisors assisting them, due to their high degree of work autonomy. They will primarily exchange thoughts on application ideas, goals, successes, and possible obstacles with their colleagues – as with other matters. Narrow and highly standardized transfer interventions do not have much effect on workers with high autonomy.[6] In these cases, peer support is often a more important lever than supervisor support.

A second reason why supervisor support for transfer may fail to have any effect is the supervisor's own conviction. The best transfer interventions by supervisors will fail if they are carried out only superficially and without conviction.[7] Pre- and post-training discussions can be very powerful when supervisors support them, or just annoying, bureaucratic hassles that do not produce a positive impact. Once again, it is clear that the decisive factor is less the intervention per se (how a template is structured, how the process is defined, etc.), but rather the supervisor's conviction and commitment to the chosen instrument.

Summary

If employees do not have a extraordinarily high degree of job autonomy, it is indispensable to have supervisors on board to support their transfer success. If supervisors consider transfer important, their employees are much more likely to do so, too. Supervisors who define clear expectations, create application opportunities, show interest and promote transfer intentions with praise and feedback make a decisive contribution to a trainee's transfer success. Yet, the way that they do it (whether formally using interview forms or informally over lunch) is less crucial than the degree of sincerity with which they provide their support for transfer. Accordingly, it makes sense not to implement transfer interventions "by force," but rather to create awareness of a problem through education, to develop interventions jointly as far as possible, and to win supervisors over as partners for transfer success.

HOW TO STRENGTHEN SUPPORT FROM SUPERVISORS

At a glance:
Ideas for reflection and implementation

Win over supervisors as transfer supporters
- Convince instead of prescribing
- Tips on how to win over the supervisor

Support supervisors with guides, samples, and templates
- Plan transfer discussions connectably with supervisors (aligned with work and other events)
- Various discussion templates
- Info mails
- Guiding questions for transfer discussions
- Fill-in transfer meeting forms

Qualify supervisors as transfer supporters
- In training or workshop, discuss and agree on benefits, shared values/self-understanding, and tasks
- Develop discussion templates together

Invite supervisors to training
- Conduct transfer meetings in the presence of the trainer
- Conduct transfer meetings during training
- Win over supervisors as sponsors, mentors, co-trainers, or representatives of the organization in training

Harmonize the central training programs in your organization
- Provide as similar training as possible for the same language at all levels of hierarchy

Evaluate the support provided by the supervisor
- Make transfer support a leadership task
- Use sample questions and items for evaluation by trainees

Win over supervisors as transfer supporters

An email to all executives: "HR development has decided to include a supplemental transfer-supporting process in our trainings. From now on, each employee must have a one-hour pre-training and one-hour post-training discussion in accordance with the attached guide and the log form on Page 4. The logs must be submitted to the Human Resources Department within one week of the pre- and post-training meetings. Sincerely, The HR Department." How would you react to such an email as a manager who supervises any number of direct reports?

"What is that supposed to be about?!" Or "Not another a form to fill in!" Or "Where should I re-allocate the time for this from?" etc. – These are all common reactions when HR development introduces a new process for transfer support from supervisors. Why? The supervisors primarily think: "Oh, that's just great. They're offloading even more work on us" and understandably resist. Then it becomes difficult for HR development. At best, the new process works when it is tightly controlled - make a follow-up call, write reminder mails, create sanctions – how tedious and how uncomfortable! It doesn't have to be like that. The resistance arises because managers see no personal benefit and advantage. And that's exactly what is needed to make it transparent. It's about getting supervisors on board and making sure they understand the purpose and benefits of transfer, training, and their role as transfer supporters. All this is much more important than the question of what the form for the transfer discussion looks like or what should be included in the accompanying e-mail. So far, so good. The only question left is: How does it work? How do you convince managers? How do you get them interested in transfer?

What can we do, what can we focus on? Here are the key points summarized for you:

Winning over supervisors as transfer supporters

- **Make transfer a topic supervisors care about.** Not all supervisors have the topic of transfer on their radar. Make transfer a topic that supervisors care about; bust the learning-as-refueling myth
- **Emphasize the importance of their leadership.** Many supervisors are unaware of how important and indispensable they are to transfer success. Demonstrate the importance and role of supervisors in transfer success and convince them of the need for and importance of their support
- **Highlight the benefits to management.** Emphasize the very personal benefit of the trainees' transfer success to supervisors. ("If your staff apply what they have learned to their work, you and your department benefit because ...")

- **Give examples.** Show supervisors concrete implementation examples of what transfer support means and what it can look like. Support them with appropriate tools (guides or sample topics for transfer discussions, best practices in transfer support, etc.)
- **Sharpen transfer goals.** Establish clear transfer goals. If possible, even agree to these in consultation with the supervisor. Only with clear goals can the supervisors know what they should support
- **Counter the fear of bureaucracy.** Avoid framing transfer interventions as bureaucracy and paperwork for supervisors, but as support and guidance. Avoid compulsory forms as much as possible, and make better use of smart, compact guidelines, tips, examples of best practice, etc.
- **Start where the shoe pinches (pain points).** Start implementation of transfer interventions where supervisors themselves have a strong interest in achieving the transfer goals (for example, for a particular academy or specific training). If they have a strong commitment to achieving the transfer goals and to the training, supervisors are also more willing to try new transfer interventions
- **Involve and engage.** Involve supervisors in developing and deciding on transfer interventions. Self-/co-developed interventions are much more convincing than "imposed" ones.

To win over supervisors as transfer supporters, it is particularly helpful and effective to actively involve them in the design process. If a manager wants training for their department, carefully review the needs and/or invite them to the selection and assignment clarification discussions with the trainer. Advise the supervisor on which transfer-promoting activities are useful for the training and, if possible, develop them together (e.g., transfer tasks, follow-ups, ...). It is "their" training and "their" transfer success; your role as a human resource developer and/or trainer is as an enabler, consultant, expert, and sparring partner! The same applies if the initiative for the training or the program does not come from a supervisor (e.g., section head or department manager, but from another, typically more "top-down" source (e.g., a request from senior management to set up a management program or an initiative by your HR development unit to establish a trainee program). Make training a matter of importance to the organization, or, better yet, a key topic for supervisors that they personally care about. Involve them in the needs assessment, ask what matters, what is important to them, and what they value. Have them decide on and participate in the selection of trainees and, optimally, in the development of the transfer support activities. Depending on organizational culture, time issues, and the scope of the training or training program, the possibilities for involving supervisors can range from multi-day or multiple conceptualization workshops to meetings, surveys, and interviews or may be limited to brief and informal discussions at the coffee machine. Whatever your organization can handle, make sure that supervisors feel involved, consider training useful and beneficial, have a personal interest in making the transfer work well, and, as a result of their commitment and involvement, want to support successful transfer.

Support supervisors with guides, samples, and templates

With the will now there, the most important and challenging part is already done. Now it's about making it as easy as possible for managers to be good transfer supporters. What helps? Appealing templates, practical guides and examples for the various transfer-supporting discussions between supervisors and trainees. A study showed that the number of preparatory interviews held using interview templates increased from 15% to 85%, and follow-up talks from 25% to 45%.[8] How to start transfer discussions? The first step is to determine how many and what types of meetings should be conducted. From a transfer perspective, of course, it is beneficial for supervisors and trainees to talk to each other as often and as intensely as possible. But, again, you need to take the organization's wishes into consideration. When planning, be aware of the amount of time a supervisor must spend with each trainee, and how many trainees a supervisor must supervise. Is the time planned realistic for the supervisor? The following table can help you to determine the nature and duration of transfer-related meetings.

Number	Planned transfer meetings	Max. Duration in min.
	Pre-training discussion – before the training / program (benefits, goals, focus, application opportunities)	
	Intermediate meeting(s) – during the training / program (showing interest, progress, focus, application opportunities)	
	Post-training discussion – immediately after the training / program (showing interest, insights, implementation plans, application opportunities)	
	Implementation meeting(s) – in the implementation phase subsequent to the training / program (showing interest, results, implementation projects, application opportunities)	
	Evaluation / final meeting – after the implementation phase (review of benefits and reflection on the development process, reflection on support, optimization opportunities)	
	Other/additional planned meetings:	
	TOTAL EXPENSES per supervisor per trainee	

Connectedness with existing culture and ways of working is also the mantra when it comes to the design of the templates and guides. Again, the following is advised: aim less at a confining "Just do it like this" approach and more at a convincing "This is what works well" guide. It is thus often more amenable to go beyond strict questionnaires and forms and to focus more on key questions, reflection questions, topic guides, discussion guidelines, etc. Aim at giving convincing recommendations instead of issuing directives or regulations! It is important that we do not lose clarity. Documents that force supervisors to do all the work of figuring out how their transfer support talks with trainees should proceed are of little help! Formulate the documents so that they are concise, simple, clear, understandable, and can be used immediately without any additional input. And last but not least, make sure that the documents are relevant to the organization in question. This can be, for example, through the language, the graphic presentation, the scope, or the type of template. If, for example, an organization is more conversational, informal, and makes its important decisions around the water cooler, there's little sense in sending out templates for a learning contract – that would not be compatible with the culture. With these three points in mind (1) a recommending style, (2) clear and simple, and (3) culturally compatible, let's now look at various complex possibilities.

Types of transfer discussion guides (examples)

A list of possible questions or topics that could/should be discussed

For employees: Discuss the following points with your supervisor before the training:
- How could I tell from my day-to-day work that the training was successful?
- What will be the most important and relevant content and topics of the training?
- How and where should I apply what I have learned? (Discuss concrete situations, tasks, projects, etc.)
- Make an appointment for the post-training discussion!
- etc.

A sample conversation

1. Clarify the goals of the program: "What we want to achieve is ..."
2. Agree on application opportunities: "I expect you to apply what you have learned to ..."
3. ...

Checklists to tick off

These topics were discussed
- ☑ Program goals
- ☑ Application opportunities and situations
- ☑ Support from supervisor
- ☑ ...

Questions / topics with blank fields for notes

For employees: Discuss the following questions with your supervisor:
- Where do you see your development potential? What do you want to work on?
- What do you expect from the training? How do you see it contributing to your professional performance?
- Which content and topics in the training are particularly crucial for you and your job?
- In what situations will you apply what you have learned? Which tasks will you take on?
- How will your supervisor support you in applying what you have learned?
- etc.

Notes / Agreements

```


```

Questions or topics with blank fields to fill in

Agreed goals, quantified targets

```


```

Agreed upon support from supervisor

```


```

An informational email with topics and questions for the discussions between supervisor and trainee is the "entry-level model." In the info email (or, more traditionally, in the information letter or informational brochure), trainees will find not only detailed information about the training, but also a list of possible questions to be discussed in advance between trainees and supervisors – essentially as an integrated preparatory task. This can be handled as a trainee-led task, i.e., asking trainees to take the initiative. In this case, only trainees receive the mail, in which they are asked to discuss the appropriate questions with their respective supervisor. Or it can be supervisor-led. In this case, supervisors also receive an email in which they are provided wth compact information about the upcoming training (an important prerequisite for supervisors to becoming increasingly active in transfer support) and possible questions for a discussion.

The other meetings (interim discussions, post-training meeting) work similarly "on the side." Trainee-led set-ups could have the participants receive questions for the meeting with their supervisor together with the flip-chart-protocol or summary of the training. For a supervisor-led set-up, supervisors get this mail, edited accordingly.

The *transfer discussion guiding questions* may be sent to trainees and/or supervisors separately, or as an attachment to other information about the training or training program. This serves as an orientation for both parties and shows what should be discussed and agreed upon in training- and transfer-related meetings (pre- and post-training discussions and ongoing implementation meetings, etc.). Templates for this are provided in the previous section.

Fill-in transfer meeting forms are designed to prompt trainees and their respective supervisors to make notes or record agreements in them, or mark tick-boxes or rankings. What is spoken is thus recorded and becomes more binding and permanent. It is also possible to ask the trainees to bring these records with them to the training or to send them in copy to HR development (this may also be handled as a task for the supervisor) or bring the completed sheet to later discussions (e.g., to the post-training meeting or an evaluation meeting). It has also proved useful to have the record signed by both the trainee and their supervisor. In addition, separate sheets can be developed for supervisors and trainees, with which they can prepare themselves for their meetings, as is often done for employee (performance) appraisals. All these things increase the level of care taken and the necessity to conduct such discussions. In addition, they create opportunities for HR developers and trainers to check whether the pre- and post-training discussions were carried out, and how seriously. Also, for the control options, the spectrum ranges from a (more or less formalized) simple feedback stating "Discussion conducted / not conducted" to the return of a completed form, i.e., answers to individual questions (as is the case with most employee appraisals). Depending on the degree of control, it can provoke resistance. Again, it is important to consider what is appropriate for the relevant corporate culture.

If you have the supervisors on board the (transfer) boat and the supervisors have already experienced for themselves how valuable and effective all these interventions are, then you can turn to working on gradually expanding supervisor support as a *process*. As before, only go as far as the supervisors (and the organization) will tolerate and support – commitment and conviction must have utmost priority. How can you specifically expand the process of supervisor support? Andrew Jefferson and his colleagues have written a whole book about this and have compiled a comprehensive process plan with a variety of tools to assist you with transfer support from supervisors, including templates and models for each step of the process.[9]

Qualify the supervisors as transfer supporters

When the importance and benefits of supervisor support are clear and have been internalized, and/or the supporting processes become more complex, there is often good news in practice: supervisors generally want to learn how to support the transfer of their employees. It is in their own interest to optimally fulfill their role and to help shape the transfer success. At this point, congratulations! You've done a brilliant job of persuasion, you've got the executives on board, and taken transfer effectiveness a big step forward! Supervisors who want to become better transfer supporters: What a luxury for HR developers and trainers! Take advantage of this luxury and comply with their wishes. One of the key interventions in transfer promotion is to qualify supervisors in their role as transfer supporters. Organize a workshop or training that addresses and deeply anchors the benefits, the shared values or self-image, and the tasks of a supervisor as a transfer supporter. Develop and discuss the support processes and the corresponding guides, sample topics, and templates together. Discuss possible concerns and uncertainties and practice the individual support steps with supervisors (for example, by role-playing or rehearsing a pre-training meeting), etc. More and more companies are choosing to include a module on this topic (e.g., "Leadership as Personnel Developers and Transfer Supporters") in their internal leadership programs. An investment that pays off!

Invite supervisors to training

Perhaps neither the qualification nor the carefully prepared templates for pre- and post-training discussions are currently capable of catching on the organization. Perhaps you have a very specific training program for which you want to be absolutely certain that support from supervisors will be available and want to intervene more forcefully to. Or you might need something like a precedent, a program in which supervisors experience for themselves how significant a difference it makes when they act as transfer supporters – this would then trickle into other programs by itself. In an investment-intensive training program, you may want to make sure that discussions between trainees and supervisors are conducted seriously and with meticulous attention to detail. Let's discuss what this might look like.

Conduct the transfer discussions in the presence of the trainer. Strive to make it part of the training program to have three-way conversations in advance: with the trainer, supervisor, and trainee. Of course, it is optimal if the trainer attending the pre- and post-training discussions plays a leading role in the training program – either because he is responsible for all the modules or because he coordinates the other trainers in the role of lead trainer. Or he looks after the trainee as a (transfer) coach beyond the training (see pages 79 ff.). What is the value in the trainer being present at discussions with the supervisor? First and foremost, discussions in this setting become more binding and meaningful. A fixed date with an external third party (which incurs a tangible financial expense) and the resulting agreements are less likely to get "lost" in day-to-day turbulence at work. In a pre-training meeting in a three-person setting, the trainer also learns first-hand what sticking points and pressing issues need to be addressed in the training – not only from HR, trainee feedback, or a completed evaluation form, but directly, with all the fine nuances and the often-so-revealing details between the lines. The same is, of course, true in a three-way post-training meeting, quite apart from the fact that it is often easier for the trainee to "sell" their transfer plans well and demand appropriate support from the supervisor if the trainer is present as a neutral advisor. Supervisors for the most part also highly appreciate it when a third party is willing to lead-moderate the discussion in the pre- and/or post-training meetings. This arrangement allows the supervisor to focus on the content; it provides relief and gives security – especially if such discussions are not yet standard practice in the organization.

A proven alternative to three-way conversations is that *supervisors join the program themselves at specific times.* In multi-module training programs, this could be for the first half day, for example. Often there's an overview of the entire program, and it's great if the supervisor gets this. A first exercise could be that supervisors and trainees mutually hone each other's individual goals as a team, agree on the desired and appropriate form of support from the supervisor, discuss possible applications, etc. – all the important things that would otherwise be individually clarified in the pre-training meeting. The advantages: Once again, the discussion in this form often benefits from higher commitment and importance and thus has a greater chance of being carried out carefully and seriously than if it simply is just another "to do" that has to be dealt with. An external person (the trainer) can also explain in a fact-based way why and how important transfer in general and support from supervisors in particular are. In addition, the group dynamics also have an effect here, because every supervisor-trainee tandem works alongside each other, and perhaps then also briefly reports in a plenary session on how this went. With a third party present, it will be difficult not to conduct the discussions! In addition to the beginning, supervisors can be integrated into the program again at different times: in a "checkpoint module" designed to reflect on progress so far and next steps, in an informal fireside chat covering one or more modules in an evening, at the very end the program for transfer planning, in a joint concluding statement, or later in follow-up format. Do you feel resistance mounting because you can see their mind's eyes totting up a threateningly long travel expense report, or because the good old "time-trouble" argument is ringing in their ears? Remember that in the era of Skype etc., physical presence is not always necessary! In addition, there is the possibility to combine elements as desired. Perhaps the pre-training discussion is in the first module, but the other conversations take place in the office! And finally, the time and resource topic is often nothing more than a matter of urgency and priority (see also pages 214 ff.).

Supervisors may also be involved in other focused roles, such as those of *sponsors, mentors, co-trainers, or representatives of the organization.* In these roles, the supervisor brings the (internal) perspective of organizational practice into the training, while the trainer takes on the (external) specialist perspective and the responsibility for process design. More concretely, and illustrated by an example, this could mean that the organization trains internal trainers. The corresponding train-the-trainer program is structured in several modules on specific topics (e.g., modules on benefits of the role as trainer, targeted application of methods and media, designing training concepts, promoting transfer, etc.). Each module is designed by an external trainer, each with a specialist within their field. But the common denominator, the individual who joins them all together, is the head of the internal training department. This person participates in every module (completely or artially) and designs individual parts of these modules. For example, an external trainer develops an idea for how to design flipcharts effectively, while the head of the training department introduces the in-house corporate identity for flipcharts. An external trainer gives examples of different methods and their effects; the internal co-trainer shows how they can be used specifically for the training topics within the organization. In addition, the head of the training department is on hand when questions about implementation or feasibility arise. And that gets many (supposed) transfer barriers out of the way on the spot.

If the trainees jointly attending a training report to two or more different supervisors respectively, then each supervisor can take on the role of mentor for a different topic or module. Then, for example, in module 1, Supervisor 1, in module 2, another supervisor, etc. This works when the supervisors know each other well and work and communicate with each other regularly.

Both options automatically encourage supervisors to show or develop an interest in training, to contribute to it, to help shape it, and to adopt it on as their own particular priority, making the training both successful and effective. Of course, this also becomes immediately visible to trainees. In addition, it is a very charming way for supervisors to learn the content of a given training without having been "officially" and "only" trainees in a training. Too often, the need for development is indeed seen in others (usually employees), but not in one's self (the supervisor). Supervisors' integration into training as sponsors, mentors, co-trainers, etc. addresses this issue tactfully but effectively.

Harmonize the central training programs in your organization

Sometimes supervisors fail to support transfer because they themselves do not know what their employees have learned in training, nor do they have much interest in finding out about it. Or they themselves act according to other models, use other instruments, or employ different terms and explanations in their everyday work than those their employees have learned in the training. One reason that such situations arise is a mostly well-intentioned misunderstanding: Higher levels of hierarchy need "better" training. In practice, this usually means the higher-level supervisors get the more expensive and renowned trainers – just as with seminar hotels, company cars, flight classes, offices, etc. From a transfer perspective, this is not a particularly good idea. If the assignment clarification is not 100 % complete – and let's be honest, when is it ever so – every trainer has their own wording. Most even have their own models, emphases, exercises, and content. Now, if supervisors at higher levels of the hierarchy learn something different from trainees and supervisors in the levels below, it is then automatically more difficult for the higher level to support and promote transfer. So, what should be done?

The tip from transfer-promotion experts: Harmonize the cross-hierarchy programs! Make sure the different levels of hierarchy learn the same models, instruments, and content and speak the same "language"! For example, if you are planning a leadership program across multiple levels of hierarchy, then you can harmonize it by using the same trainers (or by ensuring that the trainers are optimally "tuned in"). If possible, start the program at the highest hierarchical level and work downwards. Incidentally, this does not mean that all content that is relevant to upper management always has to be trained across the other hierarchy levels as well. In terms of content relevance, it makes sense for top management to attend a possible additional module on "Strategy Development" or "Managing International Teams," while such modules would be skipped for most other supervisors. However, it is important for different levels of the hierarchy to use the same concepts, frameworks, and language consistently (as is also expected for a company's products and services).

This is done through a skillful and harmonious structure of cross-hierarchy training and programs. Supervisors should optimally already know about what their employees learn in training through their own attendances at the training. They should have experienced this themselves and embody how they encourage their employees as a transfer supporter! This makes it easier and more attractive for supervisors to fulfil their role as supporters.

Evaluate the support provided by the supervisor

Supervisors at all levels typically have a lot of important and pressing tasks at hand. The mantra: Set priorities. To date, transfer support has only rarely been one of the and pressing priority tasks for supervisors. There's a simple reason for this: It isn't measured or tracked! While it is common practice to evaluate coaches, the evaluation of transfer support by supervisors has been an exception rather than a rule thus far. But it is exactly such a lack of evaluation that causes a task so decisive for transfer success to slip down or off of supervisors' priority lists. In addition, such evaluation data would allow HR developers and trainers to point out the importance of transfer support from an empirical basis and to demand it consistently. As is often the case with supervisors, "What gets measured gets done!"

What might this look like in practice? The best and most convenient way is to integrate transfer support evaluation into other systems that are already in place, rather than making it another additional element. Perhaps you are already evaluating the transfer effectiveness of your training (or perhaps will start doing so after reading Lever 12 – Transfer Expectations in the Organization)? Simply integrate a corresponding question or a suitable item there.

> **Evaluating support from supervisors**
> Sample questions and items for evaluation by trainees
>
> - My supervisor supported me well with the implementation of what I learned! (Scale: 1: Does not apply at all, to 5: Completely applicable)
> - For the practical application of what I learned, I found my supervisor to be: 1: very supportive, to 5: very inhibiting

- My supervisor
  - ☑ finds training important and meaningful
  - ☑ is interested in what I have learned in training
  - ☑ notices if I use what I learned in training
  - ☑ encourages me to apply what I have learned
  - ☑ finds what I've learned in training useful
  - ☑ acts in alignment with what I've learned in training
- I had a pre-training meeting with my supervisor (yes / no). I found this meeting to be highly beneficial (1: Agree strongly, 5: Disagree strongly). Please give reasons for your evaluation for this point (open answer field)
- How did you feel about your supervisor's role in the learning process? How did he or she help or hinder you in implementing what you had learned? Please give your impressions using keywords (open answer field)
- How did your supervisor assist you with the practical implementation of what you learned in training? (open answer field)
- What additional support would you have liked from your supervisor? (open answer field)

Another possibility is not to link the quality of the transfer support from supervisors to a specific training itself, but to treat it as part of the supervisor's assessment as a manager. Perhaps there are already some forms of this in your organization – an employee discussion in which the supervisor also receives feedback from the employee, a staff survey on leadership quality, a 360-degree feedback, etc.). Here you can easily query how well the employees who attended a training have felt their supervisors supported them on transfer. You will see that such data is incredibly valuable when it comes to winning over supervisors as transfer supporters!

Time for transfer!

Now it's your turn. How could you encourage support from supervisors? How could you get the leaders on board and motivate them to demand and promote the implementation of what has been learned? What is the next step that you would like to implement? Spontaneously write down your ideas and thoughts.

This is how I will encourage support from supervisors:

[1] For the correlation between transfer and support from supervisors, see, for example, Blume, B. D., Ford, J. K., Baldwin, T. T., & Huang, J. L., "Transfer of Training: A Meta-Analytic Review" in *Journal of Management,* 2010, 36(4): pp. 1065 –1105, or Brinkerhoff, R. O., & Montesino, M. U., "Partnerships for Training Transfer: Lessons from a Corporate Study" in *Human Resource Development Quarterly,* 1995, 6(3): pp. 263 –274, or Broad, M. L., & Newstrom, J. W., *Transfer of Training: Action-Packed Strategies To Ensure High Payoff from Training Investments,* Basic Books, 1992, or Colquitt, J. A., LePine, J. A., & Noe, R.A., "Toward an integrative theory of training motivation: A meta-analytic path analysis of 20 years of research" in *Journal of Applied Psychology,* 2000, 85(5): pp. 678 – 707.

[2] These and other results on the practice of transfer promotion in Austrian companies can be found in Weinbauer-Heidel, I., *Transferförderung in der betrieblichen Weiterbildungspraxis: Warum transferfördernde Maßnahmen (nicht) implementiert werden,* Wiesbaden: Springer Gabler Verlag, 2016, pp. 120 ff.

[3] These and other interesting facts, as well as an extremely helpful model for training transfer can be found in the highly commendable work of Wick, C. W., Pollock, R. V. H., Jefferson, A. M. K., Flanagan, R. D., & Wilde, K. D., *The Six Disciplines of Breakthrough Learning: How to Turn Training and Development Into Business Results:* Wiley, 2006, p. 128.

[4] Among the reasons why supervisors (don't) support the transfer, see Weinbauer-Heidel, I., *Transferförderung in der betrieblichen Weiterbildungspraxis: Warum transferfördernde Maßnahmen (nicht) imple- mentiert werden,* Wiesbaden: Springer Gabler Verlag, 2016, pp. 160ff.

[5] On transfer-supporting behaviors of supervisors, see Govaerts, N., & Dochy, F., "Disentangling the role of the supervisor in transfer of training" in *Educational Research Review,* 2014, 12: pp. 77 – 93.

[6] The issue of transfer support through supervisors and autonomy is dealt with, for example, in Axtell, C. M., Maitlis, S., & Yearta, S. K., "Predicting immediate and longer-term transfer of training" in *Personnel Review,* 1997, 26(3): pp. 201 – 213.

[7] For the conditions under which supervisor assistance is transfer promoting, see, for example, Van Der Klink, M., Gielen, E., & Nauta, C., "Supervisory support as a major condition to enhance transfer" in *International Journal of Training and Development,* 2001, 5(1): pp. 52 – 63.

[8] For the effect of discussions with supervisors, see Rank, B., & Wakenhut, R., "Bildungscontrolling: Erfolg in der Führungskräfteentwicklung," conference paper, Expertentagung, Munich and Mering: Rainer Hampp Verlag, April 1996, pp. 95ff.

[9] A detailed supervisor support process and much more about the role of supervisors in transfer success can be found in the highly commendable work of Jefferson, A. M., Pollock, R. V., & Wick, C. W., *Getting Your Money's Worth from Training and Development: A Guide to Breakthrough Learning for Managers,* Wiley, 2009.

LEVER 11 – SUPPORT FROM PEERS

Two practical examples

Andrea and Tobias attended a "Stress Management" training six weeks ago. Read the comments they made after today's follow-up meeting.

Andrea, 32, graphic designer in the advertising industry

Nothing but pipe dreams, just as my colleague had predicted. All those ideas and methods for coping with stress, great as they may sound, don't work for the creative industry. After the first two training days, I was surprisingly optimistic. I let myself get swept away by the others. Although I was very skeptical, I switched off my phone because everyone did. No calls or mails for two days, plus a nice little walk after lunch. I really enjoyed that, and I was determined to continue with that routine once I got back to the firm. How naïve I was! The moment I got to the office on Monday, my colleague started bombarding me with accusations. "I called you like a hundred times! We had an emergency and you weren't available!" – Well, good morning to you, too! At noon, I got up from my desk as planned, to warm my lunch and actually eat at the lunch room – for the first time in years. Nobody said anything, but I did get some strange looks. I don't even want to think about what would have happened if I had taken my after-lunch walk … At today's follow-up round, everyone was supposed to report on implementation progress. To be honest: It's nil at my end. Not because I don't want to, but because it just doesn't work at our firm. But, of course, I wasn't upfront with the group.

Tobias, 38, web designer in the advertising industry

I had high expectations! The other team that had attended the training before us had raved about it. And they were right. It really made a difference for our department. It was noticeable right there at the training how everyone got on board, one by one. It all became very clear in the evening, when our whole department sat down together and finally did some straight talking. For example, each of us was fed up with eating at our desks or over the computer, but no one wanted to go to the cafeteria on their own. Then other things came up that we should have discussed long ago ... Today, it's normal for almost everyone at the agency to take a lunch break. What's more, now it's the people who stay at their desks who get the funny looks. What a change! Also, my transfer partner was an incredible help. It's great to have someone that keeps checking whether my inner perfectionist is about to take over again. I'd always thought that only professional coaches could coach, but my transfer partner is pretty good at it. Today at follow-up, some people said they had got themselves private mobile phones to put an end to constant accessibility, and lo and behold, nothing happened to them. So, I'm going to get me one, too.

What is your impression? What is the difference between the two stories?

We humans are social beings. What people in our environment do, think, and perceive as good or bad affects our own thoughts and actions – including those related to training and transfer. Andrea received a lot of encouragement and confirmation in the training group. Unfortunately, her colleagues at work did not respond the same way; their looks and reactions said: we don't like at all what you're planning to do. It's quite the opposite with Tobias. His transfer intentions matched the department's new standards and values. They were appreciated and embraced, both in training and at the workplace. A key trigger for his transfer success.

There are two basic human needs which are addressed in almost every motivational theory: the need for growth and the need for connectedness. Growth means: We humans want to learn and develop further, that is, successfully apply what we have learned. Connectedness refers to our desire to be accepted by those around us, to get praise, attention, and encouragement. For our subject, transfer, these needs for recognition and growth can complement each other perfectly. This is the case whenever trainees' environment appreciates and supports what they've learned in a training. So, they can satisfy two needs in one go: They develop further by applying what they have learned, and they get recognition from those around them. This is the ideal case for transfer success. In a worst case, however, the two needs get in each other's way. The trainee wants to learn and apply what he or she has learned, but the team and/or supervisor is far from pleased. There is no social recognition. As a result, even though the trainee is willing, the odds are against transfer success. Especially in companies with flat hierarchies, support from peers can be even more important than supervisor support. Other people's opinions regarding the training and transfer plans have a strong influence on transfer. As transfer researchers Brinkerhoff and Gill succinctly put it, "The workplace can untrain people far more efficiently than even the best training department can train people"[1] – simply because people are scared of violating the rules, not fitting in, and therefore not being accepted anymore. This is something even the best training with the most convincing trainers and with optimally prepared transfer plans often cannot avoid. Support from peers is a crucial ingredient to transfer success.[2]

SUPPORT FROM PEERS – OTHER PEOPLE'S INFLUENCE

☕	Support from peers in a nutshell	
Trainees say	"My colleagues are backing me on implementing what I have learned."	
Definition	Support from peers is the extent to which colleagues help trainees with transfer	
Guiding question	What can you do to encourage trainees' colleagues to welcome transfer and support it?	

Groups and group situations affect individuals in incredibly powerful ways. Not only do we witness this every day with different topics in the media; we also observe or experience it in our own everyday lives. Groups and group phenomena are a huge and very exciting field of scientific research, which we can't cover here and won't even attempt to outline. Once again, from a plethora of exciting research results I'll pick out just a few that might be of particular use to our transfer subject. So, be amazed at two group phenomena you are probably familiar with, and to which we are all subjected – not only in the context of transfer effectiveness: the striving for conformity and for consistency.

We are swarm-stupid

A test subject enters a room. There is a conference table where other people are already sitting, who are all going to participate in the same experiment – or so the person thinks. In fact, everyone but our subject is privy to and part of the legendary experiment created by Solomon Elliot Asch.[3] The subject sits down. On a screen, a line appears, and next to it, three lines for comparison.

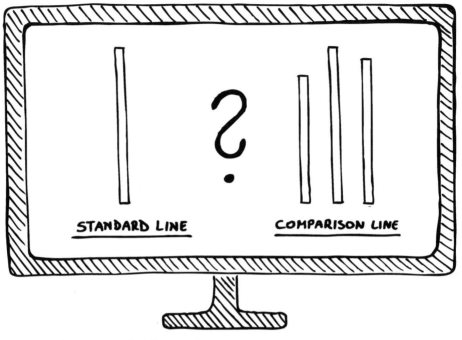

Fig. 9: *The line experiment by Solomon Asch*

The (alleged) test subjects are now given the following task: State which of the three lines of comparison is exactly the same length as the standard line on the left. Since this is relatively easy, most subjects make no mistakes (less than 1 %) – this was the control condition. Now get ready for this: The actual experiment comprised a total of 18 of these length estimates. In six of them, the pre-informed trainees all gave the correct answer. In the other twelve, they unanimously gave a wrong answer. And what was the effect on test subjects? 76 % of them let themselves be influenced by the group at least once. Although it was fairly obvious that the answer was wrong, they went along. They conformed and suddenly saw what the group saw. This impressive experiment was repeated in numerous variants. It turned out that the larger the group was, the greater the conformity. If only one of the pre-informed individuals gave a different (correct) answer, the subjects made significantly fewer mistakes; that is, with one more person agreeing, they were more likely to defend their minority opinion. This, by the way, also worked when one of the pre-informed people agreed with the test subject – this, too, would usually make them stick to their correct assessment.

Why do subjects choose to give a concurrent but wrong answer, if it doesn't even express their own opinion and perception? Solomon Asch explored their motives.

Here's what they said:

- I was unsure at the beginning, but the majority seemed certain, so I concurred with them
- I was hesitant or afraid to contradict the majority
- I did not want to stand out from the group because of my different opinion
- I actually saw it the way the majority said they did

When it's only about the length of lines, we may marvel at the effect of striving for conformity, and perhaps it makes us smile. In the following experiment by Latané and Darley, however, the consequences of conformity are rather shocking.[4] The purpose of the experiment was to find out to what extent the desire for conformity can lead individuals to risk their own health. The subjects were placed alone in a room and given tasks (e.g., filling in questionnaires). After a short while, acrid white smoke would begin to escape from the ventilation shaft and gradually spread throughout the entire room. This smoke was no danger or health hazard, but of course the subjects did not know that. So, what do you do when you think you're in mortal danger? You get out of that room as fast as you can and find help. After six minutes, 75 % of the test subjects had left the room to alert the experiment leader. Things were quite different, however, when subjects were not alone in the room, but with two of the experiment leader's assistants. When the smoke started spreading, these two merely glanced at each other briefly, shrugged, and continued to work. You guess what happened: 90 % of the subjects stayed in their seats. They didn't want to appear cowards, even in the presence of a probable health hazard.

The pursuit of conformity makes us succumb to "swarm stupidity," as Professor Gunter Dueck puts it in his bestseller by the same name.[5] We make obvious mistakes, and even endanger our health, to conform to the group's opinion. Why on earth do we do that? One reason is that we don't know for sure what the right answer is or what to do in the given situation. The group's opinion is a plausible and convenient source of information for us – so we simply agree. This is the informative influence of a group over the individual. The other factor is its normative influence. When we misjudge lengths and endanger our health, it's not only because we don't know any better but also because we want to come across as a likeable person and be accepted by the group. Having a different opinion always involves the risks of not being a part of the group anymore – a nightmarish for us humans, as we are social beings.

We act consistent with the group because 1) we want to be accepted by the group, even if that means we have to deviate from our own beliefs, and 2) we consider the majority opinion to be a reliable source of information.

So, if we even let ourselves be duped into behaving in ways harmful to our health (or even worse than that, as shown in the Milgram Experiment or the Stanford Prison Experiment), it comes as no surprise that in training, too, groups have a remarkable influence on individuals. Even before a training, participants-to-be are acutely aware of exactly what their work colleagues think of the training and its effects, or what the general opinion is in the organization regarding that training. Then, during training, they observe meticulously and explore, overtly or covertly, what the others think: How useful do they find what we are learning here? How seriously do they take the exercises, the discussions, the trainer? How much do they intend to implement? Are the others really going to try out what we've learned in training? And if so, will they stay on the ball? What are they achieving? What do my immediate work colleagues think of my transfer plans? Do they think they're good? Do they support me or oppose my plans? By observing and conversing before training, in training (especially during breaks) and back at the workplace, trainees perceive their colleagues as setting benchmarks, unspoken standards, and norms for behavior. Their desire for conformity then leads trainees to not act according to their own views (at least not exclusively) but to also do what others do and what others think is right.

Security for your next visit to the beach, free of charge

Many self-help manuals tell us we should communicate our intentions to others. When we publicly declare what we intend to do, the argument goes, we miraculously put more power into implementing ring it. Why is that so? Why do we strive harder when we tell others about our intentions? Researchers describe this phenomenon as pursuit of consistency. Some renowned theoreticians consider this striving to "walk the talk" to be so essential a human need that they call it a basic psychological motive.[6] Studies from a wide range of fields show how reliably this consistency principle works.

Here is a practical example for your next visit to the beach. Do you know how to get complete strangers to watch your bag for you while you take a swim? Thomas Moriarty looked into this on a New York beach.[7] One member of the research team pretended to be an ordinary beach-goer. He spread out his towel next to a randomly selected person – the test subject. After spending some time listening to music from a portable radio, he got up and strolled along the beach without taking his belongings with him. After a short while, another member of the research team appeared, who played the role of a thief. He grabbed the radio and took off. Well, what would you do in such a situation? Would you try to step the thief? Out of 20 subjects, only 4 did that. After a small change in the experimental setup, however, it was 19 out of 20 subjects! 19 out of 20 confronted the thief, demanded an explanation, or even detained him using physical force. How come? What made these subjects security guards all of a sudden? It was the consistency principle: Before the "beach-goer" left his place, he asked the subject if they'd watch his belongings. The subjects agreed. And the desire for consistency began to take its effect. The subjects felt they had an obligation to keep their promised, so most of them confronted the alleged thief.

NGOs also take advantage of that principle. I suppose you've been approached in the street before, by people working for Greenpeace, Caritas, Amnesty International, or some other charitable organization. They often start by asking something like, "Are you concerned about human rights?" or "Do you endorse the protection of our environment?" Of course, most people would answer Yes. And there we have it: the consistency principle. When the next question is whether we'd like to sign a standing order for donations, saying No is much less easy. By then, most people experience the unpleasant feeling of having to justify themselves. Why? Because they initially said that the topic was important to them, so they feel they ought to act consistently. Even with a simple greeting (such as "How are you?"), seasoned fundraisers take advantage of the consistency principle. You tend to reply with an equally common phrase like "I'm fine, thank you." And the asker will immediately pick up on that: "Glad to hear that, for I'd like to ask you whether you'd consider a donation for those who are less fortunate ..." Addressed like this, many find it hard to keep walking, undeterred.[8]

What's this desire for consistency all about? Why is it so important to us to stick to our word? In a broader sense, it is another form of peer pressure – the pursuit of conformity we have discussed earlier. Consistency is a social norm. This means that in our society, "being true to your word," "keeping your promises," and "walking the talk" are highly valued ideals. From an evolutionary point of view, this makes perfect sense and helps to preserve our species. Back in the time of the saber-tooth tiger, it could be life-endangering if a fellow hunter failed to appear from the other side precisely as agreed to kill the quarry. Today, it may annoy us when someone doesn't do as they said – back then it could have killed us. No wonder, then, that consistency is in such high regard in our society. A high level of consistency is considered a personal and intellectual strength, which we associate with reason, stability and honesty; all things that are highly valued in our culture. Conversely, when a person's beliefs, statements, and actions contradict each other, this person is considered confused, phony, or even mentally ill. People who don't do what they've announced are often described as untrustworthy, "blowing with the wind," or "all hat, no cattle." Inconsistent behavior makes us find people dislikeable and untrustworthy and can lead to their no longer being accepted in the group, even excluded from it – which is one of the great fears of our species.

In addition, consistency also has a very practical, even economic, background. A public announcement is usually preceded by a complex process of weighing different options and pros and cons. If we didn't have a desire for consistency, we would have to restart this thought process every single time, which would be time-consuming and inefficient. So, consistency is both a social norm we want to fulfil in order to be considered a valuable member of society, and a practical mechanism that keeps us from repeatedly reviewing decisions made earlier, and thus save time. Essentially, it's a shortcut that reduces complexity.

Of course, for our subject – transfer, the human pursuit of consistency comes in very handy. In training, it takes effect in the very moment that trainees commit to a transfer intention, in writing and in front of a group. Which illustrates, once again, how important transfer planning modules are for transfer-effective training (pages 171 f.) and how valuable transfer exercises are that involve the entire group (pages 176 ff.). But even before the training, actions such as specific agreements with the supervisor or self-commitments in the form of completing a preparatory task, can help promote transfer after training.

> The pursuit of consistency causes participants who have committed to a transfer plan to make an effort to fulfill this commitment.

The pursuit of conformity and of consistency are phenomena that can significantly influence and promote transfer but may also inhibit it. The group's opinion and actions have a decisive influence on individual trainees' transfer success or failure. But who exactly is "the group" in a training or transfer context? Who are we referring to when we talk about peer support? And what exactly do transfer researchers mean when they talk about the critical transition between two social systems? Let's take a closer look.

Re-socializing the renegades – fighting transfer

The term "peers" means "equals" or simply "colleagues." Looking at our training context, there are at least two peer groups whose opinions have a decisive influence on people's thoughts and actions, whose rules we want to conform to, or from whom we may or may not receive recognition: the training group and the colleagues at the workplace. The need to feel connected is equally present in both groups.

In special cases, these two groups can be composed of the same people: when people attend training with their work colleagues. Then, training peers are either direct colleagues (co-workers) or colleagues who have the same function in the organization.

(Examples include management training for executives from across the organization, or sales training for sales staff from different departments). Transfer researchers call this "training in natural groups." "Natural" in the sense that the groups also work together in everyday life, rather than being brought together "artificially" in the training context. A key advantage of intercorporate training is that individuals gain insights into other companies, exchange ideas, opinions, and experiences, make new contacts, and thus get to leave their filter bubble. From a transfer perspective, however, it is considered highly effective to conduct training in a natural group.[9] The advantage has been illustrated by the character called Tobias in our case example: He attended stress management training with his entire department; the result was a common awareness of the problem and a commitment to implementing stress-reducing behavior in the whole department. After the training, when they went for a beer together, they were able to address some unspoken rules for the first time, and thus change them. The training created a new common ground everyone committed to. This facilitated transfer, as the new behavior made sense not only to Tobias but also to his colleagues, who appreciated and embraced it.

Andrea, on the other hand, was not that fortunate. She attended the training without her natural group. While she critically reflected on certain stress-supporting behaviors with her training peers and, with their approval, recognized how destructive these routines were and developed new behavioral ideas for herself, when she got back everything at her office continued as before. No one there had developed the same awareness of the problem; no one else knew the terms and behaviors that, in training, were associated with certain meanings and values. Her training group formed its own culture of values and norms, in which certain things were considered good and desirable, and appropriate thinking and acting were welcomed and acknowledged (e.g., a lunch in peace was considered important because people's well-being and health had to have priority over work and performance, even under time pressure). These rules did not apply at her workplace. There, the norm that is generally rewarded is: "We are high-flyers; we meet every deadline for our customers; going to lunch is a waste of time!" No wonder Andrea's "pipe dreams from training" were a cause of irritation and therefore rejected more or less openly, and as a consequence, her odds for sustainable success with her transfer projects were quite low.

Transfer researchers even speak of resocialization in this context.[10] When trainees return to their "old culture" with new knowledge, new ideas, new rules, new values, and new norms, in a worst-case scenario they are resocialized as though they were some kind of renegades. They are re-educated by means of conformity pressure, so they can fit into the old and established culture again. In cases like these, a frequent comment is, "The approaches from the training weren't really that bad, but they don't work here." The culture that prevails in training can be quite different from the one trainees encounter in their everyday life – like the cultures of two completely different countries. In one country, people take the time to listen to each other, they value reflection and acknowledge the willingness to admit to one's weaknesses. In the other country, it's all about speed, power, dog-eat-dog, and being an individual – these are the things you get applause and respect for. The further apart the two cultures are, the more difficult it usually is for trainees to live the new culture in the midst of the old one, or even to change the old culture. And yet it is not completely impossible, as research has shown. If someone has a relatively high hierarchical or social position in the organization, they may well be allowed to set new cultural standards in the group that did not exist before – simply because they make themselves heard and persuade the others by virtue of their position or their persuasive skill. Prospects can be similarly good if someone works so independently and autonomously that their colleagues don't even notice they suddenly do things differently. And, as mentioned in the beginning, there is also the option to train not just a single person from a department or function, who will then be exposed to the risk of re-socialization, but the entire natural group, which lays the basis for cultural change. Yet another option is to install additional groups that give trainees peer support:

What we can learn from Alcoholics Anonymous.

While the support provided by the groups mentioned so far emerges (or doesn't emerge) rather naturally, there is also a tried-and-proven system for generating peer support artificially, so to speak. We know it by names such as peer groups, peer teams, buddy systems, learning partnerships, learning tandems, etc. All of these are constellations in which two or more peers work together and support each other. These kinds of constellations – let's just call them "peer groups" for the moment – are increasingly employed in training contexts as well. Experiences with them have been mixed. Participants often report that peer group meetings did not take place because other things were considered more important in everyday work, or because they were not really considered helpful. Are peer groups effective? And if so, under what circumstances? Let's take a closer look.

Peers as learning supporters.

The insight that peers can be incredibly helpful for successful learning primarily stems from the school context. You've probably benefitted from peers' learning support yourself in your school years, even though back then there wasn't such a snappy term for it. This would have been the boy or girl sitting next to you, whom you asked when you had no idea what the teacher had been trying to explain for the past twenty minutes. Or the fellow student with whom you studied when an exam was coming up, as with just two sentences out of his or her mouth the penny suddenly dropped – an effect that hadn't materialized in five sessions with the prof.

While peers – such as the person sitting next to you in school – are not exactly experts, they are like us, and that is a key advantage. They have a comparable level of knowledge and experience, which enables them to convey knowledge on an equal footing. Peers also speak our language. In the past few years, a distinct branch of scientific research has developed that focuses on this subject: expert and novice research. Experts (such as the university professor) who teach novices (such as students) are unconsciously competent.[11] Often, they can't even explain how they do something or what makes their actions successful. We know that all too well from our own experiences. For example, try to explain to a complete beginner how to drive: not easy. As experts are often unconsciously competent, they find it difficult to explain things in simple ways, the right order, and the right words (see also pages 136 ff.). Peers, on the other hand, find that easy. They are in the process of learning or have recently learned themselves, and therefore know much better what's particularly important and what words are needed to express it. In addition to easier-to-understand explanation, learning from and with peers has the advantage of communication among equals. You probably know how difficult it can be to ask an expert at a lecture or training a seemingly trivial or possibly "stupid" question. After all, you don't want to be viewed as ignorant or dense. With the colleague from your office or the person sitting next to you in the seminar room, it is much easier because the absence of hierarchy takes away much of your uneasiness. Learning with peers makes sense not only for the listener, but also for the one that explains. In the process of explaining and discussing, the subject is repeated, and the fresh knowledge deepened, and this greater processing depth enhances internalization and sustainable memorization (see pages 135 ff.). Learning and consolidating knowledge with peers is a standard element in most trainings today. In group work, trainees discuss and refine what they have learned, enrich it with their own experiences, and explore possible applications. Which is fine. But artificially formed peer groups can do more: They can also support transfer, and in very effective ways.

Peers as transfer supporters.

When we talk about effective further education for employees, and look for ideas for enhancing training transfer, different examples and role models spring to mind. Alcoholics Anonymous isn't very likely to be among them, and it may appear rather strange to compare transfer promotion in employee education to the treatment of addicts. But if we dare to take this step, we can learn a lot. Alcoholics Anonymous creates impressive and visible transfer success through its concept – despite the tougher conditions. After all, combating an addiction is generally much tougher than the transfer goals we face in company-based training. One of AA's pillars of success is the buddy concept, which we also find in smoking cessation programs, athletics, and the Weight Watchers. In the health sector, the buddy – a peer who helps trainees persevere – is a firmly established concept. So why not learn from AA? It's not without reason that leading transfer researchers such as Mary L. Broad and John W. Newstrom recommend using peers not only for learning but also for transfer.[12]

So how do buddy systems work in the health sector? What makes them successful? Buddies provide emotional, functional and affirmative support outside the seminar or conference room. Your buddy is a partner or friend who cares about how you feel, what progress you are making, what motivates you, what obstacles are in the way, and what partial successes you have achieved. This support can be provided through a range of communication channels: face-to-face meetings, phone calls, emails, text messages, or various social networks. In their communications, buddies express interest in your progress and well-being, exchange experiences and information with you, discusses tips, ideas, and problem-solving approaches with you, provide feedback and helps you practice. All of these are things we know from those of our closer relationships with friends that we experience as being supportive. So, the buddy is an additional friend for a specific (transfer) topic.

What happens when partners (and also self-help groups, by the way) help each other that way? Why is this helpful for both people being helped and those helping? Reverting to learning theory and psychotherapy research, Jürgen Matzat identifies a series of action mechanisms, including the following [authors' translation]:[13]

- Learning from role models. Watching each other, both partners see how things work (or don't work) in practice, and learn for themselves
- Getting reinforcement, praise, and recognition. Both partners reinforce each other's goal-oriented behavior through their mutual attention and their commitment (see also the urge for consistency)
- Being able to verbalize emotional content. As both partners are "affected" or "learners," it is easier to address their emotions, fears, weaknesses, doubts, and thoughts openly since both are more or less affected by those same emotions
- Getting a response that signals "I identify with you." Due to their own personal connection with the topic, the partners often show exceptional persistence and interest while listening and manage to be very empathetic.
- Developing positive feelings thanks to the "Helper Therapy Principle." Supporting their partners gives supporters a sense of competence and self-confidence as well as the feeling of being needed.

These mechanisms of action enhance trainees' self-efficacy and volition. They reduce mental stress and make it easier to stick to the target behavior. All of these things can also help trainees implement their transfer plans, so consider using this valuable resource and using a peer system to support not only learning but transfer as well.

> Peer constellations are helpful to support trainees' learning progress and maximize transfer success.

Summary

We humans strive for connectedness and growth. With regard to transfer, these two needs can mutually exponentiate or block each other. They exponentiate each other when trainees feel they and their transfer intentions are accepted and valued in their peer groups both in training and at the work place. By contrast, transfer success is blocked when trainees come back determined and able to apply what they've learned but don't get any support – or even meet with resistance – from their colleagues. Especially at the workplace, conformity pressure can be so high that trainees drop their transfer plans – they are resocialized. The (often unspoken) social norms they need to adhere to in order to belong are just too strong.

To promote the support that's so important for transfer success, we can take advantage of group phenomena such as the desire for consistency. We can create a space in which trainees publicly announce their transfer plans and get appropriate recognition (such as transfer exercises during training or return meetings with supervisors). With support from senior managers and supervisors, we can create platforms on which trainees can win their colleagues' attention and appreciation (such as presentations at regular meetings). We can conduct training in "natural groups," thus encouraging the group to build a common mindset, problem awareness, and level of knowledge during the training. We can also create new and additional support systems by establishing peers not just as co-learners, but also as transfer supporters, and much more. Let's see how all of this looks in practice.

HOW TO PROMOTE SUPPORT FROM PEERS

At a glance:
Ideas for reflection and implementation

Encourage support from co-workers who did not attend the training
- Involve work colleagues in trainee tasks by giving practical examples for tasks before, during, and after training
- Promote support from co-workers through management

Bring trainees together outside the training
- Peer groups – with tips and practical examples for work tasks
- Peer-to-peer consulting
- Exchange of experiences and networking formats

Create transfer partnerships
- Tips for successful creation and practical examples for supporting documents

Encourage support from co-workers who did not attend the training

Due to the pursuit of consistency, what co-workers think about the training and about trainees' transfer plans is crucial. The path to transfer success is smooth when colleagues are interested and do not belittle or block trainees' change initiatives and transfer projects, but show an interest in them, support them, and help create optimal conditions. But how can we ensure that if work colleagues don't attend the same training? The answer is: indirectly, via the trainees or their supervisors.

Are you the group's trainer? Involve trainees' co-workers indirectly through the assignments you give to trainees before, during, and after the training. This will arouse their colleagues' interest and help start an exchange with them about the training. Below are a few examples for your inspiration:

Get work colleagues involved via trainee assignments

Example of assignments before the training
- Presentation training: "Interview two of your work colleagues. What are the do's & don'ts of presentations from their point of view?"
- Conflict management training: "Ask your colleagues what the three biggest challenges are in conflict management in your department."
- Leadership training: "Collect examples of different leadership role models from across your department."
- Universally applicable: "Find a work colleague with whom you will discuss, reflect on, and challenge the training content. Arrange a time window of at least 15 minutes after each module."

Example of assignments during the training
- "Call a colleague tonight and tell him or her what you learned and experienced in training today. Ask them to be critical and challenge everything. Bring the questions and insights to class tomorrow, so we can discuss them together."

Example of assignments between modules or after the training
- "Present the top three insights and ideas gained during training in your next team meeting."
- "Tell two colleagues about the training and report on their reactions at our follow-up meeting."

Of course, you can also bring the colleagues into the seminar room, fictitiously, especially in the transfer planning module – for example, via transfer exercises such as: "How do you convince your colleagues?" or "Which colleagues will support the transfer? Who could pose an obstacle?"

Supervisors are also good points of contact with trainees' work colleagues, and they have excellent leverage to help foster support from peers. Imagine a team meeting in which the team leader announces an employee's training participation by saying, "Social media marketing is one of our main topics this year. It is crucial that we stay up to date in this field. That's why Angelika will attend a training on the subject next week and present her insights and ideas at the next team meeting. If you have topics or questions you want her to take to the training, please tell her. And please make sure to have her back while she is in training!" An announcement like this by the team leader signals that training is important to the entire department. It shows the other employees that the supervisor supports the training and expects appropriate implementation results. This causes the other employees to take the training seriously, too, while strengthening general motivation and the reputation of this and other trainings.

Even after training, the supervisor can publicly highlight the importance of the transfer plans and the ideas gained in the training. A brief presentation and discussion at the next regular meeting, or even a separate appointment in which the ideas are discussed and possibly a corresponding project is launched, makes everyone in the team aware: "Our boss takes the training very seriously as well as the ideas our colleague developed there, and expects us to do the same – with regard to this and to future trainings!"

Bring trainees together outside the training

Peer groups are a common design element, especially for longer training programs and academies. The statement "Let's set up peer groups!" alone often suffices to produce positive reinforcement in (expert) discussions – "Yes, peer groups are great!" Trainees, by contrast, are divided – their opinions on peer groups range from "awesome and enriching" to "waste of time." What do you think of when you hear "Let's set up peer groups!"? Perhaps a group of three to five trainees, who meet outside the training, self-organized, to jointly ... do what? The term doesn't specify that. All this means is that a group of equals is put together. Aha – but for what purpose? In most cases, it is the answer to this very question that determines whether trainees will find peer groups useful or not. Too often, there is no clear mandate. Trainees are left with vague instructions such as "Discuss in your peer group what you've learned!" It comes as no surprise, then, that peer group meetings outside the actual training are perceived as being of little use, or even degenerate into informal coffee klatsches, which are then dropped when "more urgent matters" come up. After all, these meetings – especially when they are face-to-face – take up lots of time. So, what should peer groups do when they meet outside the training? What's a good format, what's their purpose and, above all, their value for trainees? Specify these things beforehand and communicate them to your trainees. Here are some concrete examples of work assignments and tasks for peer group meetings. As always, they refer to a very specific example: a multi-module training for coaches.

> **Some ideas for work assignments for peer group meetings** and practical implementation in a coaching training
>
> **Compiling.** Trainees create content in the peer group meeting that they will present in the next module
> - *Example:* Each peer group gets a different description of a coaching intervention. This intervention will be presented in the next training module, including possible advantages and disadvantages.
> - *Purpose:* Participants develop content themselves and discuss it in advance. This increases processing depth and saves time during the actual training.

Practicing. Trainees practice what they've learned in training independently in the peer group meeting
- *Example:* A complete coaching session is conducted in the peer group meeting, using an actual, real-life concern of a peer group member, and then reviewed and discussed.
- *Purpose:* Trainees have more practice opportunities. In addition, time is saved in training.

Solve transfer tasks. Trainees carry out transfer tasks as a group
- *Example:* In the peer group meeting, the marketing tools for future coaches are planned and written down.
- *Purpose:* Working on transfer tasks together enhances motivation and self-efficacy. It's easier in the group! In addition, the pressure to complete the tasks increases.

For peer group meetings to be successful and useful, you need clear work orders and instructions. You can specify these work orders as a trainer or HR person, or you can let the peer group define what would be useful for them. This step should absolutely be completed in training – because no one likes driving to a meeting without knowing its purpose and agenda. But you can also get some inspiration from proven formats and processes, such as peer-to-peer consulting, discussed below.

Peer-to-peer consulting

Peer-to-peer consulting is a collaborative approach to getting work done. In this approach, peers search together for solutions to a concrete, practical, current professional problem. Sometimes it makes sense to have an external person (for example, a business coach, the trainer, or the HR developer) act as a facilitator, depending on the situation and the group. In any case, peer-to-peer consulting should take place in a voluntary but binding setting and have a clear structure. If you don't have any practical experience with this setting, simply follow a proven process described in the literature.[14] In general, the same principle applies for peer-to-peer consulting that we've also addressed for peer groups: There must be a convincing and personal benefit that is communicated clearly beforehand.

Experience exchange and networking formats

Less formal and structured approaches, which are geared specifically towards exchanging experiences, include various networking formats, such as round-tables, facilitated transfer-focused breakfast, joint excursions, or various other forms of regular virtual or physical meeting. Such formats are usually designed so as to last beyond the transfer phase, which is why the entertainment- and continuous-learning element is of key importance (joint dinners, sailing trips, inviting experts in, etc.). The heart of the matter and the link among trainees is the common (training) topic, so it will automatically come up once and again in the conversations, along with people's implementation experiences. As a side effect, things will happen that foster transfer effectiveness. Trainees' attention is redirected to the training content; the jointly developed concepts, norms, and ideals are cultivated further; implementation successes and challenges are exchanged and applauded; and mutual advice is exchanged; further ideas are generated and promoted around the training topic; and personal ties are strengthened. This usually happens with just a loosely defined structure, or even no structure at all. But there is a high failure rate as well, especially when these formats are completely self-controlled.

Create transfer partnerships

We've discussed earlier what transfer partnerships are and why they work so well. Now let's talk about what such transfer partnerships look like and how you can create them. So, the question is, how can you connect two peers as transfer partners and what assignments should you give them?

Transfer partners can find one another or be assigned. One key criterion, in addition to personal sympathy, is local and professional proximity: The closer the two partners are – in terms of their workplace and their position (hierarchical position, area of responsibility, industry, etc.), the easier it is to support transfer. There are several points at which you can set up transfer partnerships: towards the end of the training during the transfer-planning phase; during the training (for instance, on the first evening – at this point, trainees have gotten to know one another, and spontaneous sympathies can be taken into account). Or you can set up transfer partnerships right at the beginning of the training: In that case, transfer partners will have frequent opportunities to get to know each other in advance through partner discussions and joint work, and even to discuss transfer options for the contents covered. There is even a possibility to set up transfer partnerships before the training. This can create a strong signal effect (expressing that transfer is a key issue in this training and transfer partnerships are taken seriously). It can also increase some trainees' comfort level, as they will already "know" someone when they first enter a seminar room full of strange faces. But watch out: It can always happen that trainees call in sick at short notice and their transfer partners are left on their own, in which case you'll need to find another solution (for example, forming a team of three).

Quite informally, the task in the transfer planning module at the end of the training could be: Now look for a partner in the group, with whom you will talk about what exactly you intend to implement and achieve over the next few days, and exchange email addresses. Three to six weeks into the implementation face, you'll have an important task: You'll email to your partner and ask them whether they managed to complete what they had set out to do.

In some groups, an informal invitation like this may be just the right approach. In many other cases, however, it is advisable to offer transfer partners a bit more structure, clarity of roles, and orientation. Below are a few ideas for your inspiration.

Successfully create transfer partnerships These documents will help your trainees

Contact datasheet
The transfer partners exchange their contact data using a prepared contact datasheet, so as not to forget anything important (e.g., name, organization, telephone number, email address, Skype name, preferred form of contact, usually available between the hours of … and …, etc.)

Written agreements
The transfer partners prepare themselves for a successful partnership using worksheets (e.g., completing filling out the names of the partners and contact details, the three most important transfer intentions including timeframe, motivating goal, when and how to re-establish contact, signatures of both partners, etc.)

Discussion guide to sharpen transfer plans
The transfer partners help each other at the training to effectively formulate their transfer plans. A discussion guide laying out a possible discussion flow, sample questions, examples of good/less well-worded transfer plans, a checklist, etc. will help

Priority assistance worksheet
The transfer partners tell each other how they would like to be supported. A worksheet on "How I would like to be supported by you" with different ideas, hints, and/or a checklist can help

Tips for transfer partners
The transfer partners receive written tips during or after the training for their work as transfer partners (for example, "10 golden rules for successful transfer partnerships" or "How to give your transfer partner optimal support")

Conversation guides for discussions with the transfer partner
During or after the training, the transfer partners receive a guide for the first conversation after the training

When setting up transfer partnerships, it is important to find the right level of orientation, structure, and support for each group. If you give them insufficient specifications, the risk is that trainees are uncertain what to do or fail to recognize the benefits. Transfer partnerships would then become an informal, not very goal-oriented chat, or never be launched in the first place. A lot of structure means a lot of work for the trainer or the HR developers (after all, assignments have to be defined and templates created); also, some target groups might perceive them as patronizing and overly controlling rather than supportive. Again, consider the need for self-determination – for example, by communicating guidelines as an option rather than a binding specification (see pages 29 ff.). As always there is no good-for-all solution. As with any transfer-promoting measure, it all depends on your ability to engage with trainees, the culture of the organization, and your own preference.

Time for transfer!

Your turn: How can you foster peer support? What could you do to make trainees feel supported by their peers in implementing what they've learned? What is the next step you intend to implement? Write down the ideas and thoughts that spontaneously come to mind.

This is how I'll drive peer support:

[1] Brinkerhoff, R. O., & Gill, S. J., *The Learning Alliance: Systems Thinking in Human Resource Development,* The Jossey-Bass Management Series, 1994, p. 9.

[2] On the influence of peer support on transfer success and its determinants, see, for example, Blume, B. D., Ford, J. K., Baldwin, T. T., & Huang, J. L., "Transfer of Training: A Meta-Analytic Review" in *Journal of Management,* 2010, 36(4): pp. 1065 – 1105, or Burke, L. A., & Hutchins, H. M., "Training Transfer: An Integrative Literature Review" in *Human Resource Development Review,* 2007, 6(3): pp. 263 – 296, or Chiaburu, D. S., & Marinova, S. V., "What predicts skill transfer? An exploratory study of goal orientation, training self-efficacy, and organizational supports" in *International Journal of Training and Development,* 2005, 9(2): pp.110 – 123, or Colquitt, J. A., LePine, J. A., & Noe, R. A., "Toward an integrative theory of training motivation: A meta-analytic path analysis of 20 years of research" in *Journal of Applied Psychology,* 2000, 85(5): pp.678 – 707, or Kontoghiorghes, C., "Reconceptualizing the learning transfer conceptual framework: Empirical validation of a new systemic model" in *International Journal of Training and Development,* 2004, 8(3): pp.210 – 221.

[3] On famous conformity experiments, see Asch, S. E., "Effects of group pressure upon the modification and distortion of judgments" in H. Guetzkow (Ed.), *Groups, leadership, and men. Research in human relations,* Oxford: Carnegie Press. 1951, pp. 177 – 190. Also: Asch, S. E., "Studies of independence and conformity: A minority of one against a unanimous majority" in *Psychological monographs: General and applied,* 1956, 70(9): pp.1 – 70.

[4] For the experiment with the white smoke, see Latane, B., & Darley, J. M., "Group inhibition of bystander intervention in emergencies" in *Journal of personality and social psychology,* 1968, 10(3): p. 215.

[5] Interesting, provocative reading on the swarm stupidity keyword, especially in the field of economics, can be found in Dueck, G., *Schwarmdumm: So blöd sind wir nur gemeinsam,* Campus Verlag, 2015.

[6] For example, the following well-known theorists consider the quest for consistency as a basic motive: Festinger, L., *A theory of cognitive dissonance.* Stanford: Stanford University Press, 1957, or Heider, F., "Attitudes and cognitive organization" in *Journal of Psychology,* 1946, 21: pp. 107 – 112, or Newcomb, T., "An approach to the study of communicative acts" in *Psychological Review,* 1953, 60(6): pp. 393 – 404.

[7] The beach robbery experiment can be found in Moriarty, T., "Crime, commitment, and the responsive bystander: Two field experiments" in *Journal of Personality and Social Psychology,* 1975, 31(2): p. 370.

[8] These and more examples and background on the pursuit for consistency are provided in Chapter 3 of the highly valuable book by Cialdini, R. B., *Die Psychologie des Überzeugens: Wie Sie sich selbst und Ihren Mitmenschen auf die Schliche kommen,* Bern: Verlag Hans Huber, Hofgrefe AG, 2013 (3rd edition). p. 288.

9 On training in groups as a transfer-enhancing measure, see, for example, Saks, A. M., & Belcourt, M., "An investigation of training activities and transfer of training in organizations" in *Human Resource Management,* 2006, 45(4): pp. 629 – 648.

10 A sociological perspective on the transfer problem (including the argument of re-socialization) can be found in, for example, Köster, M., "Warum Training selten funktioniert. Über die Notwendigkeit von soziologischer Perspektive in einer boomenden Branche" in *Sozialwissenschaften und Berufspraxis,* 2003, 26(3): pp. 255 – 267.

11 For research around the issue of experts and novices, see, for example, Gruber, H., & Ziegler, A., *Expertiseforschung. Theoretische und methodische Grundlagen,* VS Verlag für Sozialwissenschaften, 1996.

12 These, and other tips & transfer interventions, can be found in Broad, M. L., & Newstrom, J. W., *Transfer of Training: Action-Packed Strategies To Ensure High Payoff from Training Investments,* Basic Books, 1992.

13 Matzat, J., "Selbsthilfe als therapeutisches Prinzip" in P.Günther & E.Rohrmann (Eds.), *Soziale Selbsthilfe. Alternative, Ergänzung oder Methode sozialer Arbeit?* Heidelberg: Winter, 1999, pp. 105-126.

14 For research on the course of collegial (peer-to-peer) consulting, visit the Knowledge Forum of the Ekeberger Coaching Days (www.coaching-globe.net) and enter the German search term *Kollegiale Fallberatung* (8 December 2016). Or simply search Wikipedia or Google, and you'll soon find what you're looking for. If you want to delve deeper into the method, you can find extensive information here (in German), for example: Lippmann, E. D., *Intervision: Kollegiales Coaching professionell gestalten,* Germany: Springer, 2013 (3rd Edition).

LEVER 12 – TRANSFER EXPECTATIONS IN THE ORGANIZATION

TWO PRACTICAL EXAMPLES

Susanne and Peter both visited their companies' internal leadership academies. Read what they tell us as they proudly hold their certificate in their hands.

Susanne, 43, manager in the healthcare sector

> *I did it! I've got the certificate in my hand! It was an intense year: 8 modules with 2 days each of leadership training. I've learned a lot of new things and met great people. I'll certainly implement a lot of it in my everyday work – as far as that is possible in our company. I was extremely satisfied with the modules – straight A's in my evaluation! I'm so grateful to my company for making the investment, and I really look forward to more valuable input from more training programs!*

Peter, 52, executive in public services

> *I did it! My implementation success has been impressive! It was an intense year: 8 modules, the preparation exercises, the talks with my manager, the jour-fixe presentations, the interviews with my partner for the transfer newsletter, the transfer coaching, and the practical project. It was the first time I attended a training in which I wasn't just given inputs and new knowledge. No, I've changed, really developed further. The term "transfer" was not just a phrase – they were serious about it. Even our board had pointed that out in the kick-off meeting. All the transfer-supporting elements really paid off. When we did the evaluations, but especially today in the presentations on implementation successes and practice projects, it became very clear to me how much I've already achieved in practice. I can see tangible evidence of my transfer success, which benefits not only me but my company, too. That makes me really proud – of myself, my company, and of our HR people.*

What do you think of these stories? What is the key difference?

Susanne and Peter took part in a comprehensive leadership program that both of them really liked. But their accounts immediately show that the program Peter attended involved much more than just being present at 8 modules. In "his" program, both his company's board and the program design signaled very clearly from the outset that this was about much more than attendance at training sessions. While Susanne's transfer success seems more like a "nice to have," in Peter's case, transfer is a clearly communicated expectation, a necessity that is emphasized strongly. The transfer expectation is communicated, and its importance stressed through the clear words from management, various transfer-promoting elements, the program evaluation, and a series of implementation presentations and practical projects. Peter knows that, if he implements what he's learned – or if he doesn't – it will be noticed in his company. That's exactly what it takes to promote transfer success.

Transfer expectations in the organization are defined as the extent to which trainees expect positive consequences from applying what they've learned, or the absence of negative consequences from non-application. So, it's about the question of whether their organization notices and pays attention to their success or failure in transfer. Is transfer just a nice-sounding buzzword, mere lip service, a "nice to have" – or indeed an aspiration in the company, which is pursued and tracked accordingly? Is there any data on how transfer-effective trainings are? Is there any information on transfer barriers and funding factors? Is this data used to increase transfer success? When trainees realize that transfer is expected by their company, this increases transfer success.[1] And I am not referring to some words in brochures, but to concrete actions that signal how sincerely an organization expects trainees to work on and succeed at transfer.

TRANSFER EXPECTATIONS IN THE ORGANIZATION – TRANSFER RESULTS AS A NEW FINISH LINE

	Transfer expectations in the organization in a nutshell
Trainees say	"People in the organization notice when I (don't) apply what I have learned."
Definition	Transfer expectations in the organization are the extent to which trainees expect positive consequences from applying what they've learned or the absence of negative consequences as a result of non-application.
Guiding question	How can you ensure that trainees' application (or not) of what they've learned is urgent, attracts attention in the organization and has positive (or negative) consequences?

Corporate training is a billion-dollar business. And why do organizations take the associated effort and enormous costs upon themselves? Why are there HR development departments and a booming training industry? Why do we continue to send executives and employees to trainings? The answer from companies usually is: We invest in training because we expect these investments to produce positive results for us. We expect trainees to learn, and then apply what they've learned to their work. So, successful transfer is the goal and the key expectation behind the investment. But are trainees aware of this? Do organizations manage to communicate their expectation clearly? Do we really live up to this expectation, or is it nothing but a vague declaration of intent? Are transfer expectations matched by concrete actions? And is transfer effectiveness something that is measured and optimized in the organization?

We know from signal theory that organizations often say one thing[2] and do – or signal with their actions – quite another (whether consciously or unconsciously). The latter is clearly more credible. So, what do we really do about transfer? And what do we signal through our actions? Let's take a critical look at this.

Flying blind

"What gets measured gets done." So goes the famous observation by transfer researchers Lisa Burke and Holly Hutchins.[3] It is universally applicable to all organizations. Whatever is important and meaningful is relevant for control. It is discussed, measured, and optimized. Of course. How else would an organization know whether it is on the right path or how close or far it is from achieving its goals? We establish sales figures to determine sales success and take action if the figures are not up to our expectations. We measure the number of delayed deliveries to determine delivery timeliness, and take action when customers have to wait too long too often for their products, and the number of complaints increases. The same applies, of course, for HR development. Transfer is the declared goal. So, we measure the transfer to determine training success, and use that data to further promote transfer effectiveness. We do that, right? Or don't we actually? What exactly do we measure to determine the success of our trainings?

A study by the American Society for Training & Development (ASTD Research) shows that 92 % of companies use feedback forms to evaluate their trainings.[4] These standardized sheets are usually issued at the end of a training and filled out by the trainees. Such feedback forms are somewhat provocatively referred to as "happy sheets" in transfer research, because they often contain a scale based on smileys showing different levels of happiness. Why the provocative name? Because they usually measure nothing but trainees' satisfaction. Typical questions include "How much did you like the training?" Or "How satisfied were you with the training, the seminar documents, the seminar hotel, the trainer," etc. And the data from these sheets is often the only criterion we use to judge whether the training was successful or not. It's like measuring our sales performance by asking salespeople how satisfied they were with their customers. Kind of absurd, right?

Now you could argue that this is different in the field of training. After all, trainees use much more of what they've learned when they were satisfied with the training. Even scientific research long worked on that assumption. See, for instance, the most popular and widely used evaluation model, developed in the 1960s by Donald Kirkpatrick: It describes four levels of evaluation: (1) reaction, (2) learning, (3) behavior, and (4) results.

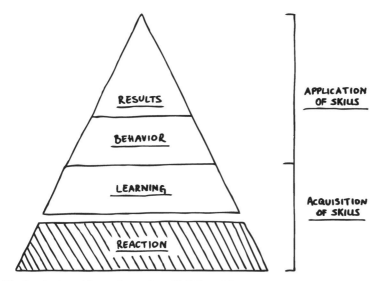

Fig. 10: The four-level model according to Donald Kirkpatrick

The bottom evaluation level is reaction: It represents trainees' satisfaction with the training. It is followed by the learning level, where the increase in knowledge is determined. The third level refers to behavior in the workplace. Only if there is a change, or a widening of the behavioral spectrum, can we actually speak of transfer. The results level at the top of the pyramid expresses the extent to which the change in behavior has had a positive business impact for the organization. For many years, experts assumed that the levels built on one another. The more positive the reaction, so we thought, the more knowledge is acquired. The more knowledge, the more transfer success. The greater the transfer success, the better the results the training produces for the organization. According to that logic, while evaluating trainees' satisfaction would not represent a direct measure of transfer success, it would be meaningful as a basis for the following levels. Well, this assumption was wrong, as a study by a group of transfer researchers showed.[5] They performed a meta-analysis of Kirkpatrick's model to find out whether satisfied trainees actually apply more of what they've learned. The answer is No. Satisfaction is not linked to transfer success. Or in other words, when we measure satisfaction, all we find out is just that: how satisfied trainees are with the training. That can be quite an interesting piece of information, but it doesn't allow any conclusions as to how great transfer success will be. And how could it? Most trainees don't know either at this point in time. So if we want to measure our goal – the transfer success of our training programs – happy sheets are the wrong tool. They don't measure what we want to measure. And if we use these reaction measurements as a criterion for designing or managing our training programs, we actually risk flying blind.

> If we use the results recorded in "happy sheets" as our only tool to measure transfer effectiveness, then we are flying blind.

So, should we completely abandon evaluations at the end of a training? Might it perhaps be too early to draw conclusions about its quality? No, not really. It is possible to derive at least initial indications of future transfer successes at the end of a training. The key difference lies in the questions we ask. The transfer researchers were able to show that different types of reactions correlate to varying degrees with transfer success. One reaction is the satisfaction response ("How satisfied were you with the training?") It has no significant correlation with future transfer success. Another type is the utility reaction. Here, a typical question in the evaluation form could be, "How useful was this training for your everyday work?" Or, phrased more specifically, "How useful was model X / exercise Y for your practical day-to-day work?" In this case, there is a correlation with transfer success, although the coefficient is still not very high[6] – simply because when we feel that something is helpful and meaningful, the probability that we will put it into practice is much higher. So, if we ask utility questions at the end of the training, at least we'll have a first indication of future transfer success.

Consequently, adapting evaluation sheets to allow a shift from satisfaction towards utility can be a quick and easy first step. According to the motto, "What gets measured gets done," however, in the long run, we should strive to measure transfer success directly. It is an important, meaningful, and thus control-relevant parameter. Only if we have concrete data on transfer success can we determine whether we are on the right path and how close we have come to our goal: transfer success.

What we can learn from annoying teachers

If transfer is the goal of our training programs, there is no way around evaluating transfer success. This valuable data is crucial for controlling transfer-effective HR development. But that's not all. With the evaluation, we send signals to the trainees and the trainers that can strongly influence the focus and design of the training, and thus increase or decrease the probability of transfer.

As we already know, the vast majority of companies assesses the success of their training programs based on happy sheet evaluations. Most trainees know that, at the end of the training, a standardized evaluation-form will be distributed in which they are to indicate their satisfaction with the trainer, training, content, seminar hotel, etc. Trainees also know that the results of this evaluation will determine whether this trainer will work for the organization again. What kind of signal is this? And what are the consequences of this form of evaluation?

To put it bluntly, this suggests that trainers ought to make trainees as "happy" as possible. Because when they are, there'll be positive reviews, and positive reviews – or the absence of overly critical ones – increase the odds for follow-up engagements. No doubt, ensuring trainee satisfaction does sound like a sensible approach. But should it really be trainers' first priority? We all know that learning and developing often means that you need to leave your comfort zone. We also know it isn't always pleasant or satisfying to do that. Learning and developing often means intense bouts of work, staying on the ball, persisting, and venturing out into unfamiliar territory. Perhaps you've experienced this in your own school days? Did you also have a teacher there who was popular among the students? Perhaps this was the teacher who preferred to keep his or her classes a bit more comfy: not being so strict, letting the class watch a film every now and then, nothing but play and excursions in the last week before vacations? That was nice! As students, we might be really happy with that teacher. And perhaps you also know the other extreme: the dedicated teacher who really took his or her subject seriously. Someone that really challenged their students. Where did you learn more? With which teacher did your learning last? With the popular, "laid-back" instructor or the dedicated, demanding one? I'd assume it was the second. If someone had asked you back then how satisfied you were with that teacher, you probably wouldn't have been full of praise. But with hindsight, your learning success may have proved that satisfaction isn't everything, and sustainable learning means making an effort and leaving one's comfort zone.

It is the extraordinary and dedicated trainers who, contrary to the "Make them happy" motto, dare to do exercises that take trainees out of their comfort zones, provide constructive-critical feedback, stimulate their actual development, and proactively address resistance and conflict rather than sweeping them under the rug for harmony's sake. All these behaviors, which are so valuable for trainees' sustainable development, involve the risk of getting lower satisfaction rates and thus not failing to get follow-up engagements. It seems much safer to make the content and exercises pleasant and less demanding, add a "feel-good exercise" at the end, and in the feedback round start with the most sympathetic trainees, who will then influence the group's opinion. This way, trainers can increase the odds for a positive evaluation result and follow-up work. So, when trainers discuss methods and exercises among themselves, it's understandable that descriptions such as, "Trainees really like this exercise!" are more common than "This exercise is really effective!" How could it be otherwise when satisfaction is key in their business!? It's also very understandable that trainers consider their assignment completed at the end of a training course. After all, the time is up, and the trainees are satisfied, so the goal has been achieved. No wonder, then, that the willingness to send out reminder e-mails, ask trainees about their implementation progress, or support them after training is limited. It's satisfaction that counts! What do you think would happen if, instead, the key selection criterion was utility or transfer success? Even I find it amazing every time how much the concepts, focus, and effectiveness of trainings can change when organizations decide to change their evaluation methods. It is also impressive and profoundly gratifying to see how trainers increasingly gain a competitive edge when they raise this topic in client organizations and proactively offer to use effectiveness, not only satisfaction, as an evaluation criterion. It's a small intervention with a tremendous impact for all parties involved.

Beware, however, of reversing the logic! Satisfied trainees are no guarantee for transfer-effectiveness, that much is understood. So, are poor satisfaction rates a sign of transfer-effective training? Of course not. And yet, you do find people that would argue that way. A trainer who is confronted with low satisfaction rates will then tell you: "I've taken the trainees out of their comfort zones and really challenged them. They don't like that, of course, but it's the only way they will really learn!" Is that so? The Study Zone model, created by the German adventure pedagogue Tom Senninger illustrates the matter pragmatically.

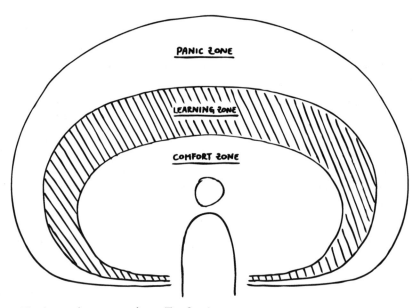

Fig. 11: The three study zones according to Tom Senninger

Within their comfort zone, learners feel safe and free. This is where they have experiences and proven strategies they resort to, this is where they have self-confidence and routine. In the learning zone, they set foot on new territory with which they have no previous experience. It is a venture associated with some uncertainty and heart-beating, but also with curiosity and positive tension. This is where learners develop new strategies and grow. In the panic zone, it all feels "one step too many or too far." Uncertainty turns into anxiety. Developing strategies is no longer possible. There is frustration and resignation, but also resistance and aggression. It is obvious, then, where trainees learn best: in the learning zone – between the comfort and the panic zone.[7]

For trainers (and teachers, too, by the way) it is therefore important to find the optimal level of challenge for trainees. In terms of transfer effectiveness, neither "feel-good" or "comfort zone" trainers nor "panic" trainers lead the pack. It's simply not possible to draw conclusions on transfer success from the level of satisfaction or dissatisfaction of trainees. It is much more helpful to ask trainees about how usefulness and effective the training or individual contents and exercises are. When we do that, we will usually find that the best rates are achieved in the learning zone.

Another factor to be considered is that the still-prevailing satisfaction-based evaluation has a signal effect not only for trainers but also for trainees. As you probably know, when a training receives good ratings, it is placed on the "good/successful" pile by the organization. This signals to employees that the organization arranges trainings to satisfy its employees. Their satisfaction, the message says, is its priority goal – just as general employee satisfaction is a high-priority goal for the organization. What seems questionable here, however, is whether satisfaction should be the only and ultimate goal for training. If so, HR development would basically be an incentives function. (Although that is also questionable, in view of increasing signs of seminar fatigue across organizations.) If, however, the purpose of HR development is developing people for the good of the organization, the goal of training must be transfer. Consequently, we should start sending a corresponding signal to trainees in our evaluation design. When we evaluate transfer effectiveness, what we signal to trainees is this: the aim of our trainings is for you to put into practice what you learn!

> When we evaluate satisfaction, we signal, "Our goal is to make you happy." When we evaluate utility and effectiveness, the signal is, "Our goal is for you to apply what you've learned to your work."

"You name it – we play it"?

Often, making trainees happy isn't only the (unconsciously) communicated signal of an evaluation but also an integral part of the training needs assessment. Critical voices sometimes refer to their organization's practices in this field as "popular-request shows," as they record employees' wishes rather than the training needs of the organization. Here are some real-life anecdotes:

- An employee enters the HR office with a glossy brochure saying, "It's been a while since I last attended a seminar. Here's one I'd really like to attend ..."
- In the cafeteria, the sales manager convinces the HR manager that "It's time to reward the top sales people with another seminar."
- In his sales pitch, a trainer claims: "This training is a big hit with employees."
- An employee complains because her colleague from the other department was sent to seminar X this year. "Why can't I go? I haven't been to a single seminar this year!"
- In the employee performance report, the supervisor fills in the field "further education needs," asking her team member, "Which seminars would you be interested in?" – without even asking whether or how this particular program could benefit the organization.
- At an HR development fair, a member of the company's HR department has learned about the latest trends in training. "We should include topic X in our training program," he tells his boss, "I bet we'll get 'sold out' in no time for that one!"

The result of such "needs assessments" is usually a colorful collection of training courses in an impressive-looking and very thick catalog. Employee training according to the scattershot approach.

Digging deeper into the matter, we find that there is usually an absolutely praiseworthy aspiration behind it: a high level of service and customer orientation. The only question is, who is the customer that HR development is supposed to serve? Is it just the employee – or is it the buyer, i.e., the organization? And what is the task of HR development: Making employees happy? Or contributing to the organization's success by developing employees? You see, it is a question of people's understanding of their roles, and of how HR development is positioned within the organization.

What if you're a training provider or trainer? Again, you can ask yourself the same question: Who is my client? The trainees or the organization? And what will strengthen your customer relationship and your competitive situation more sustainably: Trainings that only make trainees happy? Or trainings that also enhance the organization's performance? Does the former suffice?

> Don't just ask about employees' training wishes but also about how the training contributes to the organization's success.

Perhaps you are still feeling some resistance deep down inside. It's still important for you, your organization, or your client to make trainees happy? Well, good! As mentioned before, transfer effectiveness is not about making trainees unhappy or disregarding their wishes and needs. Nothing could be further from the truth. All I am saying is that fulfilling wishes is not the only criterion for transfer effectiveness. And even if you are concerned with employee satisfaction, you should reconsider (merely) fulfilling wishes. Imagine, for instance, that an employee wants to attend an expensive MBA program. You are an HR developer and you advocate that employee's request to go on the program. It takes you quite an effort to get that person onto the program. He or she is happy – at least for now. But what happens when they return to the organization with transfer plans, high levels of motivation, and lots of new ideas? A survey among MBA graduates revealed that 41 % of those that graduated recently were frustrated and considering a job change – in part, because they couldn't apply what they had learned (see pages 190 ff.). No transfer expectations, no transfer opportunities in the organization. Happiness: none.

Hence, it makes sense in terms of both employee satisfaction and successful transfer to conduct only such trainings that are clearly connected to a corporate objective. Transfer-effective trainings need to contribute to a specific outcome. It is only when it is clear what the transfer goal is, and how it serves the organization, that the training can be transfer-effective and make trainees happy in the long run.

> Transfer-effective training needs a clear transfer goal that helps achieve a specific organizational result.

As an HR developer, you should make sure that every training course you offer serves a corporate purpose. Only conduct a training if there is a clear-cut link with a result aspired to by the organization. For each training in your employee education program, ask yourself: Why are we offering this training? Which corporate objective or result does it serve? And what's the transfer goal for this particular training – what's the success-critical behavior that this training is supposed to produce? For each request you receive, find out whether it's just an employee's "wish" or actually addresses a real "need" in the organization.

Congratulations! You were physically present!

Do you remember your school or university graduation? When you were proudly holding your certificate or diploma in your hands? It was a moment when you had completed a crucial phase in your life. You had crossed the finish line. You had successfully mastered everything that was required. Reached the goal. This – though not always as intense – is what trainees feel when they leave a training with their certificate of attendance in their hands. They've complete everything that was required – goal achieved! The certificate is often issued at the end of the program or training. But what do we confirm or certify – transfer success? Successful implementation? No. In most cases it is simply a trainee's physical presence during the training. Most certificates include the content that was covered and the training period. There is usually nothing about implementation or transfer success. Anyone that attended receives a certificate. So, the signal is that the end of the training is the finish line. But what about transfer? If transfer is the goal and the company's expectation, we need to make transfer success the finish line. Instead of issuing certificates of attendance at the end of a training, thereby – provocatively speaking – rewarding physical presence in training, we could move to making transfer success the finish line, which is acknowledged with a certificate. Certificates of transfer success instead of attendance – that would be a very clear signal of what the organization expects.

> Redefine the finish line. Reward transfer success instead of physical presence.

What we say unintentionally

Companies send a whole lot of other signals that, intentionally or not, indicate to anyone involved in company training whether transfer is a nice-sounding buzzword or a clear expectation. Once sensitized, you will be amazed at how many signals you find in your organization and others. The following table shows a small selection.

Strong signals of transfer expectations in the organization	Signals that weaken transfer expectations in the organization
Training participants are required to attend follow-up sessions (or other transfer interventions) **What it indicates:** Once I decide to participate in a training, I also commit to implementing and reflecting on implementation	Attending the training is compulsory, but participating in follow-up sessions (or other transfer interventions) is voluntary **What it indicates:** The key factor for me as a trainee is that I attend. Implementation or its reflection is an optional add-on
The training description specifies transfer goals (e.g., "Trainees increase their sales success by using closing techniques in sales negotiations") **What it indicates:** The organization has a clear vision and expectation of what the training should accomplish	The training description roughly outlines training goals (e.g., "Trainees improve their sales skills") **What it indicates:** The company has only a vague idea of what the training should accomplish
Supervisors take time to support transfer (e.g., through pre- and post-training meetings). Transfer support is part of supervisors' regular agendas **What it indicates:** Transfer is considered important in the company and supported by supervisors and managers, all the way up to the top.	Supervisors don't invest time in transfer support. Transfer support is not part of the supervisor role **What it indicates:** Transfer is not considered very important in the organization. Mangers have more important things to do.
Each training ends with careful planning of individual transfer intentions. **What it indicates:** Defining transfer intentions is a central component of the training.	Transfer planning at the end of a training does not take place or only sporadically **What it indicates:** Defining transfer intentions is not (or not an essential) part of the training
Goal achievement is evaluated. **What it indicates:** Achieving a business impact as well as the transfer and training goals is important to the organization	Trainees' satisfaction with the training is evaluated **What it indicates:** It is important to the organization that the training is popular.

Certificates are awarded for the presentation of implementation results **What it indicates:** To successfully complete the training/program, it is important to achieve implementation success	Certificates are "automatically" issued at the end of the training **What it indicates:** With completion of the training, the job is "done"
After the training, trainers stay in touch with trainees and/or client contacts to discuss transfer progress **What it indicates:** The training as such is only a part of the journey; the goal is transfer effectiveness and business impact	After the training, there is no more contact between trainer and trainees, or the client contact, to discuss transfer effectiveness **What it indicates:** Upon completion of the training, the engagement is "over"
The organization pays trainers not only for training but also for transfer interventions **Interpretation:** Transfer effectiveness is crucial; the organization is willing to invest in it.	The organiztion pays trainers for training, but not for transfer interventions. **Interpretation:** The training itself is crucial for the organization; transfer is less important
HR's steering-relevant key indicators (KPIs) include transfer rates or number of transfer projects implemented **What it indicates:** Transfer effectiveness is a central and steering-relevant parameter.	HR's steering-relevant key indicators include, for example, the number of training sessions held or trainee satisfaction **What it indicates:** Transfer effectiveness is not a central or steering-relevant parameter.

This is just a small collection of typical signals usually sent unintentionally. So how about your organization and your training programs – what signals have you been sending to your trainees? Do they indicate a transfer expectation?

Summary

In our organization, will anyone notice when I don't apply what I've learned? Is transfer really considered important here? Or is it "nice to have," just a phrase, or even a non-issue? What are the roles and tasks of HR and/or trainers? To work towards trainee satisfaction or to contribute to the organization's success? Why do we have trainings at our organization at all? These are all questions to which trainees and all transfer-relevant stakeholders seek answers, consciously or subconsciously. They won't usually find them in snappy slogans or glossy brochures, but in the organization's, HR development's, and the trainers' actions. They automatically decode the signals (unintentionally) sent, which show how serious everyone is about transfer.

What is it like when something has top priority in the organization? Think, for instance, of sales figures, customer satisfaction, certain cost items. When something is really important to the organization, it is measured, discussed, supported with tangible actions, and optimized with a lot of commitment. Everyone works together in a joint effort to achieve the defined goals. So, if transfer is really important there will be metrics to provide that data. Transfer effectiveness (not satisfaction!) will be measured and optimized. It will be addressed and discussed at various points and repeatedly. There will be clear transfer goals and training programs serving an organization-wide goal. Trainees will be expected to do more than attend training, as the finish line for a training won't be trainee satisfaction; it will be achieving transfer goals that help to create business impact. So, make sure you send clear signals! Show that your task and your aspiration are not just to fulfill wishes and satisfy trainees but to make a crucial contribution to the organization's success.

HOW TO SIGNAL TRANSFER EXPECTATIONS IN THE ORGANIZATION

At a glance:
Ideas for reflection and implementation

Make transfer effectiveness part of the management steering system
- Identify the metrics for currently managing your HR development
- Implement metrics related to transfer effectiveness

Measure transfer effectiveness
- Measure transfer effectiveness – in connectable and practical ways
- Have transfer effectiveness evaluated by trainees (with sample questions and items)
- Evaluate factors promoting and inhibiting transfer
- Evaluate the 12 levers by means of a Transfer of Training Analysis (TTA) check-up

Make your feedback sheets transfer-relevant
- Evaluate utility rather than satisfaction (with sample questions and items)

Make transfer success the finish line
- Reward and certify transfer rather than attendance (with examples from practice)

Implement transfer interventions of your choice
- With every transfer-promoting measure and every discussion around transfer, strengthen the transfer expectation in the organization

Make transfer effectiveness part of the management steering system

How do you make transfer effectiveness in the organization relevant to management's steering duties? The first step is to look at the key performance indicators or factors that steer or direct your activities, as an HR developer or training provider. What key figures do you currently monitor? What key figures do you record? What do you report to your management, customers, or trainees? What do you present and what do you talk about when you discuss training success? Which data do you communicate with pride and which key figures do you use to optimize this? Typically, these are numbers such as the number of trainees or training days, costs or sales per training day or year, number of training courses offered, average number of trainees in your trainings, etc. Such quantitative information may be quite interesting. But they don't tell you anything about transfer effectiveness. Does your organization use quality metrics, such as ratings from feedback forms? Do they really provide information about transfer effectiveness, behavioral change, or the results achieved? Or are they – as in the vast majority of organizations – primarily statements about how satisfied trainees were with the training and its organization? Imagine that your management or a huge potential client directly asks you how transferable your trainings are and what their business impact is: Would you have a convincing, clear answer at hand? Do you have key figures that attest to transfer effectiveness?

Remember the saying, "What gets measured gets done"? One of the first and most important steps to promote transfer is to *implement transfer effectiveness metrics.* Figures you can proudly communicate to the outside world. Figures that allow you to identify optimization approaches. Figures that illustrate to other key stakeholders (executives, supervisors, trainers, trainees, etc.) not only the success of your training but also their co-responsibility. To manage transfer, we need data that says: this is the status quo, the success we can all be proud of – and this is where we face a need for improvement. And this need for improvement concerns you, Mary Manager, Tom Trainee, etc.

Measure transfer effectiveness

So, we need a measure of transfer effectiveness. So far, so good. Well, let's get down to implementation then. Once the decision is made to include such a key figure, the next question naturally is, how do we track this key figure? How do we even measure transfer effectiveness? Well, the answer to this question about the "correct" evaluation of training and its transfer effectiveness is not quite that clear – on the contrary, it fills entire libraries. At this point, I actually believe it is best not to give you an overview of all the approaches and models that exist,[8] let alone recommend a "right" or "best" approach. As with all transfer-promoting measures, a single "right" way simply does not exist. There are only criteria such as "connectable" (e.g., with other initiatives) "feasible," suitable for your training courses, your trainees, and your organization. Let's get our inspiration from practice. Let's look at how other companies *measure transfer effectiveness* to find out what might be fitting, workable, and connectable.

A simple, inexpensive, and therefore popular form of transfer evaluation is to send a questionnaire to trainees. I don't mean the feedback sheet but a separate questionnaire that measures transfer success sometime after the training. What "sometime" means in your case – well, there is no easy answer to that. It's the period of time that elapses by which sustainable transfer successes materialize. In a PowerPoint course where the transfer goal is "trainees use PowerPoint to create their bids and offers," a month might be enough. In a leadership training with the transfer goal "trainees use their own resources deliberately by delegating tasks to their team," it probably makes more sense to wait six to nine months or even a year to see whether trainees have adopted the desired behavior successfully and sustainably. To determine the appropriate length of time, it helps to look at the transfer goals.

Which questions or items could be included in a trainee questionnaire to evaluate transfer effectiveness? Here are some examples for your inspiration:

Evaluating transfer effectiveness
Questionnaire for self-assessment by trainees

General questions about transfer success
Create a questionnaire for trainees, which includes one of the following questions or items:
- How well have you succeeded in implementing what you have learned in your day-to-day work?
- What I learned in training has proved effective in my daily work
- I often apply what I've learned at the training to my work[9]
- Training has changed my behavior at work / has improved how I work[10]
- I'm very good at applying the training content in my daily work[11]
- I can successfully apply what I learned from the training to my work[12]

Note: General questions are universally applicable to any training. The advantage is that you can use the same questionnaire for each transfer evaluation. A disadvantage is that the answers do not allow any conclusions as to what exactly has been implemented or what exactly is meant by "implementation."

Individual transfer plans questionnaire
Create a questionnaire in which trainees indicate their individual transfer plans and their degree of implementation.[13]

Instructions: You attended the [insert training name] training some time ago. What did you want to implement from the training? How successful was the implementation? Please specify your implementation plans as exactly as possible and rate them on a scale from 0% = "not successful at all" to 100% = "totally successful."

I wanted to implement this	Success of implementation					
	0%	20%	40%	60%	80%	100%
	0%	20%	40%	60%	80%	100%

Specifically request transfer goals / behaviors

Create a questionnaire for the trainees that lists the transfer goals (behavioral goals) for the training attended. Trainees individually assess how well they have achieved these transfer goals. Depending on the scale, a wide variety of data can be obtained. Here are two variants as examples:

Variant 1

Instruction: The training you attended should have supported you in reaching the following goals. Please rate how often you succeed in taking the following actions.

1 – never
2 – rarely
3 – occasionally
4 – often
5 – always

[Insert Transfer Goal 1]	1	2	3	4	5	Note:
[Insert Transfer Goal 2]	1	2	3	4	5	Note:
[Insert Transfer Goal 3]	1	2	3	4	5	Note:

Variant 2

Instruction: Please use the following scale to evaluate how the following statements apply to you

1 – I have never tried this in my daily work
2 – I tried this in my daily work, but unsuccessfully
3 – I have tried this successfully in day-to-day work, but not kept it up
4 – I still do/use this occasionally
5 – I do/use this regularly

[Insert Transfer Goal 1]	1	2	3	4	5	Note:
[Insert Transfer Goal 2]	1	2	3	4	5	Note:
[Insert Transfer Goal 3]	1	2	3	4	5	Note:

Before-after comparisons

Create a questionnaire for the trainees that lists the transfer goals (behavioral goals) for the training attended and ask for a rating before and since the training.

Instruction: The training should help you to achieve the following goals. Please use the following scale to rate how well you succeed in the following points in your day-to-day work.

none or very low level   1 2 3 4 5   very high level

Please use the left-hand column for how you would rate yourself before the training; the right-hand column for the time since the training.

Before the Training						Since the Training				
1	2	3	4	5	[Insert Transfer Goal 1]	1	2	3	4	5
1	2	3	4	5	[Insert Transfer Goal 1]	1	2	3	4	5
1	2	3	4	5	[Insert Transfer Goal 1]	1	2	3	4	5

With questionnaires like these, you can ascertain the magnitude of the transfer success in the trainee's eyes; so we now have data on "how much" or "how transfer-effective." What we still need is the data on "why (this much/little has been done)." When we send out a questionnaire, it makes sense to also ask about transfer-promoting and transfer-inhibiting factors to reveal strengths and possible optimization potential. Then you'll be able to see where you can and should start, and to argue and convincingly prove where stakeholders (such as supervisors) haven't played their important roles as transfer sponsors and promoters.

In formulating the questions and items on factors that drive or limit transfer success, you also have various possibilities. For instance, you can rate them qualitatively by providing an open "free text" field in the questionnaire for:

- "This helped me implement what I learned" and
- "This made it difficult for me to put into practice what I've learned" or
- "This would have helped me with the implementation"

You can also ask whether certain transfer-promoting measures were actually carried out (e.g., "I had a pre-training meeting with my supervisor") or how trainees experienced these measures ("The pre-training meeting was very helpful/not helpful/ not held"). Or you may want to lay out the transfer-promoting and -inhibiting factors in quantitative form (e.g., "My supervisor assisted me with the implementation of what I have learned - applies/doesn't apply"). When asking about or formulating items, use the 12 levers as a guide. Or use available, science-based questions about the 12 levers to get a valid picture of the transfer drivers and limiters in your training (for example, the TTA check-up, see page 313).

The form of evaluation discussed so far – self-assessment by the trainees – is quick, inexpensive, and simple to administer and fill in. One possible criticism, however, is that self-assessments tend to be subjective. Then again, one could argue that this is also true for the "happy sheets" so widely accepted today, and that the distortion is minimized if surveys are anonymous. You'd still like a more objective picture? Then you should find the following ideas and possibilities inspiring:

Evaluating transfer effectiveness
Examples of (supplementary) assessments by others

Self-assessment and supervisors' assessment of transfer goals
Trainees and supervisors conduct an evaluation meeting after the transfer phase where they jointly assess the achievement of the transfer goals (see pages 101 ff.).

Quantitative or qualitative feedback from supervisor
Supervisors gather evidence of and evaluate the transfer effectiveness of the training in talks with their staff and/or by observation, and report back to HR development

Implementation presentation
Trainees present their implementation results (e.g., to management, supervisors, HR development, trainers, and training peers, etc.)

Completion of practical projects
Transfer success is evident from the successful implementation of practical projects. It is assessed by, for example, the person that commissioned the projects.

External observation
"Mystery shopper" style: an external person working "under cover" observes to what extent trainees implement the desired behaviors in their everyday work. Alternatively, this monitoring can be done overtly, and trainee behaviors can be observed "officially."

Simulations and demonstrations
As with observation, implementation is assessed by external observers. The difference is that, in a simulation or demonstration, the practice situation is created artificially (Example: a training for advisors in the public sector. Transfer effectiveness is determined by simulating a counseling session in a role play.)

As you see, the approach to assessing transfer effectiveness can be as comprehensive and sophisticated as you want it to be. Make sure you keep it pragmatic, though. There must be a sound cost-value balance that is appropriate for that particular training. In the case of a one-day training, multi-day "mystery shopping" or an elaborate simulation would probably be bit over the top and not very pragmatic. However, in this case, the effort entailed by filling in a standardized questionnaire is appropriate. It is quite a different story, of course, if you run an investment-intensive sales academy, perhaps even several times a year. In that case, it may be worthwhile to design a more elaborate evaluation. The key here is that designing training should always include designing its evaluation. It is only when we measure transfer effectiveness that the transfer aspiration will become a tangible and measurable parameter. It is only when you make transfer a success criterion to be assessed that everyone involved will make an effort to make transfer happen, allowing you to prove your success instantly at any time.

Making your feedback sheets transfer-relevant

Does this whole transfer evaluation topic seem too much for a first step? Isn't there something smaller you can start with? After all, relevance and feasibility are paramount. So what would be a small, relevant first step for transfer evaluation? A practical start would be to adapt your current feedback forms. As the saying goes, every great journey begins with a first step, so just start on the feedback sheets you hand out at the end of your training courses and develop them further. Edit them so that, at the end of a training, they will allow you to learn as much as possible about the prospects for transfer success. Integrate questions and items that let you draw conclusions about transfer effectiveness. What could those be? We've learned earlier that the popular happiness questions don't tell you anything about transfer effectiveness (see pages 282 ff.). Utility-related questions, on the other hand, are more suitable, plus they send different signals. Happiness (satisfaction) questions say, "We want you to be happy." Utility questions say, "We want what you learned to be useful in practice." So how could you rephrase your happiness questions? What utility questions could you include in your feedback sheet? Here's a selection to spark ideas:

From satisfaction-oriented questions, items, and rating scales ("We want to make you happy") ...	... to utility-oriented questions, items, and rating scales ("We want you to be able to implement and use what you've learned")
How would you rate the training as a whole? (excellent – unsatisfactory)	How useful was the training for your work? (very useful – not useful at all)
How satisfied were you with the contents of the training? (very satisfied – not satisfied at all)	The contents of the training were relevant to my work (agree strongly – disagree strongly)
How satisfied were you with the methods used? (very satisfied – not satisfied at all)?	The methods used have supported my learning success (agree strongly – disagree strongly)
Please rate the trainer on the following scale: 1 – excellent, 5 – unsatisfactory	The trainer's approach has supported my learning success (agree strongly – disagree strongly)
What is your overall impression of the training? (0 % unsatisfactory – 100 % excellent)	How confident are you that you will be able to apply what you have learned? (0 % not at all – 100 % extremely confident) Why/why not?
Open questions: What did you like the most/least? What else would you have expected?	Open questions: What supported or limited your learning progress? What would help you or make it easier to implement what you have learned when you get back to your workplace?

As these examples show, if you use the right wording for the feedback forms at the end of your training you can use them to get valuable information on (expected) transfer effectiveness, and also to send the right signals. Should you want to dig deeper and learn how to gather comprehensive information across all four levels – reaction, learning, behavior, and results – at the end of a training session, you should take a look at the hybrid evaluation sheets developed by Kirkpatrick,[14] who, it is fair to say, is one of the grand masters of training and transfer evaluation.

Making transfer success the finish line

Transfer is the official finish line for your training. A program has not been completed until the things taught have successfully been applied. This refers not only to HR development and trainers, to key performance indicators and evaluations, but, above all, to trainees. So, if you want to claim "success," then presence in training should not be the criterion; instead, the metric should be successful implementation. What exactly can this look like in practice? When and how can transfer be rewarded and certified? Here is an inspiration for you:

Demanding, rewarding and certifying transfer
Examples from practice

Confirmation by the supervisor
After an appropriate period has passed following the training, the supervisor conducts an implementation review with the employee. After the supervisor has confirmed with his/her signature that the agreed transfer goals have been achieved, HR issues a certificate (and only after receiving confirmation).

Transfer report
Each trainee writes a transfer report that describes their implementation successes. Again, a certificate is issued only after this report has been signed by the supervisor and/or sent to the HR development department or trainer.

Implementation presentation
Trainees each present their implementation successes and what they learned to a suitable committee (e.g., supervisors, the management/management team, HR development, the trainer, colleagues, ...).

Completion of the practice project
Trainees receive their certificate of completion once their practice project has been successfully completed or implemented. This is ascertained by the person who sponsors the practice project and/or by a presentation to a suitable committee.

Transfer review with the trainer
Trainees go through an implementation review with the trainer in which they report on their transfer successes and learnings. If they have achieved their goals, then they receive a certificate.

Transfer targets as part of employee appraisal
The transfer goals from the training are included as part of the employee appraisal (e.g., as an additional standardized sheet). Achievement (or not) of these goals is handled in the same way as for all other defined performance goals.

Transfer as a prerequisite for further training
Here, confirmed achievement of the agreed transfer goals is the admission ticket for applying for and attending further training within the organization. Or trainees can earn or win additional development credits by attaining transfer goals (for more on development credits, see pages 219 ff.).

All these approaches send a clear signal: Transfer is not merely a pleasant add-on at our organization. It is what we expect, and it will be noticed whether this expectation is met. Be sure to involve supervisors or management as much as you can – not only to send a particularly strong message to trainees but also to strengthen and challenge supervisors in their crucial role in bringing about transfer success.

What if your (internal) clients are used to getting some kind of "reward paper" (i.e., a certificate of attendance or the like) at the end of a training, and don't want to give it up? Are you worried that abandoning that practice would be too radical a break from a popular routine? Then take it step by step – for example, by using a system of levels. Give out certificates of attendance at the end of your training but tell them that there will be a "Practitioner Certificate" or "Confirmation of Success" after successful implementation – which, of course, trainees will also want to have.

Implementing the transfer interventions of your choice

The 12 levers of transfer effectiveness complement and reinforce one another. This means that every transfer intervention you implement also works on several levers, automatically strengthening transfer effectiveness in various ways. This is esepcially true for Lever 12 – Transfer Expectations in the Organization: With every single transfer-promoting step you implement, you will also send a signal of transfer expectation. Every statement made about transfer, every discussion on transfer, every (employee or third-party) magazine article, every testimonial about successful implementation, every transfer success story that is acknowledged and valued, every transfer review between trainee and supervisor, every follow-up session – even the smallest transfer-enhancing action that is successfully implemented and even every critical voice and resistance that provokes a controversial discussion of the topic shows that transfer effectiveness is an important topic in the organization. Here, or so the message goes, transfer is not just a slogan or lip service but a meaningful concept, an aspiration and a goal backed by concrete actions, initiatives, and metrics. So, implement the transfer-promoting actions that seem compatible and workable in the given context – for with every single action, you strengthen the transfer expectation in the organization and thus enhance transfer success.

Time for transfer!

Your turn: How can you strengthen transfer expectations in the organization? What could you do so that the organization notices and rewards trainees who apply what they've learned? What is the next step you would like to implement? Write down the thoughts and ideas that spontaneously come to mind.

This is how I/we can strengthen transfer expectations in the organization:

[1] The transfer expectation in the organization, as a significant predictor of training transfer, has been validated multiple times, for example, in the Learning Transfer System Inventory (LTSI) in terms of the positive or negative consequences of applying what has been learned. It is also crucial that trainees are held accountable for applying what they have learned. For validation of the LTSI in German, see Kauffeld, S., Bates, R., Holton, E. F., III, & Müller, A. C., "Das deutsche Lerntransfer-System-Inventar (GLTSI): Psychometrische Überprüfung der deutschsprachigen Version" in *Zeitschrift für Personalpsychologie,* 2008, 7(2): pp. 50 – 69. For transfer responsibility or the signals of the meaning of transfer within an organization, see, for example, Baldwin, T., & Magjuka, R., "Organizational training and signals of importance: Linking program outcomes to pre-training expectations" in *Human Resource Development Quarterly,* 1991, 2(1): pp. 25 – 36.

[2] Signaling theory deals with the sending and interpretation of signals when there is an informational asymmetry (e.g., between an individual and an organization). A brief overview can be found, for example, in Connelly, B. L., Certo, S. T., Ireland, R. D., & Reutzel, C. R., "Signaling theory: A review and assessment" in *Journal of Management,* 2011, 37(1): pp. 39 – 67.

[3] Burke, L. A., & Hutchins, H. M., "A study of best practices in training transfer and proposed model of transfer" in *Human Resource Development Quarterly,* 2008, 19(2): pp. 107 – 128, p. 118.

[4] ASTD Research, *The Value of Evaluation,* ASTD Press, 2009 – available at the ATD webshop: www.td.org/Store (8.12.2016).

[5] For correlations between levels in the Kirkpatrick model, see Alliger, G. M., & Janak, E. A., "Kirkpatrick's Levels of Training Criteria. Thirty Years Later" in *Personnel psychology,* 1989, 42(2): pp. 331 – 342, and also several years later in the meta-analysis by Alliger, G. M., Tannenbaum, S. I., Bennett Jr, W., Traver, H., & Shotland, A., "A meta-analysis of the relations among training criteria" in *Personnel psychology,* 1997, 50(2): pp. 341 – 358.

[6] According to the 1997 meta-analysis, the correlation coefficient between utility response and transfer (i.e., behavior at the workplace) was 0.18.

[7] The *learning zone model* is described in, for example, Senninger, Tom, *Abenteuer leiten – in Abenteuern lernen: Methodenset zur Planung und Leitung kooperativer Lerngemeinschaften für Training und Teamentwicklung in Schule, Jugendarbeit und Betrieb,* Münster: Ökotopia, 2000.

[8] If you are interested in different evaluation models, we recommend the following works: Griffin, R., *Complete Training Evaluation: The Comprehensive Guide to Measuring Return on Investment,* Kogan Page, 2014, and also Meier, R., *Praxis Bildungscontrolling: Was Sie wirklich tun können, um Ihre Aus- und Weiterbildung qualitätsbewusst zu steuern,* GABAL-Verlag, 2008.

[9] This item has been adapted from Kauffeld, S., Brenneke, J., & Strack, M., "Erfolge Sichtbar Machen: Das Maßnahmen-Erfolgs-Inventar (MEI) zur Bewertung von Trainings" [English: Visualizing Successes: The Measurement-Success Inventory for the Assessment of Training]" in *Handbuch Kompetenzentwicklung,* 2009, pp. 55 – 78, and from Grohmann, A., & Kauffeld, S., "Evaluating training programs: Development and Correlates of the Questionnaire for Professional Training Evaluation" in *International Journal of Training and Development,* 2013, 17(2): pp. 135 – 155.

[10] This item has been adapted from Kauffeld, S., Brenneke, J., & Strack, M., "Erfolge Sichtbar Machen: Das Maßnahmen-Erfolgs-Inventar (MEI) zur Bewertung von Trainings [Visualizing Successes: The Measurement-Success Inventory for the Assessment of Training]" in *Handbuch Kompetenzentwicklung,* 2009, pp. 55 – 78.

[11] This item has been adapted from Grohmann, A., & Kauffeld, S., "Evaluating training programs: Development and correlates of the Questionnaire for Professional Training Evaluation" in *International Journal of Training and Development,* 2013, 17(2): pp. 135 – 155.

[12] This example item was taken from the trainee manual for Kirkpatrick Bronze Certification. Further information can be found at www.kirkpatrickpartners.com (8 December 2016).

[13] The idea of collecting individual transfer intentions and their degree of implementation was adapted from Kauffeld, S., Brenneke, J., & Strack, M., "Erfolge sichtbar machen: Das Maßnahmen-Erfolgs-Inventar (MEI) zur Bewertung von Trainings [Visualizing Successes: The Measurement-Success Inventory for the Assessment of Training]" in *Handbuch Kompetenzentwicklung,* 2009, pp. 55 – 78, and Jodlbauer, S., Selenko, E., Batinic, B., & Stiglbauer, B., "The Relationship between Job Dissatisfaction and Training Transfer" in *International Journal of Training and Development,* 2012, 16(1): pp. 39 – 53.

[14] Hybrid evaluation sheet templates, questions, and items (Kirkpatrick (R) Hybrid Evaluation Tool Templates) are given to Kirkpatrick Bronze Certification trainees. Further information can be found at www.kirkpatrickpartners.com (8 December 2016).

MAKE TRANSFER HAPPEN

You have read a lot and hopefully have collected many, many ideas on how to increase the transfer effectiveness of your training. Now it's time to put your ideas into action!

Let's start with the levers

So, how best to start increasing transfer effectiveness using the 12 levers? How many transfer tools do you need? Perhaps you have too many ideas for transfer actions to implement all of them in the timeframe available? Or you have so many ideas that you fear implementing all of them might overtax your organization or clients? And yet, sooner or later all 12 levers should be set to "transfer effective." So, how and where to start?

For your work with the levers, my recommendation is: Stay connected. Keep the context in mind. Don't overextend yourself. It's better to take small steps and do them right, experiencing some initial successes, than to try and implement the grand plan and fail. There is no single right way, no perfect process to pull the levers and increase transfer effectiveness. But there are several proven ways that might inspire you. At this point, I'd like to introduce three approaches that have proved effective in practice: I call them (1) the deep approach, (2) the broad approach, and (3) the toolset approach.

The *deep approach* is in action when you start a training or program – preferably one that is particularly important or urgent – and implement tools and interventions in such a way that you cover all 12 levers and set them to "transfer-effective." (The transfer design tool that I use for this is the Transfer Matrix, see page 313) If you've conducted the training a few times previously, you might want to find out before plunging in what levers are already promoting transfer and where there are still some barriers (one way to find out: the TTA check-up, see page 313). It is only when this training or program is transfer-effective across all levers, and there are corresponding high transfer successes, that you may allow yourself to proceed with the next training.

In the *broad approach,* you start with a lever or a transfer tool that you use universally across all trainings. For example, you might initiate pre- and post-training interviews for each future training session. It's best to start with a transfer tool that delivers fast results, can be implemented easily, and generates as little resistance as possible. If this first intervention works well across the board, tackle the next lever or transfer tool.

In the *toolset approach,* you put together a toolbox of ready-made transfer tools for as many levers as possible. Make sure that, besides more complex transfer tools, you always have some smaller and simpler tools available that you can apply quickly and easily.

If that sounds too abstract for you, let's look at a few success stories from the field.

How practitioners work with the levers

Stefan, 43, human resources developer
I first got interested in transfer at our internal sales academy. That's why I chose it, because sales is a hot topic for us; it's a really urgent concern for all of us. So I knew that everyone was interested in making this academy a big success. The timing was also perfect, because we had just changed our distribution strategy to make use of some new technology on the market. What's the saying? "Never let a good crisis go to waste." Well, crisis is too strong. Anyway, I grabbed it as an opportunity to realign the sales academy as well.

I brought up transfer in a workshop with the sales managers and the academy trainers. They loved it, and the sales managers themselves developed the transfer goals for the academy, based on our new sales strategy and worked pretty closely with the trainers. As a result, the sales managers themselves are now our "clients," and I, as HR manager, have the role of coordinator and moderator. We went through all 12 levers with the help of an external expert, collected ideas to promote transfer in our culture, and then took the best ideas. My HR team then designed the Transfer Matrix and developed the ideas into prototypes, which we revised again in the next workshop with the sales managers and trainers. We covered all 12 levers with our tools. And due to having both managers and trainers involved, there was full commitment. After all, it's their sales academy, so they have a vested interest in making it as transfer-effective as possible. With the success of the sales academy, the word spread like wildfire within the company, officially and inofficially – and turned "transfer" into a red-hot topic. A positive one. One by one, the other divisions started saying they wanted to enhance their transfer effectiveness, too. Next, we tackled our internal apprenticeship training. Here, again, we optimized all 12 levers and set the transfer goals in cooperation with the managers. Our leadership program is next in line. By now, it has become standard operating procedure in our organization that you have to have transfer goals, a transfer concept that covers all 12 levers (Transfer Matrix), and that managers have to be actively involved. Today, transfer isn't just a slogan but something we live by. Not only in HR but everyone!

Melanie, 37, Trainer

My goal was to really differentiate myself from all the other providers of presentation trainings. I wanted to make transfer effectiveness part of my USP. I started small. First, I introduced a very simple tool: a special transfer planning tool – it looks like a plane ticket. I took it to every training session. At the end of the training, all my participants planned their "journey to implementation success." This transfer planning tool became one of my trademarks, and my clients noticed and talked about it. Over time, I added more transfer tools. For example, I started setting up a trainer hotline before each training and sending reminder emails with copies of the participants' transfer intentions after each training course.

At first, I didn't charge anything for these transfer tools. I just mentioned in the sales talks that it's standard for me to use this-and-that tool to cover such-and-such a lever of transfer effectiveness. This was incredibly good for my positioning. When I had more transfer tools, including some that were rather complex and time-consuming, I started charging for them. Using the levers, I was always able to explain to clients why this or that tool was important and useful. Not all of my clients, but surprisingly many are willing to invest in transfer-promoting measures. Which, of course, is great for me financially. But most of all, I enjoy having made a name for myself on the market based on my focus on transfer.

Leopold, 56, Head of a training institute

During a sales talk, a potential client asked me, "How do you ensure transfer? What transfer model do you work with?" We had a few individual measures to promote transfer but, quite frankly, we didn't have an end-to-end model at the time. After that conversation, though, I knew it was high time to change that. The levers of transfer effectiveness seemed logical and useful. They are flexible, which I considered important due to our wide range of different clients.

We started out with one of our own internal programs, our leadership training. We did a TTA check-up with all previous graduates. It showed us that two levers needed optimization: active practice and support from supervisors. We developed a new trainer codex that stipulated "a minimum of 30 % active practice" and that a transfer-planning module would be mandatory for each training course. To gain support from supervisors, we needed to have everything more clearly laid out in black and white. We used this opportunity to have brief awareness workshops with all our managers to sensitize them for the transfer topic, and also to clarify their importance and role. Today, we even offer trainings that qualify executives as transfer supporters, and after each leadership workshop, we evaluate the extent to which trainees' supervisors supported the transfer. Not very surprisingly, at the next TTA check-up, we got much better scores on that. After doing our homework on transfer promotion internally, we set about offering it to our clients. We gradually tried out the tools we used internally to promote transfer with and for clients. In doing that, we kept realizing how important it is to have a solid model to fall back on – in our case, the levers –, simply to convince clients of the function, purpose, and value of the tools and provide a rationale for the associated investments. Today, we have a whole box of various transfer-promoting measures for each lever. It's actually a black-colored box that we take to sales talks: our "transfer black-box." In talking with clients, we use it to demonstrate that transfer isn't just a buzzword for us but something real, something tangible, with transfer tools for all levers, at the level of complexity that's right for each organization. So, what used to be our Achilles heel – transfer effectiveness – has become our greatest competitive advantage and my own personal transfer story.

Your turn:

What is your success story with the 12 levers of transfer effectiveness? Start now and make transfer happen.

WOULD YOU LIKE SOME MORE?

Designing a scientifically sound transfer concept with the TRANSFER MATRIX
When we design transfer concepts for our clients, we use a tool called the Transfer Matrix. It helps us, to plan the right mix of transfer tools, to ensure that we have covered all 12 levers accordingly, and to find out if we have chosen only the most powerful transfer measures.
Please feel free to use the transfer matrix as well for your next training at www.transfereffectiveness.com/transfermatrix

Analyzing transfer with the TTA-CHECK-UP®
Are you curious about how the levers are set in your training and would you like to know the exact status quo? Then the Transfer of Training Analysis (TTA) check-up is the tool for you – backed by science and time-efficient.
Feel free to contact us at office@transfereffectiveness.com

Transfer management goes digital – Transfer platforms & software
Want to implement and manage all your transfer tools and interventions digitally? Digital transfer platforms offer you this ability and much more. We are happy to recommend programs that have proved especially powerful in our and our clients' experiences. Contact us at office@transfereffectiveness.com

More about the LEVERS OF TRANSFER EFFECTIVENESS
You want to know more about the levers of transfer effectiveness? Would you like to exchange ideas with other HR development professionals and trainers, network with them, and develop transfer tools and interventions together?
Learn the latest about our certifications, courses, and workshops at www.transfereffectiveness.com/academy

LET'S TALK ABOUT TRANSFER
Transfer is my passion. And my own aspiration. I want to know what moves you. Do you have questions about the levers? Ideas? Feedback? Success stories, best practices, or teachings? Tell me about it! Let's share and talk!
Contact me at ina.weinbauer@transfereffectiveness.com

Theory makes you smarter.
Practice makes you wiser.
Sustainable success requires both.

Thank you, Ina, for our intense and rewarding collaboration that has enabled me to contribute my transfer practice expertise to this book. For more than 20 years, my work in employee education has taken me around the globe and enabling me to develop and implement transfer tools and measures. What an honor and a pleasure it has been to support the results of your scientific research.

Special thanks to my clients worldwide who are fascinated by and devoted to enhancing the effectiveness of development initiatives. With stamina and sensitivity, you are successfully advancing the cause and making an important contribution.

Many people have **given me inspiration** and helped me explore this topic further. I am especially grateful to you, Seppo Virtanen, Alexandra Singer, Jon Serrander, Gunther Fürstberger, Anna Repp, Jim Kirkpatrick, Robert Brinkerhoff, Alexandra Sock, and Tanja Ineichen.

I owe the **heart** of my passion for sustainable effectiveness to my parents as well as to Rainer and Peter; you are my daily inspiration in all walks of life, and I thank you for that.

Thank you all that we have walked this path of effectiveness together for so long now and that we will continue to journey together to new destinations.

It's all about resonance!
Masha Ibeschitz-Manderbach

Expressing thanks is just a necessary formality
That's what I often thought when I read acknowledgments in other books. Today I know how deep and honest these thanks are, and how much those who are acknowledged deserve them!

First and foremost, I thank my **clients and seminar participants** for embracing the transfer effectiveness challenge. It is only because there are people like you – people who themselves aspire to be effective and are willing to work at it actively and courageously – that this book exists.

Thanks to the publishing and graphics professionals. To my writing coach, Daniela Pucher, for her pragmatic questions and her refreshingly simple answers. To my editor, Friederike Schmitz, as well as the English editors Terry Gilman and Jutta Scherer for their remarkable quality standards and perseverance. To our layout artist, Lothar Hasenleithner from PEHA Medien GmbH for keeping an actually impossible deadline, and to my illustrator, Katharina Trnka, for gently swinging her illustrator's pen in an easy-going collaboration that can only work as it does because we have been bound for many years in a deep and unique friendship.

Thanks to the initiators, co-thinkers, and feedback providers Stephanie Kneifel, Martin Sattlberger, Petra Mitterlehner, Manfred Weinbauer, Robert Stangl, Tanja Ineichen, Clemens Strahammer, Georg Kerschbaum, Julia Bröderbauer, Axel Koch, and Ralph Sichler – each of you contributed in a very personal and crucial way to the development of this book.
Furthermore, a very special thanks to Linn Steer, Robert Brinkerhoff, Markus Zellinger, Barbara Lanzendörfer, Anja Priewasser, Seppo Virtanen, and the Promote Team who all again and again encouraged me for more than a year to publish this book in English.

A very special **thanks to you, Masha.** For sharing your immense wealth of experience so openly and concretely with me and our readers. For the many hours we spent on the phone early in the morning and late at night, discussing, challenging, formulating, and generating ideas with our shared passion for effectiveness, connectedness, and concreteness. Above all, however, I thank you for believing in the 12 levers so energetically and emphatically. Without it, this book would not exist today.

Thanks to my parents, Manfred and Margit, for always being there and supporting me. **I thank you, Martin,** for the many walks and talks, for being my sparring partner, for your perseverance in building and unraveling my thoughts, and for your unflagging and friendly encouragement, "Well, write exactly that then!" which I heard so many times. Thank you for being at my side, always having my back, and sharing your ideas and energy so thoughtfully and effectively. And, last but not least, thank you, my sweet little **Noemi,** for teaching me in your cheerfully charming and efficient way what serenity, flexibility, and taking a break all mean!

Thank you all for enabling me to be effective.
Ina Weinbauer-Heidel